RADICAL ISLAM
RISING

RADICAL ISLAM RISING

MUSLIM EXTREMISM IN THE WEST

Quintan Wiktorowicz

ROWMAN & LITTLEFIELD PUBLISHERS, INC.
Lanham • Boulder • Toronto • Oxford

ROWMAN & LITTLEFIELD PUBLISHERS, INC.

Published in the United States of America
by Rowman & Littlefield Publishers, Inc.
A wholly owned subsidary of the Rowman & Littlefield Publishing Group, Inc.
4501 Forbes Boulevard, Suite 200, Lanham, Maryland 20706
www.rowmanlittlefield.com

PO Box 317
Oxford
OX2 9RU, UK

Copyright © 2005 by Rowman & Littlefield Publishers, Inc.

British Library Cataloguing in Publication Information Available

Library of Congress Cataloging-in-Publication Data Available

ISBN 0-7425-3640-8 (cloth : alk. paper)
ISBN 0-7425-3641-6 (pbk. : alk. paper)

Printed in the United States of America

For Nora

CONTENTS

FIGURES AND TABLES

FIGURES

TABLES

ACKNOWLEDGMENTS

This book benefited from the support and feedback provided by a number of colleagues, assistants, and administrators. The fieldwork was made possible by generous financial support from the Office of the Dean at Rhodes College and the Seidman Fellowship for International Studies. The Office of the Dean also provided a sabbatical that freed me to complete the manuscript.

A number of colleagues offered insights and feedback. I would especially like to thank Kamran Bokhari, Janine Clark, and John Bowen, who took the time to read through an entire draft. For their comments on various components of the book, I would also like to thank Peter Mandaville, Charlie Kurzman, Carrie Wickham, Ellen Lust-Okar, Mohammed Hafez, Karl Kaltenthaler, Steve Ceccoli, and Larry Hamlet. In addition, the book benefited from conversations and e-mail exchanges with Olivier Roy, John Hall, and Greg Gause.

The control group survey would not have been possible without the generous assistance of my colleague Steve Ceccoli, who offered his expertise in constructing and evaluating the survey. Karl Kaltenthaler made important suggestions for the questions. Brian Hummer developed a web version of the survey.

The survey was distributed and collected by my research assistant in London, Afshan Malik, who exhibited the creativity and perseverance needed to successfully conduct a sensitive poll among Muslims in the post–September 11 era.

I would also like to thank my various research assistants at Rhodes, who helped collect miscellaneous items related to the project, especially Leslie Longtin, Katie Mullins, and Lynn Keathley, who proved to be an exceptional and meticulous copyeditor. John Sexton helped with the graphics for the book.

INTRODUCTION

Good vignette
→ or too
dramatic?

invite
a
Reg are
view

In April 2003, Asif Mohammed Hanif and Omar Khan Sharif began a historic journey of terrorism.[1] Before departing Jordan, the two men hid thin Deta sheet explosives inside a Qur'an to evade detection at the Allenby Bridge crossing into the West Bank. The border guards waved them through a checkpoint reserved for tourists where visitors receive far less scrutiny than Palestinians. On April 22 at 2:30 P.M. they passed through the Erez border crossing into the Gaza Strip to meet with members of the al-Qassem Brigade, the military wing of Hamas responsible for the majority of suicide bombings in Israel and the West Bank. While in the Gaza Strip, they took the time to visit the spot where an Israeli bulldozer crushed and killed American peace activist Rachel Corrie as she protested the Israeli army's destruction of Palestinian homes. Then on April 29 they took a taxi into Israel.

On April 30 at 1:00 A.M., the men walked toward Mike's Place, a bar on the waterfront near the U.S. embassy in Tel Aviv, popular with English-speaking Israelis and tourists. As they approached, a guard blocked them from entering, and Sharif tried to detonate the explosives strapped to his body outside the main door. The bomb failed to go off. Bystanders tried to grab Sharif as he ran, but he managed to throw off the explosives and escape into the darkness. Hanif, however, successfully detonated his bomb, killing three and injuring fifty-five.

The authorities launched one of the largest manhunts in Israeli history. Sharif's picture was plastered on the front page of every newspaper, but for more than a week, he was officially at large. Twelve days after the explosion, a body was found floating in the water near the bar, so badly decomposed that police could not use fingerprints or identify the corpse. DNA from Sharif's relatives was used to confirm that it was indeed the body of the escaped bomber.

✓

Relion =
ovnmant
-ally =
good?

Suicide bombings became tragically common after the al-Aqsa intifada erupted in September 2000, but the attack on Mike's Place marked the first case of a bombing perpetrated by foreigners: Hanif and Sharif were British citizens. Both grew up in the United Kingdom, and neither fit the profile of a suicide bomber. Sharif had a thoroughly Western upbringing in a well-respected family in Derby. He enjoyed all the trappings of a wealthy childhood and even attended Repton Preparatory School for two years, an expensive public institution with a long list of famous graduates, including children's writer Roald Dahl, playwright Christopher Isherwood (d. 1986), and Lord Ramsey, the archbishop of Canterbury (d. 1988). Neighbors, friends, and family were shocked when the news of the suicide bombing reached Derby. "Anyone who knew him would tell you," said his brother. "He was just a big teddy bear—that's what people said about him."[2]

Though from a more modest background, Hanif seemed to fit into British society as well. He lived in Hounslow near Heathrow airport and attended business classes at Cranford Community College, where he received distinction on his GNVQ (general national vocational qualifications). The headmaster at the college described him as "a model pupil." Hanif was an avid cricket fan, and friends described him as a gentle person. His interest in Islam focused more on Sufism and the mystical side of Islam, the antithesis of radical fundamentalism.

Despite these personal profiles, both men were somehow seduced by radical Islam and were willing to die for a cause thousands of miles from home. And they are not alone. Hundreds of young British Muslims, predominantly of South Asian descent, have flocked to fight against the Indian army in Kashmir. Mohammed Bilal, a twenty-four-year-old from Birmingham, blew himself up in a car outside an Indian army barrack in Srinagar, Kashmir, killing a number of Indian soldiers and several Kashmiri students returning home during Ramadan.[3] British-born Ahmed Omar Saeed Sheikh, a graduate of the London School of Economics, was arrested by Indian authorities for his role in several tourist kidnappings in Kashmir in 1994. He was freed from jail in 1999 as part of a hostage exchange after supporters hijacked an Indian Airlines plane in Kandahar, Afghanistan. In 2002, he was tried and sentenced to death by hanging for masterminding the kidnapping and brutal slaying of *Wall Street Journal* reporter Daniel Pearl earlier that year.[4] British Muslims have fought in Bosnia, Chechnya, and other conflict zones favored by radical Islamic activists.

A number of British Muslims have also been tied to al-Qaeda. Seven Britons were interned at Camp X-Ray in Guantanamo Bay, Cuba, after being captured in Afghanistan during the U.S.-led war against the Taliban.[5] The Finsbury Park mosque in London is a notorious center of support for radical Islamic groups aligned with al-Qaeda, including the Egyptian Islamic Group, the Algerian Salafist Group for Preaching and Combat (GSPC), and the Algerian Armed Islamic Group (GIA). In late 2003, a British Muslim was captured in Kurdish territory after allegedly fighting for Ansar al-Islam, an Iraqi-based movement tied to al-Qaeda.[6] In March 2004, eight British nationals were arrested by London's Metropolitan Police antiterrorist branch in the biggest antiterrorism operation since September 11. In a related raid, police seized half a ton of ammonium nitrate fertilizer, the same compound used in the bombings in Bali, Turkey, Saudi Arabia, Kenya, Tanzania, and the United States. Only a few weeks later, British intelligence thwarted a chemical bomb plot by alleged al-Qaeda sympathizers.[7] Richard Reid, the "shoe bomber" who tried to blow up a 747 transatlantic flight to Boston, is perhaps the most infamous example of a Briton affiliated with al-Qaeda. Other examples abound. Scotland Yard estimates that as many as 3,000 Britons have participated in al-Qaeda training camps.[8]

At a more local level, thousands of young Britons are attracted to the panoply of radical Islamic movements with bases or branches in the United Kingdom, including Hizb ut-Tahrir, Supporters of the Shariah, al-Muhajiroun, and al-Qaeda. Many merely listen to talks and attend events sponsored by the various groups. Others become committed activists, willing to sacrifice themselves for the cause. These groups are a small minority of the Muslim population in the United Kingdom, but an increasing number of Muslims seem attracted to their message, particularly in the Midlands and London (euphemistically called "Londonistan" by some observers because of the prevalence of Islamic fundamentalist groups in the capital).

The phenomenon of citizens from the West joining or supporting radical Islamic groups is not limited to the United Kingdom. In the United States, some estimated 1,000–2,000 Muslims volunteered to fight in jihadi causes in Bosnia, Chechnya, and Afghanistan during the 1990s.[9] More recently, a number of Americans have been charged with supporting radical Islamic causes, including "American Taliban" John Walker Lyndh, the "dirty bomb" suspect Jose Padilla, James Ujamaa, and others. French citizens have been actively involved in the Algerian GIA and GSPC and have served as recruiters and volunteers for al-Qaeda.[10] In May 2004, several French citizens were convicted of conspiring with Islamic terrorists.[11] Although his definition of "extremism" can be debated, Klaus Grünewald, the former head of the counterterrorist division of Bundesamt für Verfassungsschutz (Federal Office for the Protection of the Constitution) in Germany, claims that extremist Islamic groups had more than 21,200 members or supporters in Germany at the end of 1993, a number that has likely grown significantly over the past decade.[12] After September 11, authorities closed sixteen organizations linked to Metin Kaplan, known as the "Caliph of Cologne." Kaplan, who currently has about 1,100 followers, spent four years in jail for inciting the murder of a rival Islamic activist. In May 2004, authorities issued an extradition order to send him to Turkey on terrorism charges.[13] Hizb ut-Tahrir recruits not only in the United Kingdom, but in the United States, Germany, the Netherlands, Denmark, and Sweden as well. And individuals from Canada, Australia, and numerous other Western countries have lent support to al-Qaeda. In short, radical Islamic groups are drawing nationals from a variety of Western liberal democracies.

This is not to argue that large portions of the Muslim community in the West are joining or supporting radical Islamic groups. The vast majority of Muslims in the West vehemently reject the use of violence and the fanaticism of radical Islamic groups. Though little noticed in media reporting, moderate Muslim leaders and organizations in the West openly condemned al-Qaeda and similar groups in the wake of September 11, and they are important bulwarks against the spread of militant Islam. A number of moderate leaders, in fact, have received death threats from radicals who view them as traitors to Islam. Mainstream Muslims in the West are also victims of radical Islam in a more subtle (though no less tangible) way: the actions and rhetoric of radical Islamic groups often produce blind, visceral responses from non-Muslim communities, leading to increased racism, religious bigotry, and "Islamophobia." According to FBI crime statistics, hate crimes against Muslims in the United States soared 1,700 percent in 2001 (from 28 to 481 reported cases).[14] A similar backlash was found in Europe in the months after September 11.[15]

This makes the attraction of radical Islam in the West that much more perplexing. These movements not only face considerable constraints from law enforcement and new antiterrorism legislation, but they also operate in hostile Muslim communities determined to marginalize the radical fringe and eliminate the appeal of militancy—hardly an auspicious recruiting ground. The fact that these groups require that activists assume high costs and risks for the cause makes the decision to participate seem irrational. Yet some individuals defy authorities, confront their own communities, and willingly assume risk.

This book explains how individuals are drawn to radical groups and convinced to engage in high-risk, high-cost activism. Although there is an exploding body of scholarship about Muslim communities in the West,[16] few studies deal specifically with Islamic movements in liberal democracies. Even fewer address the radical fringe. A small handful of journalistic publications try to make the case that radical Islamic groups exist in the West but fail to explain why individuals join such groups.[17] A few others focus on the assertion of Islamic identity rather than the process that draws potential participants toward Islamic movements.[18] Suha-Taji Farouki's study of Hizb ut-Tahrir is perhaps the most detailed examination of a radical group in the West, but she devotes most of her attention to describing the history of the movement, its ideology, and its structures.[19] There are a few scholars who contextualize radical groups within the broader Muslim community in Europe, but these are important exceptions.[20]

Given the paucity of research, this book focuses on a detailed case study of al-Muhajiroun—a transnational movement based in the United Kingdom—as a starting point to develop our understanding of the mechanisms and processes that draw individuals toward participation in radical Islamic groups in the West. It is concerned with both formal members and individuals who participate in various activities without formal membership status. Al-Muhajiroun is not as extreme as al-Qaeda, but it does support a number of violent causes and is considered part of the radical fringe of the Muslim community, both in the United Kingdom and the broader global community. Since the vast majority of al-Muhajiroun activists in the United Kingdom are British citizens, it provides a good case study for exploring the rise of radical Islamic groups in the West.

To understand why individuals would engage in radical Islamic activism, we need to answer three related questions. First, what explains initial interest in such movements? This book argues that individuals are initially inspired by a cognitive opening that shakes certitude in previously accepted beliefs. Individuals must be willing to expose themselves to new ways of thinking and worldviews, and a cognitive opening helps facilitate possible receptivity. Any number of things can prompt a cognitive opening (experiences with discrimination, socioeconomic crisis, political repression, etc.), which means that there is no single catalyst for initial interest. In addition, movements can foster cognitive openings through activism and outreach by raising consciousness, challenging and debating alternative ideas, and persuading audiences that old ways of thinking are inadequate for addressing pressing economic, political, and social concerns.

For some individuals, a cognitive opening sparks a process of religious seeking in which they search for answers to pressing concerns through religious meaning. Of course, not every individual who experiences a cognitive opening will engage in religious seeking, and not every individual who becomes a religious seeker explores al-Muhajiroun or other radical Islamic groups. Exposure to radicals typically results from movement outreach and social networks that tie seekers to the movement through personal relationships (both prior relationships as well as newly constructed social ties that result from movement activism).

Second, once individuals are exposed to the movement and express initial interest, how are they persuaded that a radical group like al-Muhajiroun is a credible source of Islamic interpretation? If a movement is not seen as legitimate, initial interest will dissipate, and a seeker will either look into other groups or end the search for religious meaning entirely. Given the decentralized nature of sacred authority in Islam, a movement must convince seekers that its scholarly interpretation is not only legitimate but also more authentic than alternatives. A seeker must trust the credibility of the interpreter in order to trust the reliability of the interpretation. Once an individual accepts this credibility, he or she is more willing to experience religious education through the movement.

Third, how are individuals convinced to engage in risky activism? The key to answering this question is the process of socialization. Religious education exposes individuals to deliberate "culturing" intended to inculcate the movement ideology. Through lessons and other activities, the movement tries to shift individual understandings of self-interest in a manner that facilitates progression to risky activism. Potential participants are taught that salvation is an individual's primary self-interest. The question is then, How does an individual ensure acceptance in Paradise in the hereafter? The movement offers its ideology as a heuristic device or strategy for conforming to God's will and guaranteeing salvation. In this ideological template, high-risk activism, such as support for violence, is a necessary condition for fulfilling divine commands. For individuals who accept the ideology, risky activism conforms to the logic of self-interest and inspires participation regardless of the corporeal consequences in this life.

THE EMERGENCE OF AL-MUHAJIROUN

Prior to the British suicide bomb attack in Tel Aviv, MI5 (British intelligence) was already aware that Hanif and Sharif had attended lessons sponsored by al-Muhajiroun.[21] Sharif went to a series of lessons at the St. James Center in Derby and was active in distributing movement leaflets outside a mosque in the city. Although Hanif's connection is murkier, he seems to have met movement activists during the 1990s at the mosque in Hounslow where he and his family worshiped. Omar Bakri Mohammed, the founder and worldwide leader of al-Muhajiroun, openly acknowledged that he gave religious lessons to both men. After the attacks (but prior to finding Sharif's body), he publicly celebrated their "heroism": "These two brothers have drawn a divine road map, one which is drawn in blood. We pray to God to accept one brother as a martyr [Hanif]. I am very proud of the fact that the Muslims grow closer every day, that the Muslim land is one land and there is no more nationalism or Arabism."[22]

After September 11, al-Muhajiroun became a central focus in debates about political expression and national security in the United Kingdom because of the movement's past and current support for violence. A core tenet of the movement is the use of military coups to establish Islamic states wherever there are Muslims, including Britain. It also condones the use of violence against Western militaries operating in Muslim countries. Activists encouraged Britons to fight for the Taliban against U.S.-led forces in Afghanistan,[23] and the movement issued a statement supporting jihad against coalition forces in Iraq in 2003.[24] Omar and leaders in al-Muhajiroun have issued other controversial statements as well, including fatwas (jurisprudential opinions) calling for jihad against India, Russia, and Israel; a declaration supporting the 1998 U.S. embassy bombings in Africa; and statements condoning attacks against John Major and Tony Blair if they set foot in a Muslim country.[25]

The antecedents of the movement are rooted in Omar's history of activism in the Middle East.[26] Born in Syria in 1958, he was sent to the al-Kutaab Islamic Boarding School at age five to study Islam full-time. At fifteen, he joined the Muslim Brotherhood while continuing his Islamic studies. In 1977, he fled the Syrian security services and relocated to Beirut, where he joined Hizb ut-Tahrir (HT), a movement that, like al-Muhajiroun, is devoted to the establishment of an Islamic state (the caliphate) through a military coup. Two years later, he briefly traveled to Cairo to study at al-Azhar University, where he clashed with his professors over his activist views. In December 1979, after only six months in Cairo, Omar moved to Mecca to restart his studies at the Islamic School of Saltiyah.

When he arrived in Saudi Arabia, he started organizing a cell of HT. Through personal connections to a member of the Saudi royal family, Omar acquired the ability to move freely throughout the country and used his mobility to recruit thirty-eight activists by 1983. Because of the difficulties of recruiting native Saudis, most of the members were foreign students studying at different Islamic universities throughout the country, including a number of activists formerly affiliated with Juhaiman al-Utaiba, responsible for leading the takeover of the Grand Mosque in Mecca in November 1979.

Omar sent a request to issue leaflets and commence activism to the HT leadership of the nearest branch in Kuwait. The request was denied because of concerns about mobilizing in Saudi Arabia, where the movement was banned and activism severely repressed. Omar insisted on continuing his recruitment and activism, and his intransigence prompted the leadership to suspend his membership in the movement.

Infuriated, Omar decided to ignore the suspension order and continue his work as a member of HT under the banner *al-muhajiroun, wilayat al-Jazira al-arabiyya* (the emigrants, Arabian Peninsula region), which was established in Mecca. On March 3, 1983, the fifty-ninth anniversary of the end of the Ottoman caliphate, members of al-Muhajiroun began issuing leaflets in Jeddah in an underground campaign to directly challenge the political authority of the royal family, a risky venture in one of the most authoritarian countries in the world. Although Omar was officially suspended from HT, he told his followers that his use of the al-Muhajiroun banner was purely an administrative issue and that they were still acting on behalf of the movement. In fact, he continued to view himself as part of the movement and believed that any decision to suspend his membership had to come from the worldwide *amir* (commander) rather than the Kuwaiti branch leader.

The movement grew to seventy members and issued a total of sixty-two leaflets before undergoing a series of arrests in 1984. Omar used his position at a Saudi business to get himself and thirteen others released, but two members were remanded after they physically attacked their interrogators. Membership dropped to forty-four. In December 1985, the regime launched a second series of arrests after movement activists were seen distributing leaflets at a local market in Jeddah. During a raid, Omar was caught teaching from a book written by Abdul Qadeem Zalluom, one of the early leaders of HT, and the regime concluded that there was a connection. After a week of rough interrogation at the al-Malaz detention center, seven activists, including Omar, were deported. The movement was able to account for the whereabouts of only seventeen other members. The rest were presumed dead.

Because of previous business travel, Omar had a multientry visa for the United Kingdom and settled in London on January 14, 1986, where he helped organize an active branch of HT with the support of the worldwide *amir* and the branch leader in Germany.[27] He contacted the few remaining members of al-Muhajiroun left in Saudi Arabia and instructed them to continue their activities as part of HT.

In the late 1980s and early 1990s, HT membership in the United Kingdom grew dramatically, particularly among university students. The movement gave lessons, issued leaflets, held large public demonstrations, and drew increased attention from authorities. Omar established Fostoq Limited (Fostoq is his family name), a paper supply company, to raise money, recruit new members, and provide paper for publications and leaflets. Because the revenues were devoted to the movement, the company was unprofitable and forced to close. With partners, Omar later established a similar business, Fostoq Technology System. The partners ran the business, and Omar used his own profits for HT activities. It eventually closed as well.

By 1990, membership had grown to around 400, and the movement launched increasingly bold and controversial events. During the Gulf War, Omar organized rallies and demonstrations and issued his infamous statement that, according to Islamic jurisprudence, Prime Minister John Major could be assassinated if he went to Saudi Arabia. The media frenzy surrounding the "death threat" hurled him into notoriety. Omar had been granted political asylum in July 1990, just prior to the Gulf War, and the public was furious. After the uproar, he directed his solicitor to cancel his asylum status after deciding that he could only issue such statements if he was not "under the protection" of the British government (what he calls a "covenant of security"), and the government initiated the twenty-eight-day deportation process. Under his new Lebanese passport (his wife is Lebanese), he decided to leave for Pakistan, which he had always seen as a promising venue for a military coup and the establishment of an Islamic state, what he called his "dream land." The visa application, however, was rejected, and Omar's public statements and actions made it difficult to get a visa elsewhere. British law dictated that in the absence of a visa he would have to be deported to his country of origin, Syria, but that would have most certainly meant internment and possible execution because of his prior political activities there. After a yearlong appeals process, the government reinstated his asylum status.

Omar continued building HT and organized high-profile events that drew international attention. In August 1995 in Trafalgar Square, he called for Queen Elizabeth to convert to Islam and threatened that Muslims would not rest until "the black flag of Islam flies over Downing Street." His outlandish statements generated concern from the HT leaders outside the United Kingdom, who told him to discontinue overt activism. Specifically, they wanted him to cancel a controversial Khilafah Conference scheduled a few days later. He refused, and the HT leadership, with support from the worldwide *amir,* Abdul Qadeem Zalloum, stripped him of control of the U.K. branch in November 1995. Although Omar was formally removed from power, he claims that the new U.K. *amir* asked him to stay on as the informal leader and never informed the members of the change. He decided to resign from HT on January 15, 1996, because of continued pressure to discontinue public demonstrations and rallies.

Three days later he relaunched al-Muhajiroun with only three members. It adopted most of HT's ideology but made some important alterations. While both movements believe that the establishment of the caliphate (Islamic state) is a collective responsibility fulfilled through group work, HT limits its efforts to

particular countries and areas of the world where success is most likely. Al-
Muhajiroun, in contrast, believes that the responsibility is incumbent upon
Muslims regardless of locality: God commands the establishment of his rule on
earth and does not specify a particular location. As a result, Muslims in the
United Kingdom must struggle to establish an Islamic state in Britain. Otherwise, they violate the commands of God. In addition, HT in the United Kingdom tends to be insular and focuses on culturing members and supporters,
while al-Muhajiroun believes all Muslims must enjoin good and prohibit evil in
British society through public activism. There are also differences over jihad:
HT theoretically supports jihad but does not act on this support in the British
context; al-Muhajiroun argues that British Muslims must actively support jihad
by "hand, tongue, or heart."

The establishment of al-Muhajiroun sent shockwaves through the global HT
movement. Almost immediately, Omar started receiving phone calls from members throughout the world, and the new al-Muhajiroun movement quickly attracted disaffected HT followers and Omar's former students. It has since become the most visible Islamic movement in the United Kingdom, with branches
in thirty cities and towns. Although there are only 160 "formal members," 700
followers take weekly religious lessons with Omar and other movement leaders
throughout the country and often participate in protests and other activities.
Many of these followers can be considered movement activists, since they participate in most of the movement activities and take on risk and cost on behalf of
the cause. In this book, the term "activist" refers to both formal members and
committed followers who participate in risky activism. "Members" are committed activists who have actually gone through the formal membership process.
There are also an estimated 7,000 "contacts" at any given time, potential participants who are considering participation in lessons and events.[28] Most likely the
formal membership of the movement in the United Kingdom is smaller than HT
(numbers are not available), but al-Muhajiroun's public presence and impact on
public debates about Islam, national security, terrorism, and Muslim minorities
are far more profound.

The movement has established branches in other countries as well, including
Lebanon, Ireland, and Pakistan (this branch has recently claimed independence
from the overall al-Muhajiroun movement), which are connected through regular cyberspace meetings, lectures, and lessons. In 1996, it opened a branch in
the United States, but activists have maintained a low profile, particularly since
September 11. This branch does not operate its own website and seems to only
advertise innocuous religious lessons (particularly women-only lessons). It has
avoided the inflammatory antics and statements that have characterized the U.K.

branch and propelled al-Muhajiroun to notoriety. Nevertheless, the FBI has been interested in possible ties between the movement and groups supporting violence. In April 2004, the FBI arrested Mohammed Junaid Babar, a Pakistani American accused of running a financial operation to support al-Muhajiroun and terrorism.[29]

As discussed in chapter 1, participation in the movement's high-profile and contentious activism carries a number of costs and risks for activists, particularly in the post–September 11 period. There are enormous commitments of time and energy, including religious training, outreach projects, and public demonstrations. Activists sacrifice relationships with former friends, family, and the mainstream Muslim community. And they are subject to an assortment of laws related to terrorism, treason, public order, and inciting religious and racial hatred. Arrests are common, and activists are conscious that their participation risks legal consequences. Given that there are a number of less risky religious alternatives with similar beliefs within the Islamic fundamentalist community, it is puzzling that individuals would choose to participate in al-Muhajiroun and put themselves in jeopardy.

RATIONAL RADICALISM?

Why are individuals attracted to groups like al-Muhajiroun? Most studies of the causes of Islamism offer a grievance-based explanation implicitly rooted in functionalist social psychology accounts of mass behavior, which view collective action as derived from exogenous structural strains, system disequilibrium, and concomitant pathologies (alienation, anomie, atomization, normative ambiguity, etc.) that create individual frustration and motivation for "deviant" social behavior.[30] The model posits a linear causal relationship in which structural strains, such as modernization, industrialization, or an economic crisis, cause psychological discomfort, which, in turn, produces collective action. The implication is that participation is the result of "irrationality."

For many specialists on Islamic activism, the underlying impetus derives from the crises produced by failed secular modernization projects in the Middle East.[31] Rapid socioeconomic transformations and manipulated economic policies concentrated wealth among the westernized elites, state bourgeoisie, and corrupt government officials. Large swathes of the population, in contrast, faced housing shortages, insufficient municipal services and infrastructure, rising prices, declining real wages, and unemployment. The professional classes and lumpen intelligentsia, in particular, faced blocked social mobility

[handwritten margin notes: "Why? (attacked 2 groups like this) common view or why ←"]

and relative deprivation as a result of economic malaise and widespread employment preferences that emphasized *wasta* (connections) above merit.[32] The crises were compounded by the bitter Arab defeat in the 1967 war with Israel, the legacy of colonialism and cultural imperialism, and political repression.[33] According to this perspective, individuals responded by seeking to reanchor themselves through a religious idiom and Islamic movements as alternatives to the corruption and ineffectiveness of dominant social, political, and economic elites and practices.

Criticisms of the explanation (1)

This general explanation suffers from several critical shortcomings. First, although strain and discontent are ubiquitous and Islamic groups exist in most Muslim countries, the extent of their presence varies tremendously. In fact, many countries with severe stress and crisis, including Iraq (prior to the U.S.-led invasion) and Syria, exhibit low levels of Islamic movement mobilization. Grievances may provide impetus for joining a movement, but other factors, such as the level of repression or resource availability, influence decisions about participation. As Leon Trotsky once stated, "The mere existence of privations is not enough to cause an insurrection; if it were, the masses would be always in revolt."[34]

(2) Second, it cannot explain why some aggrieved individuals choose to join Islamic groups while others do not. Studies that detail the demographic profile of Islamic activists indicate that recruits frequently come from particular socioeconomic and educational backgrounds, but not *everyone* from that shared background chooses to join.[35] Even if one accepts the argument that particular constituencies have a greater propensity to participate because of a shared set of grievances and psychological stress, there must be other mechanisms that help explain why this commonality translates into activism in some cases but not others. → *2 much feeling for clear, delineated reasons?*

Third, the sociopsychological framework does not explain differential patterns of joining *among* Islamic movements. Why, for example, do individuals with similar experiences, levels of distress, and grievances opt to join different movements? Why do some people turn to violent Islamic groups while others join moderate, nonviolent organizations and movements? What explains variance across countries with similar structural strains?

Recent research on why ↓ rational actor model

Rather than viewing Islamic activists as grievance-stricken reactionaries, recent research reconceptualizes Islamic activists as strategic thinkers engaged in cost-benefit calculations. Lisa Anderson, for example, observes that "the closer the movements were to the prospects of sharing power, the more pragmatic they appeared to be."[36] Empirical studies of the Muslim Brotherhood in Jordan illustrate this point: the Brotherhood has demonstrated its willingness to sacrifice ideological ideals for political gains.[37] And movement activists make strategic decisions about organizational resources and relationships,[38] participation in political alliances,[39] responses to economic liberalization,[40] and intramovement competition.[41]

Even radical movements previously described as unflappable, ideological zealots trapped by rigid adherence to dogma are now analyzed as strategic thinkers. Shaul Mishal and Avraham Sela, for example, argue that Hamas strategically responds to changes in the political context.[42] Prior to the al-Aqsa intifada in 2000, growing popularity for the Palestinian–Israeli peace process challenged the viability of Hamas. Strict intransigence toward peace was likely to erode support from a population that sought an end to the economic and social hardships of occupation, thereby threatening the organizational survival of Hamas. In response, Hamas tactically adjusted its doctrine to accommodate the possibility of peace by framing it as a temporary pause in the jihad. Mohammed M. Hafez uses an implicit rational actor model to explain Muslim rebellions in Algeria and Egypt during the 1990s. He contends that violence erupted as a response to "an ill-fated combination of institutional exclusion, on the one hand, and on the other, reactive and indiscriminate repression that threaten[ed] the organizational resources and personal lives of Islamists."[43] To defend themselves against regime repression, the radicals went underground and formed exclusive organizations, leading to a process of encapsulation and radicalization. Stathis N. Kalyvas views the Armed Islamic Group (GIA)-led massacres that plagued Algeria in the 1990s as strategic assaults intended to deter civilian defections "in the context of a particular strategic conjuncture characterized by (a) fragmented and unstable rule over the civilian population, (b) mass civilian defections toward incumbents and (c) escalation of violence."[44] And Michael Doran conceptualizes al-Qaeda as a rational actor, arguing, "When it comes to matters related to politics and war, al Qaeda maneuvers around its dogmas with alacrity."[45] In this understanding, "Al Qaeda's long-term goals are set by its fervent devotion to a radical religious ideology, but in its short-term behavior, it is a rational political actor operating according to the dictates of realpolitik."[46] Some scholars now argue that even suicide bombings, once seen as the ultimate acts of irrationality, are part of a rational tactic capable of prompting concessions in asymmetrical warfare.[47]

Although studies that employ a rational actor model represent a clear departure from caricatures of zealots narrowly driven by grievances, they tend to focus on the group as the unit of analysis. Tactics and activism are usually viewed as rational in the sense that they are effective means for promoting group goals. But what about the individuals who actually engage in activism on behalf of the group? Why do individuals in these groups voluntarily engage in personally risky actions? Research on Islamic extremism has focused surprisingly little on the *individual* level of analysis from a rational actor perspective. A small handful of studies argue that individual suicide bombers can be understood as acting rationally if one emphasizes such things as the importance of solidarity,[48] contract enforcement between organizations and individual bombers (through the vehicle of the "living martyr," which makes it difficult to defect),[49] and the dynamics of the "club good model."[50] But there is still little sense of *how* individuals are initially drawn to the movements or *how* the willingness to sacrifice is developed. As a result, our understanding of the complex mechanisms and processes that draw rational actors toward risky activism is extremely limited.

THEORIES OF JOINING

For decades, the study of Islamic activism has languished at the margins of social science theory. With the exception of a small handful of scholars (particularly those focused on the Iranian revolution), research on Islamic activism has not fully engaged the broader theoretical and conceptual developments that have emerged from scholarship on social movements, revolutions, and contentious politics. Yet this large body of comparative research on non-Islamic forms of collective action provides myriad tools of analysis and theoretical leverage for many questions that interest students of Islamic activism, including issues of recruitment, joining, and participation.

Since the late 1990s, a number of Islamic movement specialists have begun to bridge the gap between the study of Islamic activism and social science theories of collective action.[51] The underlying premise is that Islamic activism is not sui generis. Rather than emphasizing the specificity of Islam as a system of meaning, identity, and basis of collective action, these scholars point to movement commonalities rooted in process: how contention is organized, the way ideas are framed and propagated, how grievances are collectivized, and tactics and strategies in response to exogenous shifts in opportunities and constraints. By focusing on shared mechanisms of contention rather than the uniqueness of Islam, such an understanding avails itself of a broader array of concepts, theories, and comparative empirics.

Students of social movements primarily emphasize three factors that facilitate participation in collective action. First, movements can offer selective incentives to attract participants. For proponents of resource mobilization theory and rational actor models, the primary theoretical conundrum is how movements that

14

provide collective goods still gain members and activists, since individuals benefit from the provision of the good without actually contributing to its production. Why do individuals join a movement when they can simply "free-ride" off the efforts of others? This is particularly pertinent for radical Islamic groups, which offer to produce collective goods that will benefit all Muslims (and even non-Muslims, according to activists), such as the establishment of an Islamic state, the expulsion of the United States from Muslim lands, and divine justice. Given the high costs and risks associated with participation, joining seems to defy the logic of collective action. Mancur Olsen and others point to the use of selective incentives—benefits individuals accrue only if they contribute to the collective goods.[52] Although early models emphasized material incentives, scholars later highlighted a number of nonmaterial incentives that also motivate participation, including a sense of belonging (solidary incentives) and purpose (purposive incentives).[53]

Second, social networks are often critical for recruitment. Perhaps one of the most consistent findings in research on social movements and cults is that personal relationships are the social pathways for joining.[54] Attitudinal affinity may predispose an individual to join a movement, but social ties are critical for transforming interest and availability into actual activism. As Doug McAdam argues, "An intense ideological identification with the values of the campaign acts to 'push' the individual in the direction of participation while a prior history of activism and integration into supportive networks acts as the structural 'pull' that encourages the individual to make good on his strongly held beliefs."[55]

Networks are especially important for high-risk activism, where personal relationships facilitate trust and commitment. In the case of Nicaragua Exchange, a group in the U.S.-Central American peace movement that sent brigades to Nicaragua to help with coffee harvests during the Contra war, social ties to activists distinguished program applicants who went to Nicaragua from those who dropped out.[56] A similar pattern was found in the Freedom Summer project, in which more than 1,000 volunteers traveled to Mississippi to register black voters and teach in Freedom Schools, among other things. Those with strong ties to participants were less likely to withdraw after applying to the project.[57] Although other studies of high-risk activism emphasize additional factors, such as identity construction,[58] biographical availability (the weight of other commitments),[59] and a belief in duty and personal efficacy,[60] the relevance of networks is a consistent theme.

Recent interest in the role of ideas, culture, and cognition has led still others to emphasize the importance of a third factor: "framing."[61] Frames represent interpretative schemata that provide a cognitive structure for comprehending the surrounding environment. They offer a language and cognitive tools for making sense of events and experiences by interpreting causation, evaluating situations, and offering proscriptive remedies. David Snow and his colleagues argue that "by rendering events or occurrences meaningful, frames function to organize experience and guide action, whether individual or collective."[62] However, only when there is "frame alignment" between individual and movement interpretive orientations is recruitment and mobilization possible. The movement's schemata must resonate with an individual's own interpretive framework to facilitate participation. This alignment is contingent on fidelity with cultural narratives, symbols, and identities; the reputation of the frame "articulator"; the consistency of the frame; the frame's empirical credibility; and the personal salience of the frame for potential participants.[63] In addition, movements must compete with frames proffered by governments, countermovements, and intramovement rivals.[64]

All of these certainly impact the recruitment capabilities of a movement, but do they effectively explain why individuals participate in radical Islamic activism in particular? Such movements demand total adherence and submission to the movement ideology, self-sacrifice in high-risk activism, and the abandonment of previous lifestyles (the suicide operation is only the most extreme example). They rarely offer selective incentives that offset the enormous costs and risks associated with participation; and while networks and frame alignment may expose an individual to a movement, alone they do not explain why the individual, after the initial exposure, decides to participate irrespective of costs and risks.

Social movement theory's relatively limited universe of cases and tendency to focus on progressive, left-leaning groups in Western liberal democracies leave it ill-equipped to address radical religious groups. As Doug McAdam, John McCarthy, and Mayer Zald note, "The new comparative riches available to movement scholars are based, almost exclusively, on research rooted in core liberal democratic polities . . . If our understanding of collective action dynamics has benefited as much as we contend by comparing cases across this relatively homogeneous set of polities, imagine what we are likely to learn from broadening our perspective to include those set in very different times and places."[65] David S. Meyer echoes this observation: "By ignoring movements from the other side of the spectrum, we collect less information on political realities, with a sampling of movements whose bias jeopardizes the generalizability of what we have learned."[66] Jeff Goodwin and James Jasper note that religious and prefigurative movements that put values and norms into action, in particular, are rarely studied by social movement researchers.[67] Perhaps the dynamics of joining are similar across movement types, but this is an empirical question and needs to be researched further.

A starting point in the development of a model of joining for radical Islamic groups is to identify the common process underlying the various social movement explanations. Incentives, networks, and frames are all part of a more general *process of persuasion* intended to convince individuals to participate in activism.[68] The specifics of the process, however, vary according to movement type. Selective incentives, for example, seem most effective in nonviolent, professional, institutionalized social movement organizations, where most members participate by paying dues. Given the low risk and cost of involvement, selective incentives such as magazines or information may be enough to persuade an individual with congruent political or social views to write a check. Riskier movements, in contrast, may necessitate a greater role for social networks to foster the trust and solidarity needed to encourage new participants. Rather than assuming a universal process of joining, it seems more fruitful to create models according to "movement families," where the dynamics are likely to follow similar patterns.[69] The objective is then to move from the more general process of persuasion to the particulars of movement types.

[handwritten margin note: → good: does not generalize social movement and seems to go further.]

THE IMPORTANCE OF SOCIALIZATION

Islamic activists operate in a world of educational social networks: radical and moderate fundamentalists alike devote the bulk of their time and energy to religious learning. Education is a central concern, since Muslims can only fulfill their duties to God if they fully understand Islam. From this perspective, a Muslim must master the commands of God, as outlined in the Qur'an and Sunna (traditions of the Prophet Mohammed), to ensure that he or she follows the straight path of Islam and does not deviate from the prophetic model. Religious training is also necessary to effectively and accurately propagate the message of God to others.

[handwritten margin note: → based on diffusive tradition of Islam the real base?]

The underlying objective of radical movements is to promote what Alberto Melucci calls "networks of shared meaning."[70] Like other "new social movements," radical Islamic activists promote a set of values and identities that challenge dominant cultural codes. In doing so, they seek to create a common community of "true believers" tied together through a shared interpretation of Islam typically characterized by high levels of tension with common religious understandings. Activist proselytizing thus focuses on teaching Muslims (and even non-Muslims) about the deviance of mainstream interpretations while offering the movement's own understanding as definitive. The resulting network of shared meaning is the basis of a common identity that frequently involves commands to risky activism in the name of God.

[handwritten margin note: creating a shared meaning & common identity]

For Islamic groups, socialization is thus critical for mobilizing support and activism in the face of extensive costs and risks. Carrie Wickham's rich study of the Islamic movement in Egypt, for example, shows how Islamists promoted a new ethic of civic obligation to encourage participation, even in the face of repression by the Mubarak regime. Activists operating in parallel Islamic institutions, such as private voluntary organizations, private mosques, and Islamic commercial and banking enterprises, "saw themselves as educating fellow Muslims of their rights and obligations in Islam and forging new kinds of communal solidarity based on Islamic principles of charity and self-help."[71] The movement propagated the new ethic of civic obligation through outreach efforts and socialization environments such as study circles and religious lessons, *tafsirs* (explanations of the Qur'an), and person-to-person conversations and discussions. Historically in Egypt, groups like the Muslim Brotherhood have been successful in attracting committed participation through these forums.[72]

A similar pattern is found for Islamic groups in other countries. Islamic Jihad and Hamas, for example, used extensive ideological and political indoctrination and training to push potential suicide bombers to actually carry out attacks,[73] though there is some evidence that indoctrination became less necessary during the al-Aqsa intifada.[74] The Salafi movement in Jordan and elsewhere uses personal interactions, mosque-related activities, seminars, conferences, and religious lessons to promote the Salafi *manhaj*, or methodology for arriving at religious "truth." Propagation efforts are used to draw individuals into the network through religious education, thereby expanding the network of shared meaning predicated upon the movement's particular *manhaj*. For violent jihadi Salafis in the movement, socialization and religious education include an emphasis on the necessity of violence regardless of personal risks and costs.[75]

Comparative social movement research, however, has little to say about the conscious and strategic efforts of movements to socialize audiences and encourage participation. Although research on framing addresses the formulation of public ideational outreach, it differs from socialization in that framing campaigns and appeals are generally intended to tap into already formed beliefs and values. The purpose is to create "frame alignment," not produce entirely new ideologies. From a framing perspective, the primary theoretical question is how movements transform ideological congruence into activism.

This is not to say that scholars ignore socialization. But they often acknowledge its importance without detailing the process or the resulting ideological content and its effects on patterns of joining and participation. Doug

McAdam, for example, argues that socialization through low-risk activism can help "pave the way" for riskier forms of contention: "These 'safe' forays into activism may have longer-range consequences . . . for they place the new recruit 'at risk' of being drawn into more costly forms of participation with the cyclical process of integration and resocialization."[76] Yet he provides few details about the process or content of "integration and resocialization." Gregory L. Wiltfang and McAdam emphasize the centrality of socialization factors to explain high-risk activism in the sanctuary movement concerned with Central American refugees, but they primarily focus on ideological congruence between movement beliefs and individual ideologies derived from *earlier* socialization experiences. They examine such socialization proxy measures as religious service attendance, the importance of religious beliefs in respondents' lives, and prior activism in other social movements—all factors that impact the development of beliefs prior to joining the sanctuary movement.[77] In a study of pacifist movements, Downton and Wehr also cite socialization as one of the most important variables for predicting continued commitment, but they too focus on the development of "peace supportive principles" prior to activism.[78] Although they recognize that "a number of these factors can be cultivated by peace and justice organizations to draw new people into commitment and to reinforce their activists' persistence and effectiveness,"[79] the central emphasis is still *socialization prior to participation.*[80] In social movement research, ideology is typically assumed constant after initial interactions with the movement,[81] and even analysts who emphasize its causal importance often view it as a mobilizing force and fail to examine the process by which individuals come to internalize the ideology in the first place as a result of movement activities.[82]

There are three central questions within the empirical context of radical Islamic activism that can help address this lacuna. First, how are individuals drawn to socialization environments where movements can expose them to religious education in the first place? This is a pertinent question, given that most Muslims reject radicals as part of the "lunatic fringe." In addition, the radical nature of such movements typically circumscribes opportunities for ideological outreach. Second, how are individuals persuaded to accept the ideology of the movement as their own worldview? And third, how does socialization overcome the free rider dilemma? If radicals are indeed rational actors, as the preponderance of contemporary research indicates, why engage in behavior that on the surface seems to violate the norm of self-interest? What is it about the content of the ideological and religious education that convinces individuals that high-risk activism in the name of the cause is worth it?

[Handwritten margin notes: "ideology & social movement research"; "3 q. that can address mu!"; "does it?"; "afterlife."]

COGNITIVE OPENINGS AND RELIGIOUS SEEKING

The starting point in addressing these questions is to identify the mechanisms and processes that initially attract individuals to a group like al-Muhajiroun. Given the extreme views of radical religious groups, a basic prerequisite for joining is an individual's willingness to expose himself or herself to the movement message. Prior socialization experiences heavily influence *a priori* views of radical groups and thus the likelihood of conscious exposure. Most individuals will reject the movement outright as "extreme," "militant," or "irrational," especially if the movement has received negative coverage in the media.

However, a crisis can produce a "cognitive opening" that shakes certainty in previously accepted beliefs and renders an individual more receptive to the possibility of alternative views and perspectives. In many cases, individuals can address and resolve a crisis or psychological distress through their current belief systems. But where these seem inadequate, individuals may be open to other views.

The specific crisis that prompts a cognitive opening varies across individuals, but there are several common types found in the literature on Islamic movements, which can be categorized as economic (losing a job, blocked mobility), social or cultural (sense of cultural weakness, racism, humiliation), and political (repression, torture, political discrimination). To this list I would add "personal," since cognitive openings can be produced by idiosyncratic experiences, such as a death in the family or victimization by crime.

In addition, movements themselves can foster a cognitive opening through outreach. Activists can use current social networks or make new acquaintances to germinate a sense of crisis among contacts in discussions and subtle interactions. Islamic activists, for example, frequently initiate innocuous discussions about Islam with congregates at the mosque in an effort to develop new relationships and instill a sense of urgency about the need to address pressing concerns. In other instances, they engage in more overt forms of activism to raise Muslim consciousness about duties to God and the plight of coreligionists. This includes appeals to Muslim solidarity by "educating" Muslims about crises in places like the Palestinian territories, Kashmir, and Bosnia. Movements engage in consciousness-raising and public campaigns to increase interest in movement issues and convince audiences that change is possible, thereby overcoming the fundamental attribution error through what Doug McAdam calls "cognitive liberation."[83] Parallels are found in the liberation theology movement in Latin America, where church activists were "concerned with the deliberate development, diffusion, and institutionalization of a change in consciousness" to empower the poor.[84]

One common movement tactic for fostering a cognitive opening is the use of "moral shock." Animal rights and anti-nuclear energy movements, for example, have made rhetorical appeals to the moral sensibilities of predisposed audiences already primed for outrage when prompted by particular events or situations.[85] Although most movement activists are recruited through social networks, moral shocks can inspire strangers to seek out movements and/or more information about the cause, thus fostering the participation of previously unconnected, concerned citizens with similar ideologies.

The dynamics of moral shock for Islamic activism, however, differ from those of nonreligious social movements.[86] In many cases, as James M. Jasper and Jane Poulsen argue, "For strangers to join a movement, they must already have opinions and feelings of their own: They already detest abortion or care deeply about animals. They are recruited to a group or movement, not converted to a belief system."[87] Radical religious groups, in contrast, seek to prompt religious ideological conversion. The moral shock is used to spark interest, prompt further questions, and initiate contact with potential joiners. The point is to facilitate a cognitive opening that renders an individual willing to listen.

Where an individual's identity is in part tied to religion or he or she desires religious meaning, a cognitive opening may lead to "religious seeking"—a process in which an individual searches "for some satisfactory system of religious meaning to interpret and resolve his discontent."[88] Although more research is needed, it seems reasonable to argue that the greater the role of Islam in an individual's identity, the greater the likelihood he or she will respond to the opening through religious seeking. This may not always be the case (e.g., friends may convince an individual to look more closely at religion as a possible remedy irrespective of prior beliefs), but prior socialization and sense of self possibly influence the consequences of an opening.

Seeking is most likely where an individual's religious views and/or established religious institutions seem inadequate in addressing concerns.[89] In the case of Islamic activism, eventual joiners may, for example, question the ability of established religious institutions to offer solutions to crises since they are generally circumscribed by governments, particularly in the Muslim world where religious institutions and figures have been incorporated into the state.[90] A perceived lack of autonomy has led many Muslims to question whether religious edicts and interpretations proffered by religious elites, such as the clerical caste in Saudi Arabia or the scholars of al-Azhar University in Cairo, represent Islam or some other interests aligned with incumbent regimes. Islamic movements offer themselves as autonomous interpreters capable of assessing the divine sources of Islam without bias. For those seeking "true" Islam, this is an attractive argument.

joining through social contacts

The typical pattern is not one of an isolated individual independently searching for religious answers. As social movement theory and studies of cults and conversion would predict, social networks are critical during religious seeking.[91] Whether prompted by an independent cognitive opening or one inspired by movement outreach, seekers do not typically seek religious meaning in a vacuum. They turn to friends and family for direction and possible sources of religious learning. If social contacts are in a movement, the seeker is likely to be drawn to that movement's activities since social ties are trusted pathways of information.[92] Activists themselves usually begin by targeting people they know, thus increasing the importance of social pathways in both directions: seekers reach out to activist friends and activist friends reach out to (and even prompt) seekers. As Wickham observes for Egyptian Islamists: "Rather than approach a stranger, such activists explained, one begins by propagating the *da'wa* [propagating religious beliefs] among relatives, neighbors and peers. Tapping into prior relationships enables the *da'i* [propagator] to build on a foundation of familiarity and trust, raising the prospects that his or her message will be well received. Graduates involved in the Islamic movement typically mentioned that they were introduced to the movement by a brother, cousin, neighbor, or friend."[93]

Activists can use these relationships to foster "guided religious seeking" and lead seekers to movement events, especially where the cognitive opening is prompted by movement outreach. In some cases, this may directly incorporate an individual into movement activities and socialization. In other instances, a movement activist may help a potential joiner "shop around" and sample different religious products while subtly guiding him or her toward the conclusion that the movement is the most reasonable and appealing choice. The latter strategy is particularly effective since individuals feel empowered in making informed decisions based upon comparisons, all the while subtly influenced so that participation becomes more likely.

these activi- ties seem being tool evil & are described quite blandly

maybe NN because it is into?

At least in the case of Islamic movements, seekers frequently "seek" with friends who are also interested in religious learning. This increases the social dimensions of the activism and the prospects for solidarity. It also means that groups of friends often participate and join together. In Jordan, for example, entire groups of friends eventually became Salafis because they were exposed to the same lessons, discussions, and thoughts. Many continued their close friendships after becoming part of the movement, intertwining religious and friendship networks to produce high levels of intragroup trust.[94] A similar pattern has been found for al-Qaeda.[95]

Activists, however, can also develop new personal ties with strangers as a tactic for recruitment. Mormon recruitment, for example, is primarily through

strangers

outreach efforts to non-Mormons and the formation of new personal relationships. A thirteen-step instructional guide published in 1974 emphasizes the importance of developing new social relationships and trust prior to discussing religion. The first four steps, in fact, revolve around getting to know people and building trust: be helpful, be good neighbors, listen to the concerns of others. The activist's religious identity is not revealed until step five and only then in a rudimentary fashion that avoids church questions and instead centers on generic religious discussions and values.[96] A similar pattern was found for the Moonies. Members would "pick up" people in public places and invite them to dinners and events while minimizing religious content. These dinners and events were then used to develop affective bonds to pull individuals into the network, where they could be encapsulated and converted into committed activists.[97] In a similar fashion, some Islamic activists, particularly jihadis, hide their movement identity until after a personal relationship is developed.[98]

For Islamic activists, an activist *da'wa* (propagation) identity mandates proselytizing to strangers and familiars alike, and this helps create new relationships. In Yemen, for example, female activists from Hizb al-Islah and the Islah Charitable Society participate in *nadwas* (Qur'anic study groups) that are not affiliated with the Islamic movement. At these meetings, they gain access to new audiences and create new social ties. In many instances, these ties prompt activism without formal membership in a social movement organization (SMO): new participants seek to reproduce and expand the network of shared meaning as part of an activist identity based on Islamic movement ideological precepts.[99] While established relationships may still represent the predominant pathway for joining, the formation of new social ties is common for Islamic movements.

To take advantage of these established and new relationships, Islamic activists create institutional networks that offer a range of activities intended to tap into the concerns of religious seekers. As resource mobilization theory argues, while grievances are ubiquitous, mobilization is not; social movements need resources and mobilizing structures to translate individual concerns into collective action.[100] For Islamic activists, these include charities and cultural societies,[101] professional associations,[102] mosques, political parties,[103] religious lessons and study circles, and a number of informal institutions.[104] These create organizational points of interaction between seekers and the movement, locales to which activists can bring seekers and introduce them to a particular ideology. Without this societal presence, whether formal or informal, there is very little to offer a seeker, at least in terms of concrete activities.

Chapter 2 details the experiences of those who are initially drawn to al-Muhajiroun. Some eventual joiners experienced an identity crisis that opened them to new perspectives about religion. Encounters with racism as well as "Islamophobia" prompted these individuals to think about how they fit into British society and the role of Islam for Muslim minorities in the United Kingdom. Others experienced cognitive openings as a result of movement outreach: activists attempt to facilitate openings through discussions with familiars and strangers alike. They challenge the beliefs of friends and family and try to generate a sense of crisis and urgency about the plight of Muslims in the United Kingdom and abroad. Activists also develop new social relationships with strangers, particularly in the mosque, and over time attempt to foster cognitive openings.

summary

Not everyone who experiences a cognitive opening is drawn to al-Muhajiroun; in fact, most never experiment with radical Islam. There is a subset, however, that is more likely to do so. Eventual joiners who responded to the opening through religious seeking found mainstream religious institutions and figures wanting. For these individuals, local imams and mosques failed to provide guidance for the specific concerns of British Muslims. As a result, they were more amenable to experimentation outside the mainstream. For disaffected seekers with social ties to al-Muhajiroun through personal relationships with activists, seeking through the movement became likely. Activists serve as guides for others in their network and direct seekers toward movement activities. These activities are strategically designed to address the concerns of seekers, thereby filling the gap left by mainstream Islam. The movement has developed a deep societal presence through an assortment of organizations to enhance the prospects that seekers will be drawn to activities that interest them.

REPUTATION AND SACRED AUTHORITY

A willingness to listen and contemplate alternative ways of viewing the world, however, does not inexorably lead to participation. These movements are voluntary in nature and, as a result, cannot rely on direct coercion to indoctrinate potential participants. In studies of cults and religious conversion, early "brainwashing" theses that invoke images of powerful coercive techniques and passive objects of indoctrination have been replaced by contemporary reconceptualizations of active agents engaged in a journey of self-transformation.[105] As Laurence R. Iannaccone argues, "Conversion includes introspection as well as interaction. People question, weigh, and evaluate their situations and options."[106] The

as compared 2

process of persuasion is characterized by debate and discussion, an exchange of

'Brainwashing' → popular in mainstream culture.

↳ maybe better for Islamophobia? removes agency?

ideas in which movement activists try to convince seekers that the movement ideology represents the "truth" and provides logical solutions to pressing concerns.

For most Muslims, however, determining the validity of a particular religious interpretation is a difficult task, since there is no central political or theological authority capable of adjudicating competing perspectives and rendering definitive decisions regarding "true" Islam. As Aziz al-Azmeh argues, "There are as many Islams as there are situations that sustain them."[107] As a result, Islamic groups like al-Muhajiroun operate in a competitive marketplace of ideas characterized by alternative religious interpretations.

The vast majority of Muslims are not trained in the complexities of *fiqh* (Islamic jurisprudence) or other Islamic sciences and are therefore ill equipped to weigh the considerable religious evidence marshaled to defend competing religious interpretations. From the perspective of the nonexpert, any number of arguments or opinions might seem reasonable and convincing. How then does a movement persuade a potential joiner that its interpretation of Islam is credible and worth following?

Within this context of interpretive pluralism, Muslims often rely on the reputation of religious authorities as a heuristic device to ascertain the authenticity and validity of a religious ruling, something seen as critical for social movement frame alignment. Religious authorities can include community leaders, mosque imams, and self-taught charismatic leaders, or trained Islamic scholars—anyone perceived as knowledgeable about Islam.[108]

Because of their training, Islamic scholars, in particular, play a critical role as intermediaries between the sacred texts and everyday religious rituals and practices. As "cultural brokers," scholars interpret religious sources in an effort to apply the immutability of divine law to rapidly changing conditions.[109] They are seen as the inheritors of the prophetic mission, intellectually equipped to pass on the message of God and guide Muslims to the straight path of Islam. Scholars provide religious lessons, sermons, books, and other outlets for religious learning. They serve as community resources and act as mediators for those seeking to properly follow Islam. While offering religious guidance, scholars are also supposed to represent models of the "good Muslim," shining examples to be emulated by others.

Given the role of scholars as sources of religious understanding and interpretation, their reputation is critical in persuasion: Muslims need to trust the credibility of the interpreter to accept the reliability of the interpretation. There is no formal instrument to force Muslims to follow one religious perspective rather than others, and whether a particular fatwa has influence is to a large extent determined by whether Muslims accept the authority of the individual issuing it. Muslims will voluntarily follow a fatwa only if they respect and trust the responsible scholar(s). The reputation of a scholar, however, is not determined by objective criteria; the term "scholar" itself (*alim*, pl. *ulama*) represents subjectively derived community recognition about an individual's capacity to render informed, accurate religious interpretations. For the seeker, then, evaluations of reputation are influenced not only by perceptions about knowledge but also other characteristics, like charisma.

Because of the importance of reputation in movement persuasion, Islamic activists frequently devote resources and energies to establish their "sacred authority"—the right to interpret Islam and religious symbols on behalf of the Muslim community.[110] This is particularly the case for radicals, who are generally seen as part of the interpretive fringe. For example, in al-Qaeda's bitter framing contest with Islamic scholars representing the Saudi religious establishment, the movement's public discourse is replete with attempts to undermine the reputation of scholars who disagree with its radical religious interpretation. In its efforts to assert its right to sacred authority, al-Qaeda portrays scholars who support its jihad as logical, religious experts of good repute while characterizing opposing clerical intellectuals as emotional, corrupt, naive, and ill informed about politics.[111] To persuade Muslims to accept a radical religious interpretation and thus spread radical networks of shared meaning, groups like al-Qaeda and al-Muhajiroun must convince audiences that they have the authority to issue and promote interpretations in the first place. Just as importantly, they must demonstrate that the quality of their scholars means that the movement interpretation is superior to competing alternatives.

Chapter 3 emphasizes the importance of Omar Bakri Mohammed's reputation for seekers who eventually became activists. Omar spoke to their concerns and seemed extremely knowledgeable. He was willing to interact and debate with seekers and always delved into the religious evidence from the Qur'an and Sunna to support his arguments, something most local imams never do. This only added to perceptions about the depth of his knowledge. Positive evaluations of Omar as a scholar were reinforced by his character and personality: he seems self-sacrificial and autonomous from external influences. And he is a likeable character, something that enhances message receptivity.

The importance of reputation for movement recruitment is exemplified by the ways in which the movement tries to manage its public persona. In particular, while it uses the media to provoke coverage, it is vulnerable to the influence of media portrayals on public perceptions about the movement, which tend to be negative. As a result, it exerts resources and energies battling media reports to protect its overall reputation. The objective is to establish the movement's reputation and sacred authority so that religious seekers are more likely to attend its religious study circles and lessons, where they can be exposed to the process of movement socialization.   *Summary* ↑

CULTURING AND COMMITMENT

Most rational actor models assume a set of exogenously given preferences, but this is problematic for understanding why individuals progress to high-risk radical Islamic activism, since it seemingly violates the core tenet of self-interest. Viewing these behaviors as the rational pursuit of self-interest only becomes meaningful if we understand the process that constructs individual interests and assessments of strategies. Interests are not static; they can change as the result of things such as political and social learning, persuasion, changes in status, and social mobility.[112]

Of particular relevance for the study of social movements is the way in which movements can use socialization to alter beliefs and perceptions of self-interest. In an essay on terrorism, Martha Crenshaw recognizes this possibility in passing: "Leaders and their organization help shape people's private preferences, through ideological indoctrination, organized group actions to impress and inspire, persuasive exhortations to change one's beliefs, and charismatic appeals."[113] Activists can use what Myra Marx Ferree and Frederick D. Miller term a "conversion strategy" in which they transmit information to persuade audiences and change attitudes, preferences, and values.[114] They can change interests through consciousness-raising and other outreach activities.[115] And they can use socialization to promote the kind of ideological congruence that is often assumed by social movement theorists.

The *da'wa* ideological outreach project of moderate Islamists in Egypt detailed by Wickham was intended to achieve precisely this kind of change—a shift in preferences from narrow self-interest to a belief in civic obligations and the desirability of working for the public good. In fact, the ascent of religion in public life was expected to "resolve society's problems by encouraging a shift from self-interested behavior toward greater concern for the public good."[116] Although a number of selective incentives initially attracted interest (health care, employment, marriage partners, etc.), Wickham sees a critical shift from behavior motivated by self-interest to norm-guided action rooted in a learning process, educational settings, and socialization.

The distinction between self-interest and civic mindedness, however, may be a false dichotomy for fundamentalist movements. Through a variety of micromobilization contexts, especially religious lessons, Islamic activists try to convince audiences and potential adherents that their primary concern should be salvation in the hereafter. Lessons explain the consequences of failing to uphold God's divine law and the benefits of proper religious beliefs and practices. Rather than seeing their own interest as material or political, individuals come to see their dominant self-interest in "spiritual terms"—saving their souls on Judgment Day. It is not simply that activists are socialized to believe in the inherent goodness of civic virtue; instead, they are socialized to believe that social activism and civic obligations are necessary vehicles to ensure salvation. Socialization *redefines* self-interest, and helping produce the collective good is a means, not an end, toward fulfilling individual spiritual goals.

Some of Wickham's own evidence indicates that Egyptian activists may have been driven by spiritual self-interest. Take the argument presented in a pamphlet from the Islamist movement about duties to God:

> He who wants to proceed on this path must prepare himself to have much patience and great stamina and realize that he may die without seeing the victory of God . . . He should know that the path is full of hardship and tears, that he may be imprisoned or fired from his work or even tortured or killed. All that may be done to him to force him to leave the path, and if he caves in, he will lose both in this world and the world to come; but if he continues on the path to the end, the outcome will be in paradise, God willing.
>
> Imagine each one of us himself in the hands of God, when God holds him accountable and asks him what he did to raise his word and achieve his reign and free the conquered land of the Muslims. Will he say— 'Oh Lord, I was not convinced that work on behalf of such goals was an individual obligation for me?' Or will he say: 'Oh Lord, I didn't have the time to work for your sake?' Or will he say, 'Oh Lord, I was a coward and afraid because I know that work on your behalf is arduous and full of thorns?' I warn myself and I warn you that if we don't work for Islam, we must expect the reckoning of God and his Prophet, and that is in this life; in the world to come, the situation is even more terrible, and the punishment even more severe.[117]

Activists engage in actions for the collective good because that is what is necessary to protect spiritual self-interest. In this sense, even seemingly altruistic behavior can be understood as the rational pursuit of self-interest. A study of Mother Teresa, for example, argues that:

While empathetic and self-sacrificial, Mother Teresa's charity . . . was not altruistic, that is, motivated strictly by the desire to benefit the recipient without expectation of external reward. 'Works of love,' she laid down, 'are always a means of becoming closer to God' . . . Closeness to God, not the alleviation of human pain itself, was the preferred religious product. Indeed in Mother Teresa's assessment, poverty, suffering, and death were positive occasions of divine contact and imitation.[118]

This is not to argue that nonspiritual incentives are irrelevant. Islamic groups in Egypt, for example, provide material incentives to attract supporters, including jobs, health services, education, day care, and financial support.[119] In Jordan, the Muslim Brotherhood's charity network provides patronage employment and selective access to goods and services.[120] Both Hamas and Hizballah provide social services and basic goods and services to communities and supporters. And there is evidence that at least some (though most likely a small minority) of those who joined the Armed Islamic Group in Algeria did so to obtain the economic benefits of insurgency produced by illicit activities like smuggling.[121] But socialization and religious beliefs can also motivate risky radicalism by prioritizing spiritual self-interest, irrespective of risks and costs.

While virtually all fundamentalist movements emphasize salvation, they differ over *how believers are supposed to pursue this self-interest.* Some emphasize propagation, others engage the political system, and the more radical elements view violence as necessary to fulfill divine obligations. A movement proffers its ideology as a strategy to pursue spiritual self-interest—what Muslims must do to ensure that they follow the word of God and reach Paradise. It also outlines the costs for disobedience to God and errant religious beliefs and practices. In short, the ideology provides a heuristic device for those interested in the hereafter. Socialization, or what activists term *tarbiya* ("culturing" Muslims in proper Islamic beliefs and practices), is intended to inculcate both interest in salvation as well as ideologically sanctioned strategies for reaching Paradise.

In the case of radical Islamic groups, audiences are "cultured" to believe that true believers must engage in (or at least support) violence because this kind of activism is a divine order: particular forms of activism are proscribed as fulfilling God's will. Just as importantly, the ideology posits things like arrest and death as benefits rather than risks, glorified sources of honor and pride.[122] Ideology thus shapes understandings of both ends and means.[123]

Culturing is used to instill a particular ideological understanding of religion that overcomes the free rider dilemma and inspires activists to radicalism, irrespective of costs and risks. Because God ordains radicalism (including violence), a failure to act is akin to violating the norm of self-interest since it jeopardizes salvation. Donald

Riddle's classic study of Christian martyrs in the Roman Empire is instructive in this regard. Authorities threatened physical punishment and even death if suspected Christians "confessed" their beliefs. Denial was certainly the easy way out and meant release. Yet numerous suspects chose to confess regardless of the immediate punishments. This act of sacrifice can still be seen as the behavior of a rational actor if one understands the preference for salvation: "It is . . . clear that the willingness to undergo punishment for the crime of being a Christian was largely induced by the fear of the consequences of failing to confess. The threat of punishment in the afterworld was urged . . . with the rewards which were at the same time promised."[124] Martyrs were socialized to emphasize divine costs and benefits, enhancing the likelihood that they would endure the consequences of the confession. Therefore, content of "culturing" matters.

fur-inkrur in the alterure As chapter 4 explains, al-Muhajiroun uses religious lessons and associated activities to "culture" students about proper Islam. As the self-described vanguard of the ideological struggle against deviant beliefs like secularism and moderate Islam, it emphasizes a strict, literalist religious interpretation that revolves around the concept of *tawhid*—the oneness of God. Lessons and circles argue that the basis of Islam is the belief that only God can be worshiped and that He must be worshiped in His entirety—Muslims cannot pick and choose to follow commands piecemeal; otherwise, they are not really Muslims. For those who are concerned about spiritual salvation, the movement ideology provides a template for adhering to *tawhid* and ensuring entrance to Paradise. Students are taught that the Prophet used three divinely mandated methods to establish the rule of God on earth and hold fast to *tawhid*. He cultured society about Islam, commanded good and forbade evil through contentious activism, and worked to establish the Islamic state through a military coup. These methods were followed, regardless of the personal consequences. Those who follow this prophetic model are the "real Salafis" (followers of the Prophet and his companions) and will be rewarded in the hereafter. All others are deviant. Those who adopt these ideological tenets become "intellectually affiliated" with the movement. For the intellectually affiliated, the ideological template is rooted in the self-interest of rational actors concerned about spiritual destiny, and it is used to overcome the free rider dilemma and encourage risky activism.

A NOTE ON METHODS

Conducting research on radical Islamic groups is inherently difficult. The primary obstacle is access, as reflected by the paucity of studies based on ethnographic fieldwork. Activists are usually suspicious of outsiders. This suspicion has become more accentuated since September 11 and the "war on terror." In the Middle East, researchers also face additional obstacles from security agencies, which have, in the past, interrogated and expelled academics working on sensitive topics like radical Islam.

Research in the West, of course, is much easier than in majority Muslim countries. There are not the same security restrictions or personal safety concerns. In addition, activists often relish the political freedoms and civil liberties of liberal democracies and are more willing to speak with researchers since they feel "protected" by the very systems they despise. Since countries like the United Kingdom host a panoply of Islamic fundamentalist movements, they serve as representative microcosms of the broader, global Islamic fundamentalist community and offer rich laboratories for exploring the mechanisms and processes of joining and activism. This is not to say that researchers can approach such movements unfettered by obstacles; suspicion and secrecy still hinder access. But there is greater opportunity.

I made initial contact with al-Muhajiroun through Mohammed al-Masari, the leader of the Committee for the Defense of Legitimate Rights (CDLR), a Saudi dissident movement. Masari is a friend and fundamentalist ally of Omar Bakri Mohammed, and his personal referral led to an initial interview with Omar. This first meeting was best characterized as an opportunity for Omar to assess my expertise in Islam and possible intentions. After a detailed conversation about Islamic law and jihad, he seemed satisfied and opened access to the movement.

During trips to the United Kingdom in March, June, and December 2002, I was allowed to conduct unfettered interviews with activists. Each activist, of course, could refuse an interview, but this never occurred (some were more hesitant than others). The real difficulty was getting activists to slow down and take the time for interviews amid the hurly-burly of activities and events. As a result, while some of the interviews were structured, others were conducted in a less organized fashion at any available opportunity: on buses, on the move (literally while walking around demonstrations and events), in cars, and before and after events when activists milled around. While I tried to ask similar questions, it was often difficult to systematically go through a checklist without breaking the flow of conversation and making it seem as though I was simply "pumping" respondents for information. Instead, I typically let the conversations naturally evolve, all the while trying to ask questions related to the project in a way that fit into each specific interview or conversation. This put activists at ease and, I believe, resulted in greater amounts of information. Because of the nature of the interview process, descriptive statistics of responses are not possible.

Thirty of these conversations were long enough to constitute interviews, ranging between twenty minutes and three hours. Certain key leaders were chosen for their broad knowledge of the movement, including Omar Bakri Mohammed, Anjem Choudary (the U.K. branch leader), and several local leaders. Rank-and-file activists were randomly approached at a wide range of movement events. Many of these interviews were tape-recorded. I also interacted with about one hundred other activists and movement "supporters." Although the pool of activists is hardly a probability sample, an ethnographic approach with small groups of respondents provides unique insights into radical Islamic groups that are virtually impossible to generate through other methods, especially given access difficulties.

In addition to the interviews, I attended an assortment of activities. These included public events, like propagation tables, demonstrations, open religious lessons, and community outreach programs. Omar Bakri permitted me to attend movement-only lessons as well, which provided a glimpse into the more specialized training of activists.

The interviews and participant observation were supplemented with hundreds of movement documents (thousands of pages in total), including protest notices, leaflets, training manuals, press releases, books, and articles. I also collected some internal movement materials, including the movement bylaws, which outline details about member responsibilities and disciplinary measures. Nearly one hundred hours of recorded lessons were collected as well, though for the most part they duplicate material already found in written documents.

To provide a control group, it would have been ideal to identify and interview individuals who defected from movement activities to help explain patterns of *nonjoining* and *nonparticipation*. This would include individuals who experienced a cognitive opening but did not engage in religious seeking; individuals who engaged in religious seeking but did not experiment with al-Muhajiroun; individuals who attended al-Muhajiroun lessons but decided against joining; and individuals who became al-Muhajiroun activists but later quit the movement. The major difficulty was locating such people. Movement activists would not identify individuals who had defected, and individuals who had defected did not identify themselves.

I did, however, collect other sources of data to provide some insights. First, I distributed a small survey to Muslims in London to provide some comparative data. Surveys of this nature are extremely sensitive, especially post–September 11. Muslims are concerned about who is conducting the survey as well as how the data will be used and whether it will adversely impact the community. As a result, many are hesitant to fill out surveys. In part to address this, I hired a research assistant from the Muslim College of London. As a Muslim from the United Kingdom, she could offer reassurances about the academic nature of the survey that seem more credible than if they came from an American researcher who is not Muslim. This did seem to help for some respondents, but the research assistant was still met with suspicion about hidden motives behind the survey. She even received threatening e-mails.

Another difficulty in surveying Muslims is locating the sample population.[125] Muslims constitute only 2.7 percent of the entire British population; although there is some geographic concentration, it is difficult to conduct random samples with any efficiency (e.g., through randomly generated telephone numbers). As a result, many polls use snowballing, in which researchers begin with a small group of Muslims and expand the sample by asking these respondents for contact information for additional interviews. This, of course, raises methodological problems because respondents will likely give contact information for friends and family, who may hold similar attitudes.

In the survey conducted for this study, I used both convenience sampling and the distribution of surveys at Muslim events and activities. In the first procedure, my research assistant contacted friends for the survey. In the second, she attended a number of activities and locales frequented by Muslims in London. These included a *halal* (religiously permitted) café, a demonstration, Islamic lectures, and an end of the year gathering of university Muslims. Surveys were randomly distributed to Muslim participants during and after functions. Some filled out the survey on the spot; others mailed it to the research assistant. The response rate was 21 percent (73 of 350). The low rate of response reflects the difficulties of getting responses for a sensitive survey that addresses Muslims in the post–September 11 period as well as the length of the survey (there were forty-seven questions, and my research assistant indicated that many people declined to respond because of the length). A hyperlink to a web version of the survey was also sent to a number of British Muslim websites and chat rooms. Thirty-one responded through the web. Combining all sources, the total sample size is 104.

The process of distribution means this is not a random probability sample and that generalizability is therefore limited. The data do offer some measure of control and comparability, but conclusions should be cautious and only descriptive statistics are used. Where possible, I also try to use the survey results in conjunction with polls conducted by MORI and other professional survey groups in the United Kingdom.

Second, I came across the former spokesperson for al-Muhajiroun in the United States, Kamran Bokhari, through sheer serendipity, and he offered an insider's perspective on why individuals leave the movement (he severed ties with the movement in 1998).[126] As a *former* activist, he was more willing to address the internal politics of the movement than current participants. Through him, I also acquired an e-mail written by the former head of the women's division of the movement, who left around 2001. In the e-mail, she outlines some of the major precipitants that led her to defect.

Third, Omar Bakri himself offered some explanation, which was partially corroborated by other Islamic activists outside al-Muhajiroun. This, of course, has to be taken with measured skepticism, but it seems consistent with other sources of data. Although it is limited, I try to use this data where appropriate to offer some controls.

The focus on a single case rather than direct comparative analysis has all the advantages and disadvantages of single-case research. On the one hand, it provides an opportunity for detail, exploratory research, and the generation of new theoretical insights. This is particularly important since access to such groups is sensitive and limited. On the other hand, a single case study limits the ability to generalize to other cases. Without more research, it is difficult to determine how well a model or theory travels beyond the particular empirical case.

The goals of this book, however, are more modest than sweeping generalizability. It seeks to offer new insights into processes and mechanisms of participation by explicitly engaging broader bodies of comparative research and theory related to social movements. Rather than functioning merely as the outcome of a single case, the study builds on (and hopefully contributes to) research on social movements as well as other Islamic groups. It also seeks to fill a gap in research by addressing radical Islamic groups operating in Western liberal democracies. In addition, although we know quite a bit about radical groups in the Muslim world, there is surprisingly little information about the specific *dynamics* that prompt individuals to participate. Though empirically situated in a non-Muslim country, this study offers some theoretical and conceptual tools of analysis that can help address participation in radical Islamic groups more globally. The book is thus offered as a starting point for theoretically informed research on radical Islam.

NOTES

1. This account is based on a number of newspaper sources, including the *New York Times*, the Associated Press, the *Guardian* (London), and the *Independent* (London).

2. BBC, May 1, 2003.

3. "British Muslims Take Path to Jihad," *Guardian*, December 29, 2000.

4. "Profile: Omar Saeed Sheikh," BBC, July 16, 2002.

5. "Camp X-Ray Britons Named," BBC, January 27, 2002.

6. *Observer*, November 23, 2003.

7. BBC, April 6, 2004.

8. See "Militant Groups in the UK," *Guardian*, June 19, 2002; Reuvan Paz, "Middle East Islamism in the European Arena," *Middle East Review of International Affairs*, September 2002, 67–76; *Christian Science Monitor*, August 5, 2002; CNN.com, "UK Muslims Urged to Fight Terror," March 31, 2004.

9. D. E. Kaplan, "Made in the USA," *U.S. News & World Report*, June 10, 2002.

10. For the connection between al-Qaeda and both the GIA and GSPC, see Quintan Wiktorowicz, "The GIA and GSPC in Algeria," in Magnus Ranstorp, ed., *In the Service of al-Qaeda: Radical Islamic Movements* (forthcoming).

11. *New York Times*, May 26, 2004.

12. Klaus Grünewald, "Defending Germany's Constitution," *Middle East Quarterly*, March 1995.

13. BBC, September 19, 2002; May 27, 2004.

14. "US Muslims Suffer Backlash," BBC, November 19, 2002. Note that most cases go unreported, and Muslim organizations indicate that the number of incidents is much higher.

15. Christopher Allen and Jørgen S. Nielsen, *Summary Report on Islamophobia in the EU after 11 September 2001* (Vienna: European Monitoring Centre on Racism and Xenophobia, May 2002).

16. See Yvonne Yazbeck Haddad and I. Qurqmaz, "Muslims in the West: A Select Bibliography," *Islam and Christian Muslim Relations* 11, no. 1 (2000): 5–49. More recent publications include Shireen T. Hunter and Huma Malik, eds., *Islam in Europe and the United States: A Comparative Perspective* (Washington, D.C.: Center for Strategic and International Studies, 2002); Shireen T. Hunter, ed., *Islam, Europe's Second Religion: The New Social, Cultural, and Political Landscape* (Westport, Conn.: Praeger, 2002); Yvonne Yazbeck Haddad and Jane I. Smith, eds., *Muslim Minorities in the West: Visible and Invisible* (Walnut Creek, Calif.: AltaMira, 2002); Nezar AlSayyad and Manuel Castells, eds., *Muslim Europe or Euro-Islam: Politics, Culture, and Citizenship in the Age of Globalization* (Lanham, Md.: Lexington, 2002); Iftikhar H. Malik, *Islam and Modernity: Muslims in Europe and the United States* (London: Pluto, 2004).

17. Anonymous [Rita Katz], *Terrorist Hunter* (New York: HarperCollins, 2003); Steven Emerson, *American Jihad: The Terrorists Living among Us* (New York: Free Press, 2003); and Daniel Pipes, *Militant Islam Reaches America* (New York: Norton, 2003).

18. Gilles Kepel, *Muslim Extremism in Egypt: The Prophet and the Pharaoh* (Berkeley: University of California Press, 1993); Lars Pedersen, *Newer Islamic Movements in Western Europe* (Brookfield: Ashgate, 1999).

19. Suha Taji-Farouki, *A Fundamental Quest: Hizb al-Tahrir and the Search for the Islamic Caliphate* (London: Grey Seal, 1996).

20. Peter Mandaville, *Transnational Muslim Politics: Reimagining the Umma*, 2d ed. (London: Routledge, 2004); Olivier Roy, *Globalised Islam: The Search for a New Ummah* (London: Hurst, 2004).

21. For the movement's response to the linkage, see al-Muhajiroun press release, "The Truth about Omar, Asif and Al-Muhajiroun," May 3, 2003.

22. *Telegraph*, May 2, 2003.

23. *Observer*, October 28, 2001; Associated Press, January 7, 2002; Agence France Presse, December 4, 2002.

24. Al-Muhajiroun, "Fight the Invaders vs. Stop the War," press release, March 20, 2003.

25. These statements were widely covered in the press and confirmed in my interviews with Omar Bakri in 2002.

26. This history is based on interviews with Omar in June and December 2002. Some additional details are provided by Maham Abedin, "Al-Muhajiroun in the UK: An Interview with Sheikh Omar Bakri Mohammed," *Terrorism Monitor*, March 23, 2004, 1–13.

27. For more details about the formation of HT in the U.K., see Taji-Farouki, *Fundamental Quest*.

28. Omar Bakri Mohammed, interview by author, London, December 2002.

29. http://www.cnn.com/2004/LAW/06/16/fbi.ny.arrest

30. See, for example, Ralph H. Turner and Lewis Killian, *Collective Behavior* (Englewood Cliffs, N.J.: Prentice Hall, 1957); William Kornhauser, *The Politics of Mass Society* (Glencoe, Ill.: Free Press, 1959); Neil J. Smelser, *Theory of Collective Behavior* (New York: Free Press, 1962).

31. Susan Waltz, "Islamist Appeal in Tunisia," *Middle East Journal*, Autumn 1986, 651–70; R. Hrair Dekmejian, *Islam in Revolution: Fundamentalism in the Arab World*, 2d ed. rev. (Syracuse: Syracuse University Press, 1995); Valerie J. Hoffman, "Muslim Fundamentalists: Psychosocial Profiles," in Martin E. Marty and R. Scott Appleby, eds., *Fundamentalisms Comprehended* (Chicago: University of Chicago Press, 1995); Mahmud A. Faksh, *The Future of Islam in the Middle East* (Westport, Conn.: Praeger, 1997).

32. Saad Eddin Ibrahim, "Anatomy of Egypt's Militant Islamic Groups: Methodological Notes and Preliminary Findings," *International Journal of Middle East Studies*, December 1980, 423–53; Hamied N. Ansari, "The Islamic Militants in Egyptian Politics," *International Journal of Middle East Studies*, March 1984, 123–44; Henry Munson Jr., "The Social Base of Islamic Militancy in Morocco," *Middle East Journal*, Spring 1986, 267–84; Waltz, "Islamist Appeal in Tunisia"; Hoffman, "Muslim Fundamentalists"; Carrie Rosefsky Wickham, *Mobilizing Islam: Religion, Activism, and Political Change in Egypt* (New York: Columbia University Press, 2002), chap. 3.

33. Yvonne Y. Haddad, "Islamists and the 'Problem of Israel': The 1967 Awakening," *Middle East Journal*, Spring 1992, 266–85; François Burgat and William Dowell,

The Islamic Movement in North Africa (Austin: Center for Middle Eastern Studies, University of Texas, 1993); Nikki R. Keddie, "The Revolt of Islam, 1700 to 1993: Comparative Considerations and Relations to Imperialism," *Comparative Studies in Society and History,* July 1994, 463–87; John L. Esposito, *Islam and Politics,* 4th ed. (Syracuse: Syracuse University Press, 1998).

34. As quoted in Jeff Goodwin and Theda Skocpol, "Explaining Revolutions in the Contemporary Third World," *Politics and Society* 17 (1989): 490.

35. Saad Eddin Ibrahim, "Anatomy of Egypt's Militant Islamic Groups," 423–53; Saad Eddin Ibrahim, "The Changing Face of Egypt's Islamic Activism," in *Egypt, Islam, and Democracy* (Cairo: American University in Cairo Press, 1996); Hamied N. Ansari, "Islamic Militants in Egyptian Politics," 123–44; Mohammed Elbaki Hermassi, "La Société Tunisienne au Miroir Islamiste," *Maghreb-Machrek,* January-March 1984, 1–54; Henry Munson Jr., "Social Base of Islamic Militance in Morocco," 267–84; Susan Waltz, "Islamist Appeal in Tunisia," 651–70; Burgat and Dowell, *Islamic Movement in North Africa;* Kepel, *Muslim Extremism in Egypt,* 220; Wickham, *Mobilizing Islam.*

36. Lisa Anderson, "Fulfilling Prophecies: State Policy and Islamist Radicalism," in John L. Esposito, ed., *Political Islam: Revolution, Radicalism, or Reform?* (Boulder: Lynne Rienner, 1997), 26.

37. Sabah El-Said, *Between Pragmatism and Ideology: The Muslim Brotherhood in Jordan,* Policy Paper no. 3 (Washington, D.C.: Washington Institute for Near East Policy, 1995); Glenn Robinson, "Can Islamists Be Democrats? The Case of Jordan," *Middle East Journal,* Summer 1997, 373–88; Malik Mufti, "Elite Bargains and the Onset of Political Liberalization in Jordan," *Comparative Political Studies,* February 1999, 100–129; Wiktorowicz, *The Management of Islamic Activism: Salafis, the Muslim Brotherhood, and State Power in Jordan* (Albany: State University of New York Press, 2001).

38. Christopher Alexander, "Opportunities, Organizations, and Ideas: Islamists and Workers in Tunisia and Algeria," *International Journal of Middle East Studies,* November 2000, 465–90; Wiktorowicz, *Management of Islamic Activism;* Ziad Munson, "Islamic Mobilization: Social Movement Theory and the Egyptian Muslim Brotherhood," *Sociological Quarterly,* Fall 2001, 487–510; Diane Singerman, "The Networked World of Islamist Social Movements," in Quintan Wiktorowicz, ed., *Islamic Activism: A Social Movement Theory Approach* (Bloomington: Indiana University Press, 2004).

39. Benjamin Smith, "Collective Action with and without Islam: Mobilizing the Bazaar in Iran," in Wiktorowicz, *Islamic Activism;* Jillian Schwedler, "The Islah Party in Yemen: Political Opportunities and Coalition Building in a Transitional Polity," in Wiktorowicz, *Islamic Activism.*

40. M. Hakan Yavuz, "A Typology of Islamic Social Movements: Opportunity Spaces in Turkey," in Wiktorowicz, *Islamic Activism.*

41. Janine Astrid Clark and Jillian Schwedler, "Who Opened the Window? Women's Activism in Islamist Parties," *Comparative Politics,* April 2003, 293–312.

42. Shaul Mishal and Avraham Sela, *The Palestinian Hamas: Vision, Violence, and Coexistence* (New York: Columbia University Press, 2000).

43. Mohammed M. Hafez, *Why Muslims Rebel: Repression and Resistance in the Islamic World* (Boulder: Lynne Rienner, 2003), 21–22.

44. Stathis N. Kalyvas, "Wanton and Senseless? The Logic of Massacres in Algeria," *Rationality and Society* 11, no. 3 (1999): 245.

45. Michael Doran, "The Pragmatic Fanaticism of al Qaeda: An Anatomy of Extremism in Middle Eastern Politics," *Political Science Quarterly* 117, no. 2 (2002): 178. In the analysis, Doran derives preferences from behaviors and violates a number of other basic rational actor principles.

46. Doran, "Pragmatic Fanaticism of al Qaeda," 182.

47. Ehud Sprinzak, "Rational Fanatics," *Foreign Policy*, September-October 2000, 66–73; Robert Pape, "The Strategic Logic of Suicide Terrorism," *American Political Science Review* 97, no. 2 (2003): 343–62; Eli Berman and David D. Laitin, "Rational Martyrs vs. Hard Targets: Evidence on the Tactical Use of Suicide Attacks," in "Suicide Bombings from an Interdisciplinary Perspective," ed. Eva Meyersson Milgrom (manuscript).

48. Ronald Winthrop, "Can Suicide Bombers Be Rational?" (manuscript, 2003).

49. Mark Harrison, "The Logic of Suicide Terrorism" (paper presented at the conference Weapons of Catastrophic Effect: Confronting the Threat, London, February 12-14, 2003).

50. Berman and Laitin, "Rational Martyrs vs. Hard Targets."

51. A few examples include Wiktorowicz, *The Management of Islamic Activism*; Wiktorowicz, *Islamic Activism: A Social Movement Theory Approach*; Wickham, *Mobilizing Islam*; Sheri Berman, "Islamism, Revolution, and Civil Society," *Perspectives on Politics*, June 2003, 257–72; Hafez, *Why Muslims Rebel*; and Janine Clark, *Islam, Charity, and Activism: Middle-Class Networks and Social Welfare in Egypt, Jordan, and Yemen* (Bloomington: Indiana University Press, 2004).

52. Mancur Olsen, *The Logic of Collective Action* (Cambridge: Harvard University Press, 1965), 133–34.

53. Brian Barry, *Sociologists, Economists, and Democracy* (New York: Macmillan, 1978); William Riker and Peter Ordeshook, "A Theory of the Calculus of Voting," *American Political Science Review* 62 (1968): 25–42; Riker and Ordeshook, *Introduction to Positive Political Theory* (Englewood Cliffs, N. J.: Prentice Hall, 1973); Anthony Oberschall, *Social Conflict and Social Movements* (Englewood Cliffs, N.J.: Prentice Hall, 1973); Bruce Fireman and William A. Gamson, "Utilitarian Logic in the Resource Mobilization Perspective," in Mayer N. Zald and John McCarthy, eds., *The Dynamics of Social Movements: Resource Mobilization, Social Control, and Tactics* (Cambridge: Winthrop, 1979); Dennis Chong, *Collective Action and the Civil Rights Movement* (Chicago: University of Chicago Press, 1991); Mark Irving Lichbach, *The Rebel's Dilemma* (Ann Arbor: University of Michigan Press, 1995); Bert Klandermans, *The Social Psychology of Protest* (Oxford: Blackwell, 1997); David Sikkink and Rory McVeigh, "Who Wants to Protest?" Working Paper and Technical Report no. 2001-10 (Notre Dame, Ind.: Notre Dame University, Department of Sociology, 2001); and Elisabeth Jean

Wood, *Insurgent Collective Action and Civil War in El Salvador* (Cambridge: Cambridge University Press, 2003).

54. A few examples include Rodney Stark and William Sims Bainbridge, "Networks of Faith: Interpersonal Bonds and Recruitment to Cults and Sects," *American Journal of Sociology* 85, no. 6 (1980): 1376–95; Doug McAdam, "Recruitment to High-Risk Activism: The Case of Freedom Summer," *American Journal of Sociology*, July 1986, 64–90; David A. Snow, Louis A. Zurcher Jr., and Sheldon Ekland-Olso, "Social Networks and Social Movements: A Microstructural Approach to Differential Recruitment," *American Sociological Review*, October 1986, 787–801; Doug McAdam and Roberto M. Fernandez, "Microstructural Bases of Recruitment to Social Movements," *Research in Social Movements, Conflict, and Change* 12 (1990): 1–33; Robert V. Gould, *Insurgent Identities: Class, Community, and Protest in Paris from 1848 to the Commune* (Chicago: University of Chicago Press, 1995); Bert Klandermans and Dirk Oegema, "Potentials, Networks, Motivations, and Barriers: Steps toward Participation in Social Movements," *American Sociological Review*, August 1987, 519–31; Doug McAdam and Ronnelle Paulsen, "Specifying the Relationship between Social Ties and Activism," *American Journal of Sociology*, November 1993, 640–67; David B. Tindall, "Social Networks, Identification, and Participation in an Environmental Movement: Low-Medium Cost Activism within the British Columbia Wilderness Preservation Movement," *Canadian Review of Sociology and Anthropology*, November 2002, 413–52; and Jenny Irons, "The Shaping of Activist Recruitment and Participation: A Study of Women in the Mississippi Civil Rights Movement," *Gender and Society*, December 1998, 692–709.

55. McAdam, "Recruitment to High-Risk Activism," 87–88.

56. Sharon Erickson Nepstad and Christian Smith, "Rethinking Recruitment to High Risk/Cost Activism: The Case of Nicaragua Exchange," *Mobilization: An International Journal* 4, no. 1 (1999): 25–40.

57. McAdam, "Recruitment to High-Risk Activism."

58. Mara Loveman, "High-Risk Collective Action: Defending Human Rights in Chile, Uruguay, and Argentina," *American Journal of Sociology*, September 1998, 477–525.

59. Gregory L. Wiltfang and Doug McAdam, "The Costs and Risks of Social Activism: A Study of Sanctuary Movement Activism," *Social Forces*, June 1991, 987–1010.

60. Steven E. Finkel, Edward N. Muller, and Karl-Dieter Opp, "Personal Influence, Collective Rationality, and Mass Political Action," *American Political Science Review*, September 1989, 885–903.

61. David A. Snow and Robert D. Benford, "Ideology, Frame Resonance, and Participant Mobilization," in Bert Klandermans, Hanspeter Kriesi, and Sidney Tarrow, eds., *From Structure to Action: Comparing Movement Participation Across Cultures*, vol. 1, *International Social Movement Research* (Greenwich, Conn.: JAI Press, 1988); Snow and Benford, "Master Frames and Cycles of Protest," in Aldon Morris and Carol McClurg Mueller, eds., *Frontiers in Social Movement Theory* (New Haven: Yale University Press, 1992); Robert D. Benford and David A. Snow, "Framing Processes and Social

Movements: An Overview and Assessment," *Annual Review of Sociology* 26 (2000): 611–39.

62. Snow et al., "Social Networks and Social Movements," 464.

63. Benford and Snow, "Framing Processes and Social Movements," 619–22.

64. Robert D. Benford, "Frame Disputes within the Nuclear Disarmament Movement," *Social Forces*, March 1993, 677–701; Benford and Snow, "Framing Processes and Social Movements," 625–27; John A. Noakes, "Official Frames in Social Movement Theory: The FBI, HUAC, and the Communist Threat in Hollywood," *Sociological Quarterly*, Fall 2000, 657–80.

65. Doug McAdam, John D. McCarthy, and Mayer N. Zald, "Introduction: Opportunities, Mobilizing Structures, and Framing Processes—Toward a Synthetic, Comparative Perspective on Social Movements," in Doug McAdam, John D. McCarthy, and Mayer N. Zald, eds., *Comparative Perspectives on Social Movements: Political Opportunities, Mobilizing Structures, and Cultural Framings* (Cambridge: Cambridge University Press, 1996), xii.

66. David S. Meyer, "Opportunities and Identities: Bridge-Building in the Study of Social Movements," in David S. Meyer, Nancy Whittier, and Belinda Robnett, eds., *Social Movements: Identity, Culture, and the State* (Oxford: Oxford University Press, 2003): 6; see also McAdam et al., "Introduction," 1996.

67. Jeff Goodwin and James M. Jasper, "Caught in a Winding, Snarling Vine: The Structural Bias of Political Process Theory," *Sociological Forum* 14, no. 1 (1999): 35.

68. For the importance of persuasion in social movements, see Charles J. Steward, Craig Allen Smith, and Robert E. Denton Jr., *Persuasion and Social Movements,* 4th ed. (Prospect Heights, Ill.: Waveland, 2001).

69. Donatella della Porta and Dieter Rucht, "Left-Libertarian Movements in Context: A Comparison of Italy and West Germany, 1965–1990," in Craig C. Jenkins and Bert Klandermans, eds., *The Politics of Social Protest* (Minneapolis: University of Minnesota Press, 1995).

70. Alberto Melucci, *Nomads of the Present: Social Movements and Individual Needs in Contemporary Society* (Philadelphia: Temple University Press, 1989); Melucci, *Challenging Codes: Collective Action in the Information Age* (Cambridge: Cambridge University Press, 1996).

71. Wickham, *Mobilizing Islam*, 102.

72. See, for example, Brynjar Lia, *The Society of Muslim Brothers in Egypt: The Rise of an Islamic Mass Movement, 1928–1942* (Ithaca, N.Y.: Ithaca Press, 1998).

73. Assaf Moghadam, "Palestinian Suicide Terrorism in the Second Intifada: Motivations and Organizational Aspects," *Studies in Conflict and Terrorism,* March–April 2003, 65–92.

74. Nichole Argo, "Understanding and Defusing Human Bombs" (paper presented at the International Studies Association Annual Meeting, 2004).

75. Wiktorowicz, *Management of Islamic Activism.*

76. McAdam, "Recruitment to High-Risk Activism," 69.

77. Wiltfang and McAdam, "The Costs and Risks of Social Activism."

78. James Downton Jr. and Paul Wehr, "Persistent Pacifism: How Activist Commitment Is Developed and Sustained," *Journal of Peace Research* 35, no. 5 (1998): 531–50.

79. Downton and Wehr, "Persistent Pacifism."

80. Eric L. Hirsch, "Sacrifice for the Cause: Group Processes, Recruitment, and Commitment in a Student Social Movement," *American Sociological Review*, April 1990, 243–54; Darren E. Sherkat and John Wilson, "Preferences, Constraints, and Choices in Religious Markets: An Examination of Religious Switching and Apostasy," *Social Forces*, March 1995, 993–1026.

81. Mayer N. Zald, "Culture, Ideology, and Strategic Framing," in McAdam, McCarthy, and Zald, eds., *Comparative Perspectives on Social Movements*, 262–63.

82. For example, Russell J. Dalton, *The Green Rainbow: Environmental Groups in Western Europe* (New Haven: Yale University Press, 1994); Gerald M. Platt and Rhys H. Williams, "Ideological Language and Social Movement Mobilization: A Sociolinguistic Analysis of Segregationists' Ideologies," *Sociological Theory*, November 2002, 328–59; Steven F. Cohn, Steven E. Barkan, and William A. Halteman, "Dimensions of Participation in a Professional Social-Movement Organization," *Sociological Inquiry*, August 2003, 311–37.

83. Doug McAdam, *Political Process and the Development of Black Insurgency, 1930–1970* (Chicago: University of Chicago Press, 1982).

84. Christian Smith, *The Emergence of Liberation Theology: Radical Religion and Social Movement Theory* (Chicago: University of Chicago Press, 1991).

85. James M. Jasper and Jane Poulsen, "Recruiting Strangers and Friends: Moral Shocks and Social Networks in Animal Rights and Anti-Nuclear Protests," *Social Problems*, November 1995; James M. Jasper, *The Art of Moral Protest: Culture, Biography, and Creativity in Social Movements* (Chicago: University of Chicago Press, 1997).

86. Jasper and Poulsen, "Recruiting Strangers and Friends," 497.

87. Jasper and Poulsen, "Recruiting Strangers and Friends," 497.

88. John Lofland and Rodney Stark, "Becoming a World-Saver: A Theory of Conversion to a Deviant Perspective," *American Sociological Review*, December 1965, 868.

89. Lofland and Stark, "Becoming a World-Saver," 868.

90. See James P. Piscatori, ed., *Islam in the Political Process* (Cambridge: Cambridge University Press, 1983); Wiktorowicz, *Management of Islamic Activism*, chap. 2; and Seyyed Vali Reza Nasr, *The Islamic Leviathan: Islam and the Making of State Power* (Oxford: Oxford University Press, 2001).

91. Max Heirich, "Change of Heart: A Test of Some Widely Held Theories about Religious Conversion," *American Journal of Sociology*, November 1977, 673.

92. David Knoke, "Networks of Political Action: Toward Theory Construction," *Social Forces*, June 1990, 1041–63.

93. Wickham, *Mobilizing Islam*, 130.

94. Wiktorowicz, *Management of Islamic Activism*, 135.

95. See Marc Sageman, *Understanding Terrorist Networks* (Philadelphia: University of Pennsylvania Press, 2004).

96. Stark and Bainbridge, "Networks of Faith," 1376–95.

97. John Lofland, "'Becoming a World-Saver' Revisited," *American Behavioral Scientist*, July-August 1977, 805–18.

98. Wiktorowicz, *Management of Islamic Activism*, 140–41.

99. Clark, *Islam, Charity, and Activism*, chap. 4; Clark, "Islamist Women in Yemen: Informal Nodes of Activism," in Wiktorowicz, *Islamic Activism*, 164–84.

100. Mayer N. Zald and John D. McCarthy, eds., *Social Movements in an Organizational Society* (New Brunswick, N.J.: Transaction, 1987).

101. Denis J. Sullivan, *Private Voluntary Organizations in Egypt: Islamic Development, Private Initiative, and State Control* (Gainesville: University of Florida Press, 1994); Wiktorowicz, *Management of Islamic Activism*; Clark, *Faith, Networks, and Charity*.

102. Carrie Rosefsky Wickham, "Islamic Mobilization and Political Change: The Islamist Trend in Egypt's Professional Associations," in Joel Beinin and Joe Stork, eds., *Political Islam* (Berkeley: University of California Press, 1997); Ninette S. Fahmy, "The Performance of the Muslim Brotherhood in the Egyptian Syndicates: An Alternative Formula for Reform?" *Middle East Journal*, Autumn 1998, 551–62.

103. John L. Esposito and John O. Voll, *Islam and Democracy* (New York: Oxford University Press, 1996); Glenn Robinson, "Can Islamists Be Democrats?" 373–88; Vicky Langhor, "Of Islamists and Ballot Boxes: Rethinking the Relationship between Islamism and Electoral Politics," *International Journal of Middle East Studies*, November 2001, 591–610; Ellen M. Lust-Okar, "The Decline of Jordanian Political Parties: Myth or Reality?" *International Journal of Middle East Studies*, November 2001, 545–69.

104. Wiktorowicz, *Management of Islamic Activism*; Singerman, "Networked World of Islamist Social Movements."

105. Lofland, "'Becoming a World-Saver' Revisited"; William Sims Bainbridge, *Satan's Power* (Berkeley: University of California Press, 1978); David A. Snow and Richard Machalek, "The Convert as a Social Type," *Sociological Theory* 1 (1983): 180; James T. Richardson, "The Active vs. Passive Convert: Paradigm Conflict in Conversion/Recruitment Research," *Journal for the Scientific Study of Religion* 24 (1985): 163–79; Laurence R. Iannaccone, "The Market for Martyrs" (paper presented at the annual meeting of the American Economic Association, 2004).

106. Iannaccone, "Market for Martyrs," 8.

107. Aziz Al-Azmeh, *Islams and Modernities* (London: Verso, 1993), 1.

108. Some Islamist leaders are what Olivier Roy terms "new Islamist intellectuals": well-educated individuals from Western-style schools and secular professions who turned to religion after facing blocked social mobility. They often have degrees in areas such as engineering and medicine. See Olivier Roy, *The Failure of Political Islam*, trans. Carol Volk (Cambridge: Harvard University Press, 1994).

109. Richard Antoun, *Muslim Preacher in the Modern World: A Jordanian Case Study in Comparative Perspective* (Princeton: Princeton University Press, 1989).

110. Dale F. Eickelman and James Piscatori, *Muslim Politics* (Princeton: Princeton University Press, 1996).

111. Quintan Wiktorowicz, "Framing Jihad: Ideology and Sacred Authority in the Muslim World," *International Review of Social History,* 49 supplement (2004): 159–77.

112. Sherkat and Wilson, "Preferences, Constraints, and Choices," 993–1026; Jeffrey T. Checkel, "Why Comply? Social Leaning and European Identity Change," *International Organization,* Summer 2001, 553–88.

113. Martha Crenshaw, "Political Violence in Algeria," *Terrorism and Political Violence,* Autumn 1994, 264.

114. Myra Marx Ferree and Frederick D. Miller, "Mobilization and Meaning: Toward an Integration of Social Psychological and Resource Perspectives on Social Movement," *Sociological Inquiry,* Winter 1985, 50–52.

115. Hyojoung Kim and Peter S. Bearman, "The Structure and Dynamics of Movement Participation," *American Sociological Review,* February 1997, 70–93.

116. Wickham, *Mobilizing Islam,* 83.

117. Wickham, *Mobilizing Islam,* 146–47.

118. Susan Kwilecki and Loretta S. Wilson, "Was Mother Teresa Maximizing Her Utility? An Idiographic Application of Rational Choice Theory," *Journal for the Scientific Study of Religion,* June 1998, 211.

119. Sullivan, *Private Voluntary Organizations in Egypt*; Wickham, *Mobilizing Islam.*

120. Wiktorowicz, *Management of Islamic Activism,* chap. 3.

121. Luis Martinez, *The Algerian Civil War* (New York: Columbia University Press, 2000).

122. Chong, *Collective Action*; Lichbach, *Rebel's Dilemma,* 123–24.

123. For a similar argument with respect to culture in general, see Jasper, *Art of Moral Protest,* 83.

124. Donald W. Riddle, *The Martyrs: A Study in Social Control* (Chicago: University of Chicago Press, 1931), 38.

125. See MORI, *Polling British Muslims,* November 16, 2001, www.mori.com/mrr/2001/c011116.shtml.

126. Kamran is currently a doctoral student at Howard University. Since leaving al-Muhajiroun in 1998, he has become an ardent critic of groups that support the use of violence. He has published widely and gives talks attacking jihadis like those in al-Qaeda.

HIGH-RISK
ISLAMIC ACTIVISM

As a researcher, I typically attempt to maintain the degree of empathy necessary to understand subjects during fieldwork. But with the memory of the September 11 attacks still fresh, it was all I could do to maintain a facade of decorum when listening to al-Muhajiroun diatribes supporting al-Qaeda and violence against the West. Anger and disgust seethed beneath the surface. In one of my early encounters with the movement, I watched as a group of activists gathered around Omar Bakri's laptop computer to see a video reenactment of 9/11 sent by al-Qaeda supporters. The video clipped together old movie footage intended to simulate the events on the plane, inside the Pentagon, and inside the World Trade Center just before and after the attacks. This was followed by actual news footage of the attacks and the explosions. Activists responded with cries of *Allahu akbar* (God is great) and *subhan Allah* (Glory unto God, used here to mean "amazing"). My initial reaction was that this was a group of fanatics, hardly the neutral observations of a social scientist.

My visceral response to the antics of al-Muhajiroun is hardly an isolated example. Journalists, academics, government officials, and the general public frequently denounce radical Islamic groups like al-Muhajiroun as irrational zealots inspired by a warped interpretation of Islam that transmogrifies edicts of peace into demands for violence. Observers who follow radical Islamic groups in the United Kingdom have used a variety of colorful pejoratives to describe al-Muhajiroun: "whack jobs," "media hookers" (referring to the movement's propensity to attract media attention), "nutters," "loonies," and "clowns," to mention only a few. Mainstream Muslim leaders routinely dismiss

[handwritten margin notes: "Honesty ↓ better than not explaining their views should be done more in research"]

[handwritten margin notes: "Negative view of their people as disturbed & completely irrational"]

45

the movement as "the lunatic fringe."[1] Such labels give the impression that participants are psychologically disturbed at the least; cynics might argue for the more aggressive term "sociopathic."

The language surrounding diatribes against the movement is, at least in part, an artifact of emotions in the maelstrom of post-9/11 global and local politics and security. But even if one rejects these diatribes as ill informed or expressing disgust against groups that espouse violence in the name of religion, questions about the rationality of participants remain. From a social science perspective, rationality is measured according to whether an individual pursues his or her self-interest in an efficacious manner, as subjectively understood by the actor. In other words, to ascertain the rationality of behavior (at least in terms of social science theory), one would ask whether an individual is engaged in action that strategically helps fulfill the individual's self-interest.

Gregory L. Wiltfang and Doug McAdam argue that in deciding whether to participate in activism, individuals are influenced by a subjective assessment of costs and risks.[2] *Risks* are threats to an individual's well-being, such as threats to employment or physical safety. *Costs* are factors associated with the demands of participation that require the sacrifice of other commitments or interests. According to rational actor models, we expect that individuals are unlikely to participate in high-risk, high-cost activism unless there is an offsetting reward.

Given this model, participation in al-Muhajiroun seems irrational. Activists are constantly investigated, arrested, and even convicted of a wide range of charges, including disturbing the public order, inciting religious or racial hatred, and supporting terrorism. Since the introduction of new antiterrorism measures after 9/11, the risks have increased significantly. Sacrifices in terms of time, friends, family, and even employment are rewarded with increased government scrutiny, public disdain, and possible imprisonment (or deportation in some instances).

And the prospects for successfully implementing the movement's agenda in the United Kingdom are minute. One of the most important ideological tenets is that Muslims must promote the formation of an Islamic state via a military coup in Britain, hardly a likely occurrence. Even Omar Bakri recognizes the futility of the effort: "Practically it is not going to happen except in a Muslim country."[3] In addition, it is unlikely that the movement will successfully transform the British Muslim community into similarly minded radicals. The costs and risks are numerous and give the general impression that activists engage in irrational behavior.

REQUIREMENTS FOR THE COMMITTED ACTIVIST

Al-Muhajiroun activists participate in a dizzying array of required weekly activities, and the tempo of activism is fast-paced, demanding, and relentless. Activists commit to an assortment of lessons, public outreach programs, protests, and countless movement-sponsored events, all of which consume tremendous amounts of time, energy, and resources. They center their lives around the movement and in the process frequently sacrifice work, friends, family, and leisure time. To put it simply, al-Muhajiroun participation is an intense experience.

Religious training lies at the core of activism: committed activists must master religious doctrine and movement ideology so that they can effectively promote al-Muhajiroun's ideological vision of an Islamic state and society. To ensure that they are intellectually equipped with "proper" (i.e., movement) religious beliefs, formal members are required to attend a two-hour study session held by the local *halaqah* (circle) every week. Attendance is mandatory, unless the individual cannot make it because of travel constraints, a sick family member, or an emergency. In each country where al-Muhajiroun is active, the country leader may excuse absences for additional reasons deemed acceptable under Islamic law.[4]

The *halaqah* is an intensive, member-only religious lesson that revolves around the movement ideology, and students must spend time preparing. Given the intensity of the session, a lack of preparation incurs the ire of movement teachers and social pressure from other participants, thereby discouraging consistent indolence.[5] The overall tone at the circle is captured in the movement bylaws: "Each member must understand that the Halaqah is a serious discussion and not a chat."[6] Members are prohibited from eating or drinking (apart from water) during the lesson and cannot hold any kind of social gathering after the session is completed.[7] Although the *halaqah* is scheduled for two hours, many last much longer. The Thursday evening lesson at the movement's headquarters in London, for example, typically runs from 9:00 P.M. until early Friday morning (some marathon sessions go until 5:00 A.M.).[8]

In addition to the administrative requirements for religious training, members are also expected to learn about the social, cultural, and political environment in which they operate. This is seen as necessary to facilitate public outreach, communication, and recruitment. Take, for example, the following dictates, as outlined in a section of the movement constitution titled "The Requirements of Every Member of Al-Muhajiroun":

- To care about the affairs of the people in society
- To have a deep understanding of the society: thought, concepts, emotions, culture, customs and public opinions

- To be well equipped with Al Muhajiroun's objective, method, concepts, thoughts, culture, work and administration
- To have a deep understanding of the groups and the parties in the society and the different types of thought and disagreements among the members of a group and among the groups

These requirements make it imperative that members conduct intensive studies and strive to master not only the movement ideology (a formally required activity), but also social and political issues. As a result, members demonstrate a voracious interest in current events, particularly concerning Muslims, such as the war on terrorism, the situation in Iraq, and the Israeli–Palestinian conflict. A penchant for staying up-to-date on contemporary news, however, does not necessarily translate into an accurate understanding of global issues. Many activists, for example, get much of their news from pro–al-Qaeda websites, which are mired in conspiracy theories woven to legitimize and glorify violence against the West.[9]

Membership also necessitates understanding the ideology of other Islamic groups. This primarily functions to equip activists with tools to effectively debate and refute alternative ideologies. Although members are educated to refute moderate Muslims, a great deal of time is devoted to understanding the ideologies of rivals *within* the fundamentalist community. In essence, the movement must convince potential recruits to join al-Muhajiroun as opposed to similar alternatives. Since these alternative groups target many of the same audiences as al-Muhajiroun, this competition can be fierce.

In addition to movement education, members are required to participate in a variety of public outreach events. Every week, members must host at least one public study circle, which is advertised at the local mosque and in the movement newsletter. The public circles are intended to disseminate the movement ideology and draw in new recruits. Other public outreach programs include movement-sponsored public talks, *tafsirs* (explanations of Qur'anic verses), and community events. Although some of these other public activities are not technically required under the movement bylaws, interviews and participant observation indicate that members try to go to as many as possible. In some cases, this necessitates traveling with Omar (usually in the evenings) to various cities throughout Britain, particularly areas with large Muslim populations, such as Birmingham, Luton, and Slough.

Every Saturday, members are required to set up a *da'wa* (propagation) stall in their local community from 12:00 P.M. until 5:00 P.M. In reality, these tend to start a bit later (usually a half hour or an hour) but generally last at least four hours. They are held outside local tube stops, public libraries, municipal buildings, and other public locales. The stalls reflect an activist *da'wa*, which centers on raising public awareness about the plight of Muslims and responsibilities in defending the global *umma* (Muslim community). Activists put up posters, chant slogans, shout through loudspeakers, and interact with observers and passing pedestrians. In effect, these are small protest rallies, usually attended by as many as twenty local activists.

Every Friday afternoon, members must participate in demonstrations that last approximately two hours (barring reasonable excuses, such as employment requirements or an inability to get to the location of the event). The particular topic of the protests varies from week to week, depending on the "pressing issue" of the day. Examples include demonstrations against India and its role in Kashmir, the government of Qatar's role in hosting a U.S. military base, President Mubarak's "un-Islamic" rule in Egypt, and Pakistani President Musharaf's cooperation with the United States in the war on terror. Generally, protesters stand across the street from an embassy, chant slogans, and wave placards denouncing any number of "enemies" of Islam.

Movement members are expected to promote al-Muhajiroun's ideology outside these movement events as well. General principles for community outreach and activism at the individual level include:

- To combine one's Belief (Iman) and sayings with action
- To be present among the masses: to interact with them, to address them and to always be in an interactive environment
- To always be in contact with Muslims whatever difficulties, obstacles and inconveniences one may face
- To receive Islam intellectually and to carry it as a Mujahid [a Muslim engaged in a jihad] not as a preacher, clergyman, MP or a philosopher
- To understand that he/she is the voice, the eyes and the ears of the Muslims
- Every member must make the people and the society feel their presence as an ideological Muslim who defends Islam and Muslims all the time
- Every member of Al-Muhajiroun must struggle against (kufr) i.e. all man-made law, thoughts and concepts and if he/she loses any battle they must organise themselves for the next battle until they win the war[10]

These principles create demands on movement members to spend time interacting with individual Muslims (and even non-Muslims) at work, school, the mosque, and other social settings. Thus members often go to the mosque and initiate discussions about Islam with others in an effort to open a dialogue and encourage "correct beliefs" (as part of *da'wa*). Others have formed organizations at colleges. Many members propagate the movement ideology at work. Any social interaction is seen as an opportunity for *da'wa*. As Janine Clark argues, this form of activist *da'wa* differs from the general Muslim obligation to proselytize in that it entails a conscious attempt to encourage an understanding of Islam that links beliefs to behavior according to a movement's ideology.[11] In other words, activist *da'wa* is not just promoting Islam; it is the promotion of an ideologically inspired interpretation of Islam that demands activism by others. In the case of al-Muhajiroun, divinely mandated activism includes such things as support for military coups to establish Islamic states and jihad against Western militaries in the Muslim world.

Although some members may do the bare minimum, most tend to do *more than is required*.[12] At lessons, for example, students tape-record the talk to review it later. And because they must come to the *halaqah* prepared, members must do homework. One student likened it to *madrasa* training (theological education at preuniversity Islamic schools for orthodox Sunni Muslims), which can be intense and time-consuming. For those who are students at universities, this creates an additional course of study (or more); and for those who are employed, this means studies in the evenings (when they are not already committed to specific movement activities). Despite these enormous requirements, members frequently expressed frustration that they could not do more because of other obligations, despite the fact that many attend al-Muhajiroun activities almost every day.

For members whose commitment begins to slip, there are a set of disciplinary measures that provide sanctions for missing required activities.[13] For example, if on three separate occasions in a single year a member fails to attend the *halaqah* or monthly gatherings or refuses to distribute movement materials or attend movement activities (without a good excuse), the disciplinary proceedings call for "complete expulsion from all Halaqah and closed monthlies and exclusion from all Administrative procedures of Al-Muhajiroun (including informing him/her about Al-Muhajiroun activities) for a period specified by the Mu'tamad [the leader responsible for the country branch of the movement]."[14] In some cases, individuals might legitimately believe they have a valid excuse. If the leadership does not agree, however, the individual is temporarily excluded from all *halaqahs* and closed monthlies for a minimum period of one month. In this case, the leader can also levy a modest fine before readmitting the offender.[15]

There is some evidence that the bylaws are enforced. In February 2000, for example, Nadeem Amin and Abdul Rashid were prevented from attending the monthly gathering of members in London after being sanctioned for administrative discipline. The movement does not expel members per se, since such a move is seen as preventing an individual from fulfilling his or her Islamic obligation to join a group and implement Islamic beliefs (as seen by al-Muhajiroun). But as the worldwide leader (*amir*) of al-Muhajiroun, Omar Bakri is recognized as the authority when it comes to administrative rules (as opposed to the divine rules of God). He therefore has the power to change the *halaqah* rules or exclude someone from participating in movement activities to protect the group "for the benefit of Dawah, the Jama'ah [group], or his members."[16] Interviews indicate, however, that disciplinary measures are rarely needed, since members willingly sacrifice time and alternative commitments for activism.

Although nonmembers who are committed activists are not subject to the same disciplinary measures, they too participate in the array of activities, indicating that it is not disciplinary sanctions alone that motivate participation and prevent free riding. Nonmember activists attend weekly lessons, public events, *da'wa* stalls, and demonstrations. In terms of activities, the only major difference between formal members and nonmember activists is that the former are allowed to attend member-only lessons. The latter can still participate in local *halaqahs*.

MATERIAL COSTS

There are a series of direct and indirect material costs related to al-Muhajiroun activism. First, members are required to pay dues and donate one-third of their salary to the movement.[17] There are several well-off members who probably provide substantial donations, but they seem to be a minority in the movement, considering that most of the activists are students or young adults. There are wealthy benefactors outside the United Kingdom as well, including some who supported the Taliban and have engaged in jihad.[18] In addition, members from other branches send donations to the London office, since this is the worldwide headquarters of the movement.

Money is also raised by selling al-Muhajiroun products, such as videotapes, books, and audio recordings. These are generally free if requested by those seeking "Islamic knowledge," but the movement also sells them at public events. This was observed at a community "bazaar," where the movement set up a table and sold reproduced copies of videos and cassettes with cheap, homemade covers. The movement also raised additional money by selling concessions at the event.

Al-Muhajiroun claims that it does not receive government funding and is thus "self-funded." According to one member, it has turned down sizable government donations, including one from the Iranian government.[19] Although this cannot be verified, government support for the movement seems unlikely given that al-Muhajiroun verbally attacks almost every regime in the Muslim world. Since the movement is trying to foment military coups to replace all of these governments with Islamic states, regimes in the Muslim world are not predisposed to offer financial support.

Given the time commitment required by the movement, a number of activists take less lucrative jobs in order to gain schedule flexibility, thereby incurring additional material costs. This is not a formal requirement, but several activists voluntarily incur the cost in order to more effectively fulfill their obligations and religious duties. Some, for example, have tried to start up businesses, risking the stability of a paycheck for self-employment.[20] Conscious decisions to become part of what Anthony Oberschall calls the "free professions" or to take part-time work for more discretionary time and flexibility is a pattern found in other social movements as well.[21]

A desire for self-employment is not unique to al-Muhajiroun activists, especially considering that most are from the South Asian community, which shows a deep appreciation for business ownership. And many in this community appreciate the flexibility self-employment provides for religious practice. In a survey in the 1990s, for example, two-thirds of self-employed Pakistanis felt that their employment choice "meant it was easier for them to perform their religious duties."[22] But the rationale is different: whereas most South Asian Muslims see self-employment as allowing them to practice their faith through prayer, attendance at the Friday *jumaa* (prayer and *khutba*, or sermon), and other religious rituals, al-Muhajiroun activists view it as allowing them to engage in protests, demonstrations, outreach programs, and other forms of collective action.

For several movement business owners, these ventures have failed dramatically. Two activists, for example, joined together to form an information technology company that specializes in IT training. The office was located in the same business park as the movement headquarters, thus offering ease of access for many movement activities and events. I visited the business when the activists were still purchasing equipment and remodeling the offices. Six months later when I followed up, there was a notice on the door indicating that the business had already closed. The activists had purchased used Pentium II computers for training, which may explain why the business never took off.

Others have sought part-time work or government assistance rather than self-employment or full-time jobs. One activist, for example, found a job working

part-time in a sports shop and was paid under the table. Another was quitting *workplace*
his job in public transportation (after thirteen years) so that he could go on welfare and free up time for *da'wa* and movement activities. Although the specific
employment choices may vary, most activists emphasize the necessity of work
flexibility and their willingness to take less lucrative jobs to pursue activism.

The activism itself presents material risks. Although current U.K. law prohibits discrimination according to race, there is no comparable legal protection
against religious discrimination in the workplace (at least at the time this book
was written).[23] A few religious groups, such as Jews, Sikhs, and Rastafarians, *acknowle-*
are classified as racial groups under the law and therefore protected, but *ages*
Muslims do not enjoy similar status, despite the fact that the majority of Muslims *changing*
favor a religious rather than racial identity. The law thus does not reflect self- *time*
identification in the Muslim community, and there are debates about making re- *care*
visions. Unless a Muslim can demonstrate that he or she was negatively affected
at work because of race rather than religion, there is no legal protection. Since
al-Muhajiroun activists vehemently reject race as their source of identity (it is
seen as a form of nationalism and antithetical to the notion of a global Islamic
community based on bonds of faith), they have actually turned down assistance
from South Asian advocacy groups in cases involving discrimination. This
opens activists to the possibility of dismissal for espousing radical religious
views or participating in the movement.

In one specific case, Islam, a movement leader of Bangladeshi descent, was
fired from his job working for the social services department at a local government council. As Islam tells the story, the council terminated his contract a
month after they learned of his radical religious views and activities, even though
he had another month left on the contract. After Ramadan and returning from
his "spiritual high," he contacted the local media about the termination. He decided to fight the termination through the employment tribunal in what could
have amounted to a landmark case about religious discrimination.[24] He lost the
case.

Activists have also been fined for their activism. In cases where they have violated local ordinances or laws related to public order, convictions are accompanied by court costs and often hefty fines. Under these circumstances, the
movement tries to pay the fines and alleviate the cost, but this may not always be
possible.[25]

The material burdens are thus engendered by the formal requirements of
membership, voluntary choices about employment, and the consequences of activism. For those who are employed full-time, these costs may be marginal, but
for others they can be quite substantial. The student base of the movement

means that many activists have no steady income, and fines and other costs may have considerable effects on individual budgets and cash flow. At a minimum, activists choose to spend money on the movement and related activities rather than alternatives.

SOCIAL COSTS

Individuals do not operate in a social vacuum. They are connected to others through dense interpersonal networks of friends, family, and acquaintances. As a result, decisions about activism are derived amid interactions and relationships. One of the most consistent findings in research about movement joining is that prospective joiners are connected by social ties to the movement. Ideological affinity may predispose an individual to join, but friends and social connections tend to pull the individual toward participation.[26] People make decisions, especially important ones, in a social context by discussing them with trusted others. If an individual's social circle objects to risky activism, participation can entail a social cost, whether this is the loss of former friends, stress with family members, or marginalization by the community. Al-Muhajiroun activists have suffered all of these consequences.

One potential social cost is related to children. Activism in al-Muhajiroun requires time away from family, which can impose a cost on the family, especially where small children who need care and supervision are involved. For women in the movement, this is an important potential cost, since they are the primary caregivers at home. They are required to fulfill their obligations to the movement, just like men, but they also must attend to their children.

The movement recognizes this potential cost and attempts to accommodate parents to reduce possible social obstacles imposed by family responsibilities. Although topics at movement events include issues of violence, members and supporters are allowed to bring their children. In one case, so many women brought their young children to a women-only lesson at the movement headquarters that the screaming and noise nearly drowned out Omar Bakri as he strained to be heard above the chaos of scampering toddlers. Though less common, men bring their children to lessons as well. At one public circle, for example, a man brought his young son, whose boisterous play in front of the podium failed to distract Omar from delivering an emotional lesson about the evils of India.

Participants even bring children to volatile protest rallies. At a demonstration against President Musharaf of Pakistan, about fifteen women brought their children, including infants. With baby strollers parked among the protesters, women screamed for jihad. A number of toddlers and younger children held up signs calling for "Jihad Now!" From the perspective of al-Muhajiroun, the women were able to fulfill both their obligations as mothers and their responsibility to serve God by publicly protesting against ungodliness.

Most members, however, face a different kind of family pressure. Although a few of the older leaders have children, the typical activist is an eighteen- to twenty-two-year-old university student without a spouse or children. For the majority of al-Muhajiroun activists, the primary social pressure instead comes from parents. Parents are predominantly from a generation of South Asians (either immigrants or recently arrived families) who believe that the Muslim community should focus on creating Islamic institutions and practices without engaging in social or political activism. Many believed that they would eventually return to their country of origin and therefore sought to transplant South Asian traditions, institutions, and community life. As a result, there was little attempt to integrate into the broader British society, and ethnic enclaves developed in cities with large South Asian Muslim populations.

More importantly, parents eschew controversial political and social activism, especially outside the South Asian community. Where collective action is acceptable, it is primarily concerned with meeting the basic needs of the Muslim community in a predominantly Christian country, such as getting *halal* (religiously permitted) food in schools or preventing religious discrimination.[27] There is a strong desire to avoid the more contentious al-Muhajiroun-style mobilization that could jeopardize stability.

Comparative research indicates that competing pressures not to participate can undermine high-risk activism. In the Huk rebellion in the Philippines, competing social ties siphoned emotional energies and commitments away from participation in the rebellion.[28] Similarly, plantation workers in the Philippines were more likely to participate in risky Marxist activism if they had already established their own household, thereby weakening the possible competing pressures from parents.[29]

This kind of pressure was found consistently among respondents in this study. Almost uniformly, respondents in this study noted their parents' opposition to activism. Parents do not object to religious education per se, but they believe in a personal, apolitical Islam and set different goals. They want their children to be doctors, lawyers, and bankers, not radical fundamentalists. This derives from a particular view of "success" defined by typical British standards of socioeconomic achievement as well as a more general concern that their children could become involved in dangerous groups and gamble their future. Al-Muhajiroun activists believe that their parents prioritize following the rituals of Islam, getting an education, and working hard. Some concerned parents even contacted Zaki Badawi, founder of the Muslim Council of Britain, and asked him to intervene after discovering their children's involvement.[30] Opposition also comes from siblings. In one case, Sulayman, a convert to Islam and leader in al-Muhajiroun, had not seen his brother in three years because his brother opposed radical activism.[31] Another member recounted a story in which his brother came to him and said, "You are here in this country, pray when you can. Just work. Don't be active."[32] This kind of family opposition creates social pressure not to participate, particularly in traditional South Asian households where respect for parents is important.

Activists in al-Muhajiroun, however, are frequently undeterred by familial opposition. As one respondent put it, "They warn you and say don't go with these people, but then they see you are firm and what can they do?"[33] A Somali member reiterated this sentiment: "If the boys are convinced, the parents can't do much. They can tell them not to go, but they can't stop it."[34] *male emphasis*

Activists commonly attempt to avoid family friction by hiding their involvement.[35] Although activists acknowledge their parents' disapproval of Islamic groups such as al-Muhajiroun, most never actually told them about their involvement (some told siblings). In one family, three brothers are active in radical groups (one in al-Muhajiroun and two in Hizb ut-Tahrir) but simply tell their parents that they are taking religious lessons without specifying sponsors or the degree of activism. Another admitted that because his mother believes such groups are divisive, he decided not to tell either of his parents.[36] Although Mohammed, a white convert to Islam and former atheist, told his parents about his conversion, he never told them he was part of al-Muhajiroun, despite the fact that he is a senior leader in the movement and gives lessons at local movement events and through Internet forums like Paltalk. When asked why he never revealed his involvement, he shrugged and mumbled, "It just never came up."[37]

This, however, does not necessarily eliminate the social cost, since the movement's ideology requires activist *da'wa*, which leads to heated debates with family members about the proper interpretation and practice of Islam. I found little evidence that traumatic altercations shattered the family or created irreconcilable differences, but there was tension. One recent joiner recalled that because his father "stands with Union Jack," they used to have rather emotional discussions.[38] Another recounted a story in which he shocked his extended family members as they discussed the standoff between Pakistan and India in 2002 by boldly declaring his hope for nuclear war. This, he argued, was a religious obligation and for the sake of Islam. God would therefore reward the Muslims by destroying "Hind" (India). His father is a staunch supporter of Britain, and this created a great deal of consternation.[39] These kinds of interactions indicate that

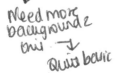
Need more background a this — Quit basic

although parental ignorance about participation may soften family pressure, it is unlikely to eliminate the cost altogether.

Members also sacrifice prior social ties where former friends do not follow strict Islamic mores. Socializing with unreligious friends is difficult since activists are constrained in terms of where they can go and what they can do. Every activity must receive divine permission from the Qur'an and Sunna. Pubs, for example, are a favored locale for socializing in British society, but there are movement edicts against patronizing establishments that serve alcohol. Most typical social scenes in Britain are also frequented by both men and women, but the movement strongly prohibits the "free mixing" of different genders (there are a few special exceptions to this rule, such as medical emergencies where there is no option but to be in the same room with the opposite gender).[40] This, in effect, is a prohibition against the pastimes and socializing activities of the dominant age cohort in al-Muhajiroun, since they typically include both genders. This means that activists cannot go out to dinner with friends from the opposite gender, attend parties where men and women mingle, or go to public "free-mixing" spaces such as movie theaters. In effect, activists can no longer be "friends" with the opposite sex, and the social scene of the past is no longer an option for activists.

Table 1.1. Social Activities Discouraged by al-Muhajiroun

1. Listening to music and radio
2. Smoking
3. Cruising
4. Watching TV
5. Running away from responsibilities to go on picnics and holidays
6. Daily socialising with the intention to have fun and kill time
7. Sleeping a lot and chilling out
8. Deserting reading serious books such as the Qur'an, Hadith and Fiqh to read cheap newspapers, novels and magazines
9. Playing games
10. Solving crosswords
11. Chatting on the phone for hours
12. Ignoring duties/responsibilities and prefer to rest, slack and be lazy
13. Exceeding ones involvement in sport activities
14. Diverting from the serious, fruitful work to wasting time
15. Playing on the internet for no need
16. Looking for excuses not to do any duties as he is bored with doing them
17. Window shopping and spending hours in the market
18. Going to cinemas and restaurants to eat out
19. Hanging out with friends
20. Joking around and being sarcastic

Source: Al-Muhajiroun, Al-Malal: Boredom, n.d.

In addition to limitations on freedom of movement and the kinds of establishments that can be frequented, al-Muhajiroun explicitly discourages leisure and social activities in general. Any spare time should instead be devoted to worshiping God and promoting the proper interpretation and practice of Islam. Socializing is seen as an unproductive and wasteful distraction that not only diverts attention away from God but also tempts Muslims to be sinful. According to the movement, these kinds of activities reflect the boredom endemic in the culture of contemporary Muslim youths. If only boredom could be transformed into activism, al-Muhajiroun argues, a proper understanding of Islam would spread rapidly throughout society. The list of typical British social activities prohibited by al-Muhajiroun is extraordinary and tends to isolate activists from their nonreligious friends (see table 1.1).

The movement ideology emphasizes that activists should avoid not only certain activities and establishments, but individuals who do not fully practice their faith as well. This includes anyone who does not follow the strict interpretation of Islam espoused by al-Muhajiroun and other radical groups. Nominal or moderate Muslims are considered heretics, and the movement has issued fatwas declaring several leaders of the mainstream Muslim community apostates (the ultimate sanction for apostasy is death). Anyone who associates with such people is liable to sin and deviate from the straight path of Islam. This is based on the Sunna of the Prophet: "beware of who you keep as your friends, for you will take the Deen [religion] of your friends."[41] Al-Muhajiroun therefore emphasizes the importance of religiously based friendships: "It is important for us to keep good company and be among people that are obedient to Allah (swt) and with people whom we can learn and benefit from. Our behavior and mentality is affected by the people we associate with."[42]

All of these ideological edicts isolate activists from social circles outside the radical Islamic community and even al-Muhajiroun itself (since other radical groups are seen as slightly deviant in their religious interpretations). While this is not the kind of isolation practiced by Takfir wal-Hijra, which charged the entire society with apostasy and sought to recreate the purity of the first Muslim community in Medina by isolating itself from the broader community, al-Muhajiroun does demand a certain degree of social encapsulation to avoid the polluting effects of non-Muslims and Muslim pretenders.

Certainly these old friendships and social ties can be replaced by new bonds of religious activism formed through the process of participation. Activists view their newfound friendships in the movement as more substantive than past relationships since they are based on fidelity to God rather than drinking alcohol, playing football, or carousing for dates. In some cases, groups of friends become involved in al-Muhajiroun at the same time, mitigating the potential social cost of participation. But this is not always the case, and many joiners sacrifice friends (and even family) for people they are just beginning to know. In other words, replacement bonds take time to develop, and there are potential social costs, at least in the short term.

Beyond the costs of individual social ties, there is a broader "pariah effect" in being associated with al-Muhajiroun: both the Muslim community and the British public in general view movement activists as part of the "lunatic fringe" and treat activists with hostility. Prior to September 11, there was a general norm among moderate Muslim leaders and organizations that they should not publicly disparage other Muslims, including radicals. This was based on an accepted tolerance of interpretive pluralism in religious doctrine, which accommodates the possibility of multiple interpretations of Islam (in contradistinction to the radicals who believe there is only one correct version and denounce anyone who disagrees with them as apostates). Zaki Badawi, a prominent moderate Muslim, was contacted by a recent Muslim immigrant who asked about locating Omar Bakri Mohammed and al-Muhajiroun so that he could take religious lessons; and rather than chastising the group or discouraging this individual from contacting the movement, Badawi actually passed along al-Muhajiroun's contact information.[43] This is despite al-Muhajiroun's public statement declaring Badawi an apostate and enemy of Islam.

Al-Qaeda's attacks in 2001 and the increased publicity and newspaper coverage of radical Islamic groups, however, eroded this norm. Mainstream Muslim leaders issued public statements deriding the radicals in an effort to distance Islam and the British Muslim community from the ideological precepts and antics of extremists. There was a general fear that the overwhelming coverage of the radicals would leave the impression that people like Omar Bakri represent the mainstream Muslim view. In a context of confusion, suspicion, and growing religious discrimination after September 11, this was considered an extremely dangerous prospect that could threaten the entire Muslim community in Britain.

As a result, the mainstream took the offensive to undermine the credibility of Omar Bakri and al-Muhajiroun. As Inayat Bunglawala, spokesperson for the Muslim Council of Britain, explained, "The Muslim Council, which normally does not criticize other Islamic groups, has given me permission to openly criticize them [al-Muhajiroun] because they are doing a lot of harm."[44] Zaki Badawi, the founder of the council, reiterated a similar point: "These people are not leaders of any group. They do not represent the Muslim community. In normal times they are just harmless lunatics but in times like these they are extremely dangerous."[45] Dr. Ghuyasuddin Siddiqui, chairman of the Muslim Parliament of Great Britain, articulated his concerns as well: "I don't want these nutters to become martyrs. Let the community reject them."[46]

The volume and tenor of Omar Bakri's statements, press releases, and fatwas, in particular, elicited snide comments from moderate leaders. Bunglawala, for example, dismissed Omar Bakri as "a clown, a loony. People must understand this. He is free to issue fatwas left, right and center. We joke that there is one a month."[47] Al-Muhajiroun was dubbed "the fatwa of the month club." Lord Ahmed, the only Muslim member of the House of Lords, referred to Omar Bakri as a "rent-a-quote publicist."[48] The verbal attacks were intended to paint al-Muhajiroun as part of the "lunatic fringe" and ostracize it from the Muslim community. Following the bombings in Madrid in March 2004, the Muslim Council of Britain urged imams and Muslims to be vigilant against groups supporting terrorism.[49]

Of course, activists might not care about the views of the mainstream Muslim community, since these are seen as the opinions of hypocrites and apostates. For al-Muhajiroun, in fact, the sense that the movement is acting against the mainstream produces the kind of excitement often found in counterculture movements rebelling against the status quo. Activists are rebelling against their parents' Islam and traditions, establishment Islam, and British culture; and there is discernable excitement when they discuss their altercations with the police and other representatives of the British government. Some of this may reflect pure bravado: an attempt to signal courage to fellow activists. Many activists, however, seem to enjoy their role as "outsiders."

Regardless of whether activists reject the animosity from the Muslim community as irrelevant or view it as a source of excitement, the social stigma attached to al-Muhajiroun activism carries tangible costs. Many Muslims are concerned that groups like al-Muhajiroun could spread their ideas and tarnish the reputation of Muslims in the United Kingdom, particularly in the post–September 11 era when society and politicians are sensitive about Islamic radicalism. This has led a number of communities to ban the movement from using community centers or local mosques for its activities. According to the chairman of the board of trustees at the Brixton mosque, for example, the community banned al-Muhajiroun members and those with similar ideologies from entering the mosque.[50] A local mosque in Luton issued a statement that clearly communicated the community's stance toward the movement: "Al-Muhajiroun have been warned in no uncertain terms that their activities will no longer be tolerated here . . . Muslims are sick and tired of their provocative remarks."[51] Religious

Community
opposition

leaders in Luton banned al-Muhajiroun and other similar groups from distributing posters and pamphlets calling for jihad against the United States.[52] The movement found it increasingly difficult to work through local community institutions.

In a few instances, community opposition to al-Muhajiroun involved acts of violence. In Luton, for example, newspapers reported that two young local men were killed fighting for the Taliban against coalition forces in Afghanistan. Local Muslims complained that al-Muhajiroun was actively recruiting British Muslims to fight abroad and inciting religious hatred. They were furious after the reports and blamed the movement for preying on vulnerable young men in the community. After the local movement leader made a public statement calling the two men heroes and martyrs, he was attacked and nearly choked to death by several irate Muslim men. The Scottish leader of al-Muhajiroun, Ifran Rasool, actually moved to England because of possible community attacks (an ongoing police investigation into his activism likely inspired the move as well).[53] Several others maintained a lower public profile for fear of community reprisals after their names were published by local newspapers.

Activists also face possible reprisals from other elements in the British public, which has become increasingly less tolerant of groups like al-Muhajiroun. According to members of the movement, they have been physically attacked on several occasions by right-wing groups like the British National Party. Anjem Choudary, the U.K. leader of the movement, has expressed concern about what he perceives as the unfettered ability of such groups to operate (and thus threaten al-Muhajiroun). Although movement activists may show a lack of concern about their pariah status, the movement's notoriety carries real costs.

Antiterrorism Laws and Increased Risk

The United Kingdom is used to dealing with radical groups and terrorism. Between 1970 and 2000, 350 terrorist attacks took place on the U.K. mainland (not including Northern Ireland). Over the years, the government has created various instruments for arresting and prosecuting terrorists. Legislation, however, was drafted to specifically combat violent Irish nationalist groups, which were seen as the primary threat to national security.[54] Earlier laws therefore failed to deal with the growing presence of radical Islamic groups in the United Kingdom.

The first piece of antiterrorism legislation was passed in 1974 after the Irish Republican Army (IRA) bombed a Birmingham bar frequented by off duty British soldiers, killing 21 and injuring more than 180. The new

Prevention of Terrorism (Temporary Provisions) Act (PTA) substantially augmented police authority and included new powers to arrest, detain, search, and conduct raids against suspected terrorists without a warrant. It outlawed belonging to terrorist groups, wearing the insignia of banned organizations, or providing words of direct support on television or radio (print was still allowed). Beyond the specifics of the act, terrorism was viewed as a criminal (as opposed to political) act and therefore subject to criminal statutes.[55] Police powers were further augmented under the Prevention of Terrorism (Additional Powers) Act in 1996, which allowed police to cordon off potentially targeted areas for twenty-eight days and stop and search any individuals in the area.[56]

Under these legal parameters, Islamic groups that supported violence operated with relative impunity. To a large extent, this was because the legal prohibitions applied only to terrorist groups that sought to launch attacks in the United Kingdom and did not specifically address the use of Britain as a safe haven to support or commit terrorism against targets outside the country. Before the emergence of al-Qaeda, most radical Islamic organizations directed their support toward external causes, particularly the Palestinian struggle. When it was first launched in 1996, al-Muhajiroun was known as the "eyes and ears" of Hamas and helped raise funds for Palestinian terrorism as part of its declared obligation to defend Muslims against Israeli occupation and aggression. The movement raised money for rebels in Chechnya and Kashmir as well. Omar Bakri and others in the movement were quite open about their fund-raising activities and support for international violent causes, openly discussing their support with the press, including the government-owned BBC. A number of governments, including Russia, Algeria, and Egypt, complained that the United Kingdom was harboring terrorists. This view was shared by the French security services, which allegedly dubbed the British capital "Londonistan" because of the prevalence of radical Islamic groups in the city. Even the United States, Britain's staunchest ally, expressed concern about the growing radical presence in the United Kingdom.

The major loopholes in the early legislation were closed after the passage of the Terrorism Act 2000, enacted in response to the "real IRA" bomb attack in Omagh, Northern Ireland, which killed 28 and injured more than 200 in an attempt to derail the 1998 Good Friday Peace Accords. The new act was intended to be permanent legislation, in contrast to the earlier 1974 provisions, which required periodic review and renewal. It was also intended to address concerns about the presence of international terrorist groups by redefining terrorism to include actions inciting and supporting violence in other countries. In the first year of enforcement, a total of 131 individuals were arrested under the act. Ninety-three of these were arrested for international terrorism (as opposed to only thirty-seven for Irish terrorism). Since the vast majority of proscribed international terrorist groups are Islamic, the enforcement principally targeted support for radical Islamic groups.[57]

The Terrorism Act 2000 effectively undermined the ability of radical Islamic groups to openly raise funds for international terrorism. After the act became effective in February 2001, al-Muhajiroun was forced to end its public fundraising activities for Hamas and other proscribed groups. Most likely the movement still raises money for violent causes, but it is collected as charity, relief funding, or support for general propagation efforts. In addition, activists who openly support Islamic terrorism risk arrest under the new law, and this consideration always looms over movement events where they address issues related to jihad and violent struggles in the Muslim world.

The legal environment became even more constraining after passage of the Anti-Terrorism, Crime, and Security Act 2001, which was rushed through following the September 11 attacks. The act gives the Home Secretary the power to deport non-British terrorism suspects without trial. Many foreign members of al-Muhajiroun live in the United Kingdom, and several expressed concern that they might be arrested under the act.[58]

The government's ability to deport individuals, however, is somewhat limited by Article 3 of the European Convention on Human Rights, which prohibits extradition to countries where individuals risk execution, inhumane treatment, or torture. Many suspects are wanted on terrorism charges and convictions in their home countries, especially in Middle Eastern countries such as Yemen, Jordan, Egypt, and Algeria, and deportation would amount to a death sentence or torture. The Anti-Terrorism, Crime, and Security Act addresses this by allowing the government to detain suspected foreign terrorists indefinitely without charges or trial. The act also restricts the right to judicial review (appeals can only be made through the Special Immigration Appeals Commission, SIAC) and the right of habeas corpus.[59] To avoid conflict with Article 15 of the European Convention on Human Rights, which prohibits indefinite detention, the British government declared a state of emergency in order to derogate from the article.[60]

Perhaps the greatest concern for al-Muhajiroun activists is the redefinition of terrorism. A terrorist is defined as any individual who "a) is or has been concerned in the commission, preparation or instigation of acts of international terrorism; b) is a member of or belongs to an international terrorist group; or c) has links with an international terrorist group."[61]

The last part of the definition includes broad support or assistance to proscribed groups, and this component of the act holds the greatest consequences for al-Muhajiroun. The movement has been consistently linked to terrorist groups in the press. In many cases, this is because Omar Bakri and other leaders try to purposefully insinuate strong connections to encourage press coverage and exaggerate the movement's role in the global Islamic movement. Prior to September 11, Omar Bakri was nicknamed "bin Laden's man in London" by the British press, a moniker he did nothing to dismiss until the attacks on the World Trade Center and Pentagon. In 1998, he issued a fatwa supporting the al-Qaeda embassy attacks in Kenya and Tanzania. Omar Bakri publicly argues that his "only ties to bin Laden are ties of Islamic brotherhood" and denies that he has ever met the al-Qaeda leader. In a private interview, he modified this position by explaining that he met bin Laden in Saudi Arabia a long time ago but did not really know who he was at the time.[62]

Most likely Omar provides only moral support for al-Qaeda's war against the United States, and this is offered with reservations because he believes that the movement can only attack U.S. government or military targets in Muslim countries. When asked about his reaction to 9/11 in the immediate aftermath, Omar responded: "I am very happy today." He quickly qualified his statement, arguing that he was indeed glad that the United States experienced the sting of defeat and humiliation suffered by Muslims for decades ("with the USA you must pay"), but that the attacks against civilian targets were religiously prohibited. The Pentagon was considered fair game, but Omar rejected tactical use of the planes since there were innocent civilians aboard.[63] His objection to the World Trade Center attacks incurred the wrath of Ayman Zawahiri (second in command of al-Qaeda), who denounced Omar Bakri as an apostate. Despite this fallout, Omar Bakri continues to publicly support aspects of al-Qaeda's strategies and tactics, and he refuses to denounce bin Laden. In fact, he argues that so long as bin Laden and the hijackers *believed* that what they were doing accorded with Islamic law, they would be rewarded in heaven. This kind of equivocation and moral support has led the general public, press, and political figures to conclude that a possible connection exists, upping the risks for al-Muhajiroun activists.

Ideologically, the movement sees no problem in cooperating with terrorist groups like al-Qaeda. Leaders routinely argue that "there is an obligation on all Muslims to cooperate on the good deeds," leaving the possibility of cooperation with terrorists where there are points of doctrinal agreement.[64] Omar Bakri has long tried to coordinate with other radical groups in protests and activism, and there was at least some contact and communication about cooperation with Abu Hamza al-Masri's radical Supporters of Shariah, which has been linked to al-Qaeda.[65]

Obfuscating = darken/ to make difficult to understand / obscuring

Al-Muhajiroun has implied a connection through its own activism by issuing statements of support for various violent causes throughout the Muslim world, but in some instances, the possible connections to terrorism have been more co-incidental. Omar Bakri's International Islamic Front was initially confused with bin Laden's International Islamic Front for Jihad against Jews and Crusaders. Omar Bakri seemed to take advantage of the confusion by obfuscating the relationship, only clarifying the distinctness of the two organizations when it became clear that there could be serious consequences.

After September 11, Omar Bakri's Hizb ut-Tawhid organization was confused with al-Tawhid (Unitarianism), a radical group uncovered in Germany. Shortly after an attack on a synagogue in Tunisia that killed a number of German tourists, German authorities arrested four members and supporters of al-Tawhid, which was formed to topple the Jordanian government and fight Jews. The detainees were charged with plotting to attack Jewish targets in Germany, most likely the Jewish Museum or other targets in Berlin as well as a Jewish-owned dance club in Düsseldorf. The movement is supposedly led by Abu Mussab al-Zarqawi, al-Qaeda's representative in Iraq[66] and is thought to be responsible for plots to attack U.S. and Israeli targets in Jordan, including the attack against U.S. Diplomat Lawrence Foley in 2002.[67] There is speculation that the movement is inspired by the radical Palestinian scholars who support al-Qaeda—Abu Qutadah (Omar Mahmoud Abu Omar) and Abu Muhammad al-Maqdisi.[68] Al-Tawhid cells were discovered in London and Luton, and similarity in names prompted police investigations into Omar Bakri.[69]

The movement was obviously concerned about the consequences of the new terrorism acts, since many of its activities fell within the purview of the laws. In December 2001, when it became clear that the government was considering enforcement against Omar Bakri, the movement went on the offensive, warning the government that it would be "playing with fire" if the police arrested their leader. Omar Bakri laid down a gauntlet: "If I am arrested, my followers are not just going to sit down and accept it. There are 800 of them and if they are provoked in this way, there will be riots."[70]

The arrest of several other key radical figures signaled that enforcement of the antiterrorism laws against al-Muhajiroun was coming. The movement was particularly alarmed by government moves against Abu Hamza al-Masri, a notorious preacher at the Finsbury Park Mosque, a known center of Islamic extremism. (His fiery sermons and radicalism eventually led the Charity Commission to strip him of his role as preacher at the mosque.) In April 2003, Home Secretary David Blunkett initiated proceedings to strip Abu Hamza of his British citizenship to pave the way to expel him under charges of terrorism and section 4 of the Nationality, Immigration, and Asylum Act 2002, which gives the government the power to "deprive a person of a citizenship status if the Secretary of State is satisfied that the person has done anything seriously prejudicial to the vital interests of— a) the United Kingdom or b) a British overseas territory."[71] There were questions about whether the removal of citizenship was legal, since it would leave Abu Hamza stateless.[72] In May 2004, after the United States handed down an indictment charging him with raising money for terrorism, supporting al-Qaeda, and trying to set up a jihadi training camp in Oregon, the British government moved to have him extradited to the United States.[73]

The government's moves against Abu Hamza had real import for Omar Bakri.[74] Even prior to 9/11, there were investigations into the possibility of expelling Omar from the United Kingdom. Donald Anderson, the Labour chair of the Common's Foreign Affairs Select Committee, called for his possible expulsion as early as 1998. In 2000, Andrew Dismore, a Labour MP from Hendon, requested that the Home Secretary look into Omar Bakri's activism and consider legal action: "I believe it is within your power to arrange for his [Omar Bakri's] removal if you consider that to be 'conducive to the public good.'"[75] Such calls became increasingly common after September 11, couched in the language of antiterrorism. Given the parallels between Abu Hamza and his Supporters of Shariah movement, on the one hand, and Omar Bakri and al-Muhajiroun, on the other, it was clear that the government could pursue a similar course of action against Omar and his followers: both sets of activists held similar ideological precepts and engaged in similar forms of activism, including demonstrations and support for al-Qaeda.[76] Abu Hamza had in fact offered to merge Supporters of Shariah and al-Muhajiroun on several occasions, though Omar Bakri declined.[77] All of these factors suggested that the movement could be vulnerable to arrests under terrorism laws.

The anticipated crackdown on al-Muhajiroun began to materialize in July 2003. On the heels of the suicide bombing at Mike's Place in Israel, which was at least indirectly linked to al-Muhajiroun, the Metropolitan Police Anti-Terrorist division launched a series of raids on the movement headquarters and homes of Omar Bakri and Anjem Choudary. It was the first time the terrorism acts were enforced against the movement,[78] which responded with a press release recognizing the risks of activism and condemning the Blair government:

> Following the 200,000 men, women and children being bombed and now either murdered or missing in Afghanistan and the recent massacre of innocent civilians in Iraq, these latest raids underline the Blair regimes insistence on targeting the Muslim community and trying to ensure that all voices of dissent are silenced . . .

The habits of non-Muslims violating the sanctity of Muslims when they have authority over them, of raiding their homes, of fabricating evidence against them, of treating them as guilty before any investigation is not a new phenomenon.[79]

The Public Order Act and Inciting Hatred

The Public Order Act (1986) provides police with wide latitude in dealing with local community disturbances. It essentially prohibits any public activism deemed threatening, abusive, or insulting to bystanders or observers. Police at the scene make on-the-spot decisions about whether an action constitutes a violation of the act.

For al-Muhajiroun, the most relevant parts of the Public Order Act are sections 17 and 18, which ban activism intended to stir racial hatred toward groups in the United Kingdom. This includes the distribution of written materials, public displays, verbal statements, plays and recordings, and behaviors that incite racial hatred. If individuals either intend to foment racial hatred or racial hatred is likely to erupt given the context of the activism, it is a criminal offense.

The 1986 act was amended and broadened by the Crime and Disorder Act 1998 and the Anti-Terrorism, Crime, and Security Act 2001. The most relevant changes for al-Muhajiroun were:

1. An expansion of prosecutable racial hatred to include hatred toward other groups outside the United Kingdom
2. An expansion of prosecutable offenses to include religiously aggravated offenses
3. A change in the maximum sentence from two years to seven

⌐→High cost

Many of al-Muhajiroun's public activities easily fall within the purview of the legal prohibitions against religious and racial hatred. Events often focus on opposition to Israel, in particular, and are filled with anti-Semitic rhetoric, materials, and displays. Frequently activists distribute leaflets quoting a provocative verse from a hadith (recorded tradition of the Prophet Mohammed): "The final hour will not come until the Muslims kill the Jews." Al-Muhajiroun's anti-Semitic public actions led Michael Whine, a member of the Board of Deputies of British Jews, to argue that "Sheikh Mohammed [Omar Bakri Mohammed] is probably the most dangerous man in Britain today."[80]

Arrests (or at least threats of arrest) under the Public Order Act and related laws most commonly occur at the *da'wa* stalls. It is generally not the act of protesting itself that raises risks of arrest, in the sense that activists are disturbing the peace. It is instead the content and message at the stalls. These miniprotests contain inflammatory language directed at Israel, Jews, Christians, Hindus, and the West in general. The language is often accompanied by outrageous posters and displays designed to elicit "moral shock" and outrage. The shock is intended to evoke emotional responses and sympathy for what al-Muhajiroun views as Western–Zionist attacks against the Muslim world, including the U.S. occupation of Iraq, Israeli repression of Palestinians, and Indian repression of Kashmiris. Pictures of mutilated and decapitated bodies are ubiquitous. Pictures of malnourished or mutilated children are common, since they evoke the most consistent emotional response, regardless of whether a person is a Muslim. The point is to demonstrate why visceral hatred toward these "oppressors of Muslims" (Israelis, Indians, etc.) is warranted. Activists argue that they are merely opening the eyes of the public to the atrocities committed against Muslims everywhere.

These pictures, more than anything else, draw the ire of police, who are often in attendance at the stall (policing protest) or are called in by local business owners or concerned citizens who have seen the images and heard the chants. Altercations with police over whether the pictures and chants are "free speech" often lead to arrests, especially if members refuse to remove the pictures.

This was confirmed by observations at a *da'wa* stall outside a public library in London. About ten activists gathered around a display table and an easel adorned with grotesque pictures of the "oppressed": mutilated bodies from the alleged Israeli "Jenin massacres" (the United Nations did not find any evidence to support the accusations). The pictures, to say the least, were shocking: images of an old man with half his face missing; children with massive injuries; and bodies with organs ripped through the skin. The graphic nature of the pictures prompted a flood of calls to the police, and six officers responded and arrived at the stall about an hour after it opened.[81] The protesters were told that they could continue their message verbally and use pictures of bombed buildings, but they had to remove the pictures of the mutilations. A heated argument ensued. The demonstrators argued that they were merely showing "the truth" (facts that the Western media refused to publish) so that people understood what was happening to Muslims worldwide. The police retorted that the pictures were offensive and because they were being displayed in a public place, bystanders (including children) had no choice about exposure. The argument was impassioned, and the police threatened arrest. In this particular case, the pictures were taken down. Al-Muhajiroun activists cited the confrontation as another example of Western repression of Muslims. Interviews with various members of the movement, a police officer at the scene, and eight participants at the stall indicate that this kind of altercation is common.[82]

*Hadith =
speech of mohammed
[person] the prophet.
(literal)*

Other examples abound. During celebrations of Israel's fiftieth anniversary, al-Muhajiroun organized a demonstration against "the pirate state of Israel" outside the Wembley Conference Centre. The demonstrations included inflammatory language, including a call for jihad against Israel. Claiming that the demonstrators were inciting religious and racial hatred, the police intervened, violence broke out, and one protester was detained. Three al-Muhajiroun activists were later arrested and prosecuted for inciting religious and racial hatred at a related rally.[83] Two activists were arrested under the Public Order Act at a protest against homosexuals because of a leaflet entitled *Gay Today, Pedophile Tomorrow?* They were both convicted and fined £160.[84]

For the movement, the most prominent case was the conviction of Iftikhar Ali. The Crown charged that he issued a "call to arms" by distributing leaflets about jihad in Palestine that included the hadith that "the hour will not come until the Muslims fight the Jews and kill them." According to press reports, when he was arrested he allegedly stated, "What is written on the paper is true. The Jewish people must die." Authorities interpreted the leaflet to be a threat against the Jewish community in the United Kingdom, and he was convicted of distributing "threatening, abusive, or insulting" material with the intent to foment racial hatred. Judge Jeremy McMullen argued that "words created 1,400 years ago are equally capable of containing race hate as words created today. Scholarly and faithful study of the texts is not unlawful but words used in holy texts are capable of inflaming race hate. That would happen if quoted in circumstances where race hate is likely to be stirred up." Because the judge accepted the defense argument that Iftikhar had primarily intended to raise public awareness about the Palestinian crisis rather than sow racial discord, jail time was avoided. Instead, the judge sentenced him to 200 hours of community service, a £1,200 prosecution fee, and a £3,000 fine.[85] Other movement activists were arrested around the same time for distributing the same leaflet throughout the country, but the charges were dropped.[86]

Al-Muhajiroun framed the trial and its results as part of a "postsecular" Crusade designed to separate politics and religion and to reduce Islam to ritual. It reminded audiences that Britain had an essential role in destroying the caliphate and "giving" Palestine to the Jews and warned that the government might further erode the ability of Muslims to practice their faith: "Under the new anti-terrorist and race hate laws in the UK, it has now become an offense to distribute or quote the Qur'an and ahadith [hadith, plural in Arabic] because they contain text that commands Muslims to fight and defend their property, honour and lives when attacked. The UK government is pursuing a course and *[sic]* may eventually lead to a ban on people from even having the Qur'an and Hadith collections in their homes!"[87]

Government officials have tried to preempt al-Muhajiroun's public activism by expressly prohibiting the discussion of particular topics or banning the group from demonstrating. Participants at one *da'wa* stall claimed that the local council put up a notice at a square listing topics that could not be discussed. The list included the movement's favored topics, such as Israel, Jews, and homosexuality. One activist claimed that when he spoke with one of the local counselors, he was told that the sign was put up in direct response to earlier al-Muhajiroun protests.[88] Another participant claimed that, according to a friend in the local counsel office, authorities put a camera across the street to zoom in on the leaflets in order to enforce the Public Order Act.

In 2002, Ken Livingstone, the mayor of London, went even further to curtail al-Muhajiroun's activism by refusing to issue a permit for the movement's Rally for Islam in Trafalgar Square. According to a spokeswoman, the government believed that al-Muhajiroun would use the rally as "a platform for homophobic and anti-Jewish sentiment that offends many people." There was also fear that the movement would use the event as an opportunity to recruit new members.[89]

Al-Muhajiroun ignored the ban and went ahead with the rally on August 25, 2002. Anjem Choudary later received an official summons from the Greater London Authority at City Hall to appear at the Bow Streets Magistrate Court on January 14. The charges included: "1. Exhibiting a notice, advertisement or any other written or pictorial matter; 2. Using apparatus for the amplification of sound; 3. making a public speech or address; and 4. organising an assembly."[90]

In 2003, the repercussions for this kind of activism became even more severe with the trial and sentencing of Abdullah el-Faisal, a Jamaican citizen living in the United Kingdom. In his talks and sermons, el-Faisal espoused the same form of anti-Semitism as al-Muhajiroun, often quoting the same hadith and using similar rhetoric. As with many al-Muhajiroun activists, he was convicted of inciting religious hatred under the Public Order Act. But the government went even further and convicted him of soliciting murder under the 1861 Offences against Persons Act, which covers threats to kill—the first such prosecution in more than 100 years. El-Faisal was sentenced to a total of nine years in prison, and the judge recommended he be deported to Jamaica.[91] The Court of Appeal upheld his conviction, though it reduced his sentence to seven years.[92]

The conviction sent a chilling message to al-Muhajiroun: the government had upped the ante for radical Islamic activists and could broaden the range of prosecutable offenses. In defending el-Faisal publicly, al-Muhajiroun reiterated the rationale it had used to defend its own members in similar cases: el-Faisal had been convicted for "quoting verses of the Qur'an concerning Jihad."[93] The movement argued that the Blair government was trying to silence the "true" voice of jihad, stomp out Islamic activism, and relegate Islam to the domain of private observance and ritual:

> The latest conviction [of el-Faisal] relates . . . to the Qur'an, which consequently gives the British Government an open precedent and a green light to arrest and convict any Muslims, lay or scholar, if they dare talk about Jihad (or other sensitive issues) without adopting the Blair definition of it as 'struggle against oneself' as opposed to *fighting to defend ones life, honour and wealth or spreading the authority of the Islamic state by removing the obstacles in the way of implementing the Shari'ah, as defined by the classical scholars of Islam!*[94]

Because of their personal experiences and the negative consequences of activism for similarly minded radicals, al-Muhajiroun activists clearly recognize that the government considers certain subjects taboo and will wield the Public Order Act against the movement. Yet they consciously choose to defy the authorities and incur the risk of arrest and prosecution anyway.

Treason and Incitement to Violence

The Treason Act of 1351 is perhaps the oldest statute still in force in the United Kingdom. The last time it was actually used was nearly fifty years ago, when William Joyce (known as Lord Haw Haw Joyce) was convicted of working for the Nazis and hanged at Wandsworth prison. A day later, Theodore S. Church was hanged under the supplemental Treachery Act passed in 1940. Whereas the prosecution was required to demonstrate that the defendant had broken his or her allegiance to the Crown under the original treason statute, the Treachery Act required that the prosecution merely demonstrate an intention to help the enemy.[95]

Although treason laws are hardly mentioned in legal textbooks or at law schools, the aftermath of September 11 sparked new interest. In October 2001, rumors circulated that British Muslim citizens were traveling to Afghanistan to fight for the Taliban against allied forces, prompting some sectors of society and the political elite to question the loyalty of the British Muslim community. Debates about the prospect of resurrecting treason as a prosecutable offense followed. Lord Rooker warned that those who took up arms could possibly be charged under the old Treason Act.[96] In a polarized environment exacerbated by the "either you are with us or against us" attitude, the Muslim community found itself on the defensive.

Al-Muhajiroun was, to some extent, responsible for the renewed interest in loyalty and treason. At a minimum, it exacerbated the situation. The movement publicly claimed that thousands of British Muslims had gone to Afghanistan to fight on behalf of the Taliban. The government vehemently disputed the figure, though it recognized that a small handful might have traveled to fight. Regardless of the accuracy of the numbers, the movement purposely conveyed the impression that Muslims in the United Kingdom were primarily loyal to other Muslims and that they would travel halfway around the world to kill British soldiers in defense of the *umma* if necessary. Certainly this was how the public interpreted the movement's claims and public statements about Afghanistan. One letter to the editor captured the general public sentiment: "It is scandalous that we allow the likes of Sheikh Omar Bakri Mohammed to reside in Britain. Give them one-way tickets to Afghanistan."[97]

It is not that al-Muhajiroun accepted the Taliban as a perfect Islamic regime. Although he respected their domestic Islamic practices, Omar Bakri had misgivings about the Taliban's international relations, particularly its interactions with the United Nations. As a result, he characterized the regime as an Islamic *emirate*, not an Islamic state. He even sent movement delegates to the Taliban to convince them to break contact with non-Islamic international agencies. The Taliban did not take kindly to the religious advice and gruffly sent the al-Muhajiroun representatives back to London. Regardless of his reservations about the purity of the Taliban, Omar Bakri felt duty bound to defend them from the U.S. and U.K. allied forces.

Throughout the country, al-Muhajiroun activists exhorted Muslims to defend their fellow Muslims against the "Crusaders" in what amounted to a recruitment drive. Although the movement denies actively recruiting fighters for the Taliban, its activities had that effect. Omar Bakri and other activists told gatherings of mostly young Muslim males about the atrocities committed by the "illegal" U.S.-led attacks against the Taliban. The movement painted a picture of hundreds if not thousands of innocent Afghanis dying at the hands of the invading Crusaders. Given the high-tech weaponry of the allied forces, civilian death could not be an accident; it was a naked attempt to cow the Muslim world into submission. Just as importantly, the invasion violated the sanctity of Islam. Under these conditions, the movement argued, Islamic law commands every able Muslim to support a defensive jihad against the Americans and their allies. Fulfilling the divine obligation to God (and other Muslims) requires that individuals provide verbal, financial, or physical support to the Afghan cause. Those who refuse are sinners (and possibly apostates), since they consciously choose to ignore clear edicts from the Qur'an and Sunna. The argument apparently worked with at least a few Muslims who went to Afghanistan to fight after attending al-Muhajiroun events.[98]

Cognizant of the possible legal ramifications, the leadership in the United Kingdom tried to make a distinction between informing individuals about their religious duty to fight and actually telling them to go to Afghanistan. It is a fine distinction, but Omar Bakri and others in the movement insisted that they were merely telling audiences what the *shari'a* (Islamic law) says about duties regarding the conflict in Afghanistan. The decision to act on that duty was an individual choice and not the responsibility of the movement. Anyone who then participated in the jihad against the allies was doing so in an individual capacity and not as a representative of the movement.

The reality of the movement campaign, however, is that some Muslims took the advice to heart and went to fight. If an individual respects an Islamic scholar and that scholar tells him or her that fighting in the jihad is a religious duty and the only way to fully please God, the advice can have an enormous effect on choices. Under such circumstances, telling a follower that Islamic law mandates fighting is the same thing as telling that individual to go fight. The fine semantic difference between offering a general Islamic principle about fighting in Afghanistan and actually advising an individual to fight is lost. One twenty-two-year-old movement activist expressed a general sentiment held by others in the movement: "I have pledged myself to what he [Omar Bakri Mohammed] says. It's a promise and one that I intend to keep. I'd do anything he'd ask me to do."[99] For the impressionable, if Omar Bakri tells you it is a duty to fight, this is a powerful edict. At a minimum, the movement was trying to inspire Muslims to wage jihad.

While the leadership in the United Kingdom emphasized the semantic difference between outlining divine obligations and facilitating participation in the war, activists abroad were far less careful in their verbiage. Hassan Butt, the movement leader of the Pakistani branch in Lahore, gave a number of media interviews that indicated a more direct tie between al-Muhajiroun and recruitment for the Taliban. He boasted of bringing 400 Muslims to the region after September 11 and claimed intimate connections to jihad training camps. Although the evidence is murky, it appears that al-Muhajiroun activists in the United Kingdom referred interested individuals to the movement branch in Lahore. One newspaper report indicated that the movement actually paid the airfare for volunteers, but this cannot be confirmed.[100] Another story cited a claim by Butt that the recruitment network included al-Muhajiroun supporters and wealthy financiers.[101] Once in Pakistan, volunteers were provided food, shelter, and contacts elsewhere in Pakistan and Afghanistan.[102] While most volunteers remained in training camps in Pakistan, the movement claimed that at least a few went to Afghanistan to fight. Al-Muhajiroun kept the public informed about British

Muslim volunteers killed in combat in Afghanistan. After public calls to investigate the movement for terrorism, Butt and al-Muhajiroun once again argued that anyone involved in the recruitment efforts was acting in his or her own capacity as an individual and not as a representative of the movement.[103] For the British public, the subtle distinction hardly mattered.

The maelstrom caused by the recruitment issue was further exacerbated by movement statements publicly rejecting loyalty to Britain. One activist argued, "If I have to fight against British troops it is because I don't see myself as a British person. I am a Muslim, that's the reality."[104] In another interview, an activist declared that his "allegiance is to Islam, not to Queen or country—if I have to shoot British soldiers, then so be it."[105] The Scottish leader of the movement claimed that killing a British soldier would "not bother [him] in the least" and that he was prepared to face charges of treason.[106] During a gathering outside the Central Mosque in London, movement activists insisted that Muslims had to choose between being Muslim and being British. One activist grabbed a megaphone and shouted his disdain for those who sought a peaceful solution to the Afghan conflict: "I am fed up with Muslims saying Islam is about peace. It is also about war. Allah will send an army of angels against the allies of the West and they will go home in bodybags."[107]

The public was furious. How could Britain allow such treason in its midst? There were calls for revisiting treason laws and possibly prosecuting al-Muhajiroun. Activists scoffed at the threats. Responding to accusations of treachery, Butt responded: "I am being labeled a traitor but I would rather be a traitor to Britain than my religion. I am a Muslim first and foremost and I have no sense of duty towards Britain."[108]

Rather than restraining his public statements in the face of growing criticism, a few months later in an interview with the BBC, Butt warned that Britons who had fought for the Taliban would likely return to the United Kingdom to fight a "new phase" of terrorism: "If they do return I do believe they will take military action [against] British military and government institutes, as well as British military and government individuals."[109] This conformed to his earlier threat that Muslim fighters had not "ruled out" the use of car bombs against government and military targets in Britain.[110] These kinds of audacious statements eventually led Omar Bakri to remove Butt from his leadership position in Pakistan.

In the end, Butt's activism caught up with him. Approximately eleven months after making statements to the press about British Muslim volunteers fighting in Afghanistan, he was arrested. Rather than resurrecting old treason laws, the government arrested him under the Terrorism Act, signaling that it would prosecute radicals who supported jihad against British targets.

Butt's outrageous and open support for violence against allied troops was not isolated. Movement activists consistently argued that anytime non-Muslims invade, govern, or occupy Muslim territory, Muslims have an individual obligation to wage jihad. For the most part, public statements have avoided calls for attacks in the United Kingdom, but a few isolated incidents did raise questions about whether al-Muhajiroun supported terrorism at home. In addition to Butt's statement about a "new phase" of terrorism in the United Kingdom by British Muslims returning from the front, Abdul Rehman Saleem (another leader) gave an inflammatory taped interview to a journalist from Agence France Presse (London office) just after the invasion took place:

> Because the allies, the British and American, have started bombing the Muslims of Afghanistan, for those people over there, the government buildings here, the military installations, including 10 Downing Street become legitimate targets . . . That includes the Cabinet and it includes the Prime Minister as well . . . If a Muslim of this country decides to do it, or if a Muslim who is over there fighting in the front line comes here and decides to do it, this person is not going to be punished for that act under Islamic law, this person is going to be praised . . . What it means is that if any Muslim wants to assassinate him [Blair] wants to get rid of him, I am not going to shed any tears for him, and from the Islamic point of view this person is not going to be chastised, this person will be praised.[111]

As per its modus operandi, al-Muhajiroun claimed that Saleem was simply explaining the Islamic legal perspective, or "*shari'a* angle," on the proper response to the invasion of Afghanistan and was not actually calling for British Muslims to kill Blair. Omar Bakri later clarified the statement, arguing that "if Blair enters a Muslim country, then he becomes one of the legitimate targets because he has aggressed against the Muslims' countries. Muslims living in the West are not in a state of war with anyone and hence they should not break the trust and charter they have concluded with the Western order under which they are living."[112] In other words, the prime minister was fair game for non-British Muslims. This was the argument used to justify a similar fatwa issued against John Major during the Gulf War.

Omar Bakri himself raised questions about possible treason during a public talk about suicide operations, caught on tape by a BBC reporter and aired on BBC Radio 4's *File on 4* in February 2004 (it was also reported in the *Sun*). After telling the audience about the virtues of suicide (or what he calls "self-sacrifice") operations and citing a number of "heroic" examples (the 1998 U.S. embassy bombings, the attack against the USS *Cole*, and September 11, among others), he used a hypothetical example of an operation: "What is self-sacrifice operation? It is going to be the following scenario. Somebody, he fly airplane and he decide to land the airplane over 10 Downing Street, for example, or over the White House. This is a form of self-sacrifice operation."[113] MP Patrick Mercer responded with astonishment: "It's absolutely astounding that these things are being said inside Great Britain today. He's clearly breaking the law. I'm sure he could probably be accused of treason." After the broadcast, al-Muhajiroun issued a press release in which it once again argued that Omar Bakri was simply "educating Muslims about the Islamic perspective" on suicide operations and never actually told British Muslims to go do it.[114] At a minimum, it was an event extolling the virtues of violence. After the talk, one listener claimed that he had trained in Pakistan and was now waiting to be called to martyrdom: "This is something as children we dream of becoming one day. Maybe in the West the dream is to become a great footballer. For us it is to become a great martyr."[115] This view is supported by Omar's fatwa about the religious permissibility of "self-sacrifice operations."[116]

Although the treason laws have not been utilized to combat Islamic radicalism, the issue of sedition underlies the government's campaign against groups like al-Muhajiroun. Public outrage over movements that support jihad against the United Kingdom or British interests has been inflamed by September 11 and the very public manner through which al-Muhajiroun, in particular, has voiced its disdain for British interests.

The risks for Islamic activists are only increasing as the government presses forward with more stringent legal and police powers to crack down on terrorism. Anjem Choudary nicely summarizes the costs and risks of activism:

> Being part of al-Muhajiroun is not really the most prestigious thing. People don't become a part and say "mashallah" [what God has willed, indicating a good omen] and go around saying I am a member of al-Muhajiroun because obviously we get attacked by the government and our members are arrested regularly at demonstrations and at stalls because they speak out openly and publicly about what they believe. They might get arrested because they talk about homosexuality or they might think he is a homophobe or think he is racist and anti-Semitic because he is talking about Palestine. We have had a number of prosecutions. Iftikhar Ali . . . is the first person in this country to be arrested for incitement to religious hatred for quoting a verse from the text [Qur'an] which was considered to be racist. This has never happened before. It is a landmark decision and he a member of our organization. If they join and stay that is because they believe in the cause, they believe in the struggle. We ask our members to interact with the culture and to go out regularly on talks and demonstrations, and they will attend weekly and monthly gatherings, and a fair amount of their time will be taken up.

And obviously they will be asked to contribute financially as well, because we don't receive any finances from the government. We contribute ourselves.[117]

RATIONAL ALTERNATIVES

Given the costs and risks for al-Muhajiroun activists, one might reasonably question why individuals decide to participate, especially when alternative movements are taken into consideration. The United Kingdom hosts virtually every conceivable Islamic fundamentalist movement in the world. Some are obviously larger than others, but al-Muhajiroun is not the only visible movement that pontificates a strict interpretation of Islam. Al-Muhajiroun admits that most of the fundamentalist groups, including itself, share 95 percent of the same ideological precepts.

In addition, al-Muhajiroun offers very few unique selective incentives that could explain the attraction (aside from "member only" lessons, but these kinds of exclusive activities are offered by other movements as well). There are no material incentives, in the sense of magazines or concrete outputs available only to formal members. The solidary incentives derived from group identity, social interactions, and religious activities are offered by other fundamentalist (and even moderate) groups. And other movements and groups offer similar purposive incentives because of their fervent religious missions.

At the same time, al-Muhajiroun is one of the riskier movements: its public and overt activism and support for violent causes draw notice from the public and authorities, raising prospects for investigations, arrests, and prosecution under a number of different laws. Other movements may indeed agree with al-Muhajiroun that jihad against Western troops in Muslim countries is a religious duty, but they do not purposely publicize these views through controversial protests, public statements, and public events.

Take Hizb ut-Tahrir, for example. Since al-Muhajiroun is a spin-off movement formed by Omar Bakri after he resigned from Hizb ut-Tahrir, ideological similarities are to be expected. Both movements believe in a strict interpretation of Islam, defensive jihad to defend Muslims in places like Palestine, and the establishment of an Islamic state through a military coup. And both movements hold similar activities: study circles, religious lessons, and campaigns to encourage military coups to establish Islamic states.

The primary difference between the movements in terms of activism is twofold. First, whereas Hizb ut-Tahrir designates specific countries as targets for military coups, al-Muhajiroun argues that Muslims must attempt to establish an

Islamic state wherever they live. This means that Muslims in the United Kingdom are required by divine law to promote a coup and Islamic state in Britain. The movement routinely issues public statements that Muslims will not rest until "the black flag of Islam is flying over Downing Street [the prime minister's residence]." Hizb ut-Tahrir, in contrast, argues that Muslims are only obligated to work for the establishment of the Islamic state in Muslim countries designated as targets by the movement leadership (presumably because some countries are more vulnerable than others). As a result, it avoids drawing the same level of attention as al-Muhajiroun, thereby reducing risks to its activists.

Second, Hizb ut-Tahrir does not believe in public demonstrations and activism, since these can incur the ire of authorities and impede the fundamental mission to establish an Islamic state in the Muslim world. This is particularly the case for Muslims in Britain: there is concern that the "host country" might crack down on the movement if it engages in the kind of activism practiced by al-Muhajiroun. Omar Bakri and his followers argue that it is a divine duty to be contentious and to act out against the authorities, irrespective of location and possible consequences. As a result, they engage in collective action that frequently results in substantial individual costs.

The major difference between Hizb ut-Tahrir and al-Muhajiroun in terms of activism thus centers on level of risk. The ideology of al-Muhajiroun demands greater levels of contention and the conscious adoption of risky strategies and tactics. Hizb ut-Tahrir shares many similar ideological principles but avoids risky contention where it can. Other fundamental movements take the same stance as Hizb ut-Tahrir, so why join al-Muhajiroun and take on the risk? For the outside observer, the decision seems a bit irrational.

CONCLUSION

Given the costs and risks of activism, al-Muhajiroun can hardly approach uninitiated strangers and successfully persuade them to engage in radicalism. During the initial process of recruitment, then, the question is how, at a minimum, the movement exposes individuals to the movement message. In other words, the movement recognizes that it needs to persuade and convince others to join in high-risk, high-cost activism but that it must first fulfill a necessary prerequisite: message exposure. In short, the movement needs to get an audience to listen (put people in the seats). This, of course, does not guarantee successful recruitment, but an inability to expose individuals to the movement's "sales talk" almost certainly guarantees recruitment failure.

Attracting initial interest, however, is not an easy task. Even if potential recruits are unaware of the costs and risks associated with al-Muhajiroun, the movement hardly enjoys a sterling reputation with the general public. It is indeed successful at attracting media attention, but this attention does not always translate into positive coverage. The average Muslim sees al-Muhajiroun as a notorious bunch of al-Qaeda–supporting "loonies." The movement "brand name" has therefore suffered serious blows.

NOTES

1. *Daily Telegraph*, September 20, 2001.

2. Gregory L. Wiltfang and Doug McAdam, "The Costs and Risks of Social Activism: A Study of Sanctuary Movement Activism," *Social Forces*, June 1991, 987–1010.

3. Omar Bakri Mohammed, interview by author, London, June 2002.

4. Al-Muhajiroun, *The Administration of al-Muhajiroun*, n.d.

5. This pressure was observed by the author at a movement-only lesson in June 2002.

6. Al-Muhajiroun, *Administration*.

7. Food and drink are allowed if provided prior to the start of the *halaqah*. Al-Muhajiroun, *Administration*.

8. Participants, interview by author, and the author's own attendance.

9. During interviews, activists routinely cited the same news sources, including az zam.com, which has since been shut down. Some activists augment this with mainstream papers.

10. Al-Muhajiroun, *Administration*.

11. See Janine Clark, *Islam, Charity, and Activism* (Bloomington: Indiana University Press, 2004), 14; Clark, "Islamist Women in Yemen: Informal Nodes of Activism," in Quintan Wiktorowicz, ed., *Islamic Activism: A Social Movement Theory Approach* (Bloomington: Indiana University Press, 2004), 168–69.

12. Interviews conducted by author indicate that members who have been with the movement for some time, in particular, attend the vast majority of activities.

13. Al-Muhajiroun, *Administration*; leaders and other members, interview by author, 2002.

14. Al-Muhajiroun, *Administration*.

15. Al-Muhajiroun, *Administration*.

16. Omar Bakri Mohammed, e-mail message posting, February 28, 2000.

17. Maham Abedin, "Al-Muhajiroun in the UK: An Interview with Sheikh Omar Bakri Mohammed," *Terrorism Monitor*, March 23, 2004, 8.

18. One of the major financiers was Isfar Ahmed. Kamran Bokhari, former U.S. spokesperson for al-Muhajiroun, telephone conversation with author, June 2004.

19. Interview by author at movement protest rally, June 2002.

20. Various activists, interview by author, 2002.

21. Anthony Oberschall, *Social Conflict and Social Movements* (Englewood Cliffs, N.J.: Prentice Hall, 1973), 152. James Downton Jr. and Paul Wehr, "Persistent Pacifism: How Activist Commitment Is Developed and Sustained," *Journal of Peace Research* 35, no. 5 (1998): 538.

22. Paper based on *Islamophobia*, Runnymede Trust, runnymedetrust.org/meb/islamophobia/Islam_in_Britain.html.

23. At the Labour Party Conference in September 2004, Prime Minister Tony Blair announced the government's intention to outlaw religious discrimination.

24. Islam, interview by author, London, June 2002.

25. Omar Bakri Mohammed, interview by author, London, December 2002.

26. Rodney Stark and William Sims Bainbridge, "Networks of Faith: Interpersonal Bonds and Recruitment to Cults and Sects," *American Journal of Sociology* 85, no. 6 (1980): 1376–95; Doug McAdam, "Recruitment to High-Risk Activism: The Case of Freedom Summer," *American Journal of Sociology*, July 1986, 64–90; David A. Snow, Louis A. Zurcher Jr., and Sheldon Ekland-Olso, "Social Networks and Social Movements: A Microstructural Approach to Differential Recruitment," *American Sociological Review*, October 1986, 787–801; Doug McAdam and Roberto M. Fernandez, "Microstructural Bases of Recruitment to Social Movements," *Research in Social Movements, Conflict, and Change* 12 (1990): 1–33; Robert V. Gould, *Insurgent Identities: Class, Community, and Protest in Paris from 1848 to the Commune* (Chicago: University of Chicago Press, 1995); Bert Klandermans and Dirk Oegema, "Potentials, Networks, Motivations, and Barriers: Steps toward Participation in Social Movements," *American Sociological Review*, August 1987, 519–31; Doug McAdam and Ronnelle Paulsen, "Specifying the Relationship between Social Ties and Activism," *American Journal of Sociology*, November 1993, 640–67; David B. Tindall, "Social Networks, Identification, and Participation in an Environmental Movement: Low-Medium Cost Activism within the British Columbia Wilderness Preservation Movement," *Canadian Review of Sociology and Anthropology*, November 2002, 413–52; and Jenny Irons, "The Shaping of Activist Recruitment and Participation: A Study of Women in the Mississippi Civil Rights Movement," *Gender and Society*, December 1998, 692–709.

27. For the typical concerns of Muslims in the United Kingdom, see Tariq Modood, "The Place of Muslims in British Secular Multiculturalism," in Nezar AlSayyad and Manuel Castells, eds., *Muslim Europe or Euro-Islam: Politics, Culture, and Citizenship in the Age of Globalization* (Lanham, Md.: Lexington, 2002).

28. Jeff Goodwin, "The Libidinal Constitution of a High-Risk Social Movement: Affectual Ties and Solidarity in the Huk Rebellion, 1946 to 1954," *American Sociological Review*, February 1997, 53–69.

29. Rosanne Rutten, "High-Cost Activism and the Worker Household: Interests, Commitment, and the Costs of Revolutionary Activism in a Philippine Plantation Region," *Theory and Society*, April 2000, 215–52.

30. Zaki Badawi, conversation with author, London, June 2002.

31. *Newsnight*, April 29, 2004. Transcript available at http://news.bbc.co.uk/1/hi/programmes/newsnight/3670007.stm.

32. Interview by author, London, June 2002.

33. Hassan, interview by author, London, June 2002. For rank-and-file members, pseudonyms or other anonymous indicators are used to protect the privacy of respondents.

34. Somali member, interview by author, London, June 2002.

35. Somali member, Kamal, and Mohammed (movement leader), interview by author, London, June 2002.

36. Kamal, interview by author, London, June 2002.

37. Mohammed, interview by author, London, June 2002.

38. Rajib, interview by author, Slough, June 2002.

39. Khalid, interview by author, London, June 2002.

40. Al-Muhajiroun, *Fiqh of Free Mixing (Hukm ul-Ikhtilaat)*, n.d.

41. Al-Muhajiroun, *Dheeq Ul-Ofouq: Narrow-Mindedness*, n.d., 2.

42. Al-Muhajiroun, *Dheeq Ul-Ofouq: Narrow-Mindedness*, n.d., 2.

43. Zaki Badawi, conversation with author, London, June 2002.

44. *Independent*, September 20, 2001.

45. *Daily Telegraph*, September 20, 2001.

46. *Independent on Sunday*, November 4, 2001.

47. *Daily Telegraph*, September 20, 2001.

48. BBC, as quoted in *The Hindu*, January 7, 2001.

49. Muslim Council of Britain, "MCB Community Guidelines to Imams and British Muslim Organisations," press release, March 31, 2004. For al-Muhajiroun's reaction to this release, see al-Muhajiroun, "MCB Calls upon Muslims to Commit Apostasy," press release, March 31, 2004.

50. *Al-Sharq Al-Awsat*, December 27, 2001, 4, in *Foreign Broadcast Information Service Daily Report for West Europe;* hereafter FBIS-WEU-2001-1227.

51. *AFP*, November 1, 2001, in FBIS-WEU-2001-1101.

52. *AFP*, November 1, 2001, in FBIS-WEU-2001-1101.

53. *Daily Record*, November 12, 2001; *Scotland on Sunday*, November 11, 2001.

54. For the history of antiterrorism laws, particularly as they pertain to Northern Ireland, see Laura K. Donohue, *Counter-Terrorist Law and Emergency Powers in the United Kingdom, 1922–2000* (Dublin: Irish Academic Press, 2001).

55. See Ian Cuthbertson, "Whittling Liberties: Britain's Not-So-Temporary Antiterrorism Laws," *World Policy Journal*, Winter 2001–2002, 28–30.

56. Cuthbertson, "Whittling Liberties," 30.

57. See various independent reviews of the antiterrorism laws at www.homeoffice.gov.uk/terrorism/reports/independentreviews.html.

58. Press Association, December 20, 2001.

59. Sebastian Payne, "Britain's New Anti-Terrorist Legal Framework," *Rusi Journal*, June 2002, 45–47.

60. Payne, "Britain's New Anti-Terrorist Legal Framework," 46–47.

61. Payne, "Britain's New Anti-Terrorist Legal Framework," 45.

62. Omar Bakri Mohammed, interview by author, London, June 2002.

63. Agence France Presse, September 17, 2001.

64. Rasool (Scottish leader of al-Muhajiroun), as quoted in the *Sunday Herald*, November 4, 2001.

65. Omar Bakri Mohammed, interview by author, December 2002.

66. Reports indicate that al-Tawhid may be a spinoff of disaffected al-Qaeda supporters.

67. *Financial Times*, April 24, 2002; Agence France Presse, July 2, 2003; Associated Press, July 3, 2003; Agence France Presse, July 24, 2003; Associated Press, September 11, 2003.

68. Reuven Paz, "Qa'idat al-Jihad: A New Name on the Road to Palestine," May 7, 2002, www.ict.org.il/articles/articledet.cfm?articleid=436.

69. *Observer*, May 25, 2003.

70. *Daily Record*, December 18, 2001.

71. www.hmso.gov.uk/acts/acts2002/20020041.htm

72. For the saga of Abu Hamza's citizenship issue, see BBC, February 25, 2003; April 5, April 6, April 15, and April 19, 2003.

73. CNN.com, "Cleric: UK Seeks Fast Extradition," May 28, 2004. In April 2003, the U.S. Justice Department cut a deal with James Ujaama, convicted of "conspiring to provide cash, computers and fighters to the Taliban" for testimony against his former mentor, Abu Hamza. In exchange, several other charges, including accusations that he attempted to set up a terrorist training camp in Oregon and kill Americans abroad, were dropped. Abu Hamza is an unindicted coconspirator in the case. See *Seattle Times*, April 15, 2003.

74. For the movement's reaction to the 2004 Abu Hamza extradition hearing, see al-Muhajiroun, "Which One Do You Prefer: Death Penalty or Life in Prison," press release, May 27, 2004.

75. U.K. Newsquest Regional Press, *This Is Local London*, October 4, 2001.

76. After several members of al-Muhajiroun defected to Abu Hamza, his Supporters of Shariah began using the same protest methods as al-Muhajiroun. The timing does not seem coincidental.

77. Omar Bakri Mohammed, interview by author, December 2002.

78. BBC News, July 30, 2003.

79. Al-Muhajiroun, "Al-Muhajiroun Raided by Blair Regime," press release, June 30, 2003.

80. *Birmingham Sunday Mercury*, December 10, 2000.

81. Lead police officer at the scene, interview by author, London, June 2002.

82. Al-Muhajiroun activists, interview by author, London, 2002.

83. Suha Taji-Farouki, *A Fundamental Quest: Hizb al-Tahrir and the Search for the Islamic Caliphate* (London: Grey Seal, 1996), 35–36.

84. Arrested activist, interview by author, London, June 2002.

85. Press Association, May 3, 2002; *Birmingham Post*, May 4, 2002; BBC News, May 3, 2002.

86. At events sponsored by the Khalifah Movement (one of the many names used by al-Muhajiroun) in 2001, participants were accused of inciting religious hatred because of leaflets that quoted the same hadith. The prosecution decided not to proceed because of insufficient evidence and the unlikelihood that the leaflets would actually incite civil unrest.

87. Al-Muhajiroun, "UK Judge Outlaws Qur'an and Hadith," press release, April 4, 2002.

88. Local leader at the *da'wa* stall, interview by author, June 2002.

89. Press Association, August 13, 2002.

90. Al-Muhajiroun, "Ken Livingstone Sues al-Muhajiroun," press release, December 9, 2002.

91. *Guardian*, March 8, 2003.

92. BBC, February 17, 2004.

93. Al-Muhajiroun, "Sheikh Faisal Conviction Part of Blair Crusade," press release, February 24, 2003.

94. Al-Muhajiroun, "Sheikh Faisal Conviction."

95. BBC, "Could UK Taliban Fighters Be Tried for Treason?" October 30, 2001.

96. Press Association, October 30, 2001.

97. News of the World, September 23, 2001.

98. See Agence France Presse, November 2, 2001; *Daily Record*, November 12, 2001.

99. *Observer*, November 4, 2001.

100. *Sunday Herald*, November 4, 2001.

101. *Birmingham Post*, November 5, 2001.

102. *Independent on Sunday*, November 4, 2001.

103. See, for example, al-Muhajiroun press release, November 5, 2001; Anjem Choudary, interview by author, March 2002.

104. *Evening Standard*, September 19, 2001.

105. Press Association, October 29, 2001. For the movement's general argument against allegiance to Britain, see al-Muhajiroun, *Our Allegiance Is with Allah, Not the Queen*, leaflet, n.d.

106. *Scotland on Sunday*, November 4, 2001.

107. *Independent*, November 17, 2001.

108. *Birmingham Post*, November 5, 2001.

109. *AFP*, January 7, 2002.

110. *Sunday Herald*, November 4, 2001.

111. *Guardian*, October 10, 2001; *The Times* (London), October 10, 2001.

112. *Guardian*, October 10, 2001; *The Times* (London), October 10, 2001.

113. BBC Radio 4, *File on 4,* February 10, 2004.

114. Al-Muhajiroun, "A BBC Christian Reporter Declares His Crusade against Islam and Muslims," press release, February 10, 2004. Omar Bakri argues that Muslims living in Britain enjoy a covenant of security (i.e., they are bound by British law) and therefore cannot themselves engage in such acts.

115. BBC Radio 4, *File on 4*, February 10, 2004.

116. Al-Muhajiroun, *The Permissibility of Self-Sacrifice Operations*, n.d.

117. Anjem Choudary, telephone interview by author, June 2002.

2

COGNITIVE OPENINGS AND RELIGIOUS SEEKING

O n the surface, a decision to join a radical Islamic group like al-Muhajiroun seems irrational. Participation entails enormous costs and risks, especially since the movement supports the use of violence and is highly contentious. And the risks are only increasing in the post–September 11 period. Activists are frequently referred to as "zealots," "fanatics," and "militants," connoting an irrational adherence devoid of reflective logic. So how are individuals drawn to the movement? (Summary or prev. chaps) Gained many times

At the heart of decisions about joining is the process of persuasion. Individuals rarely awake with a sudden taste for radicalism or an epiphany that drives them to support violence. And they rarely transform themselves from moderates one day to radicals the next. The process is more complicated and elaborate.

A necessary precondition is that individuals are willing to listen to the movement and its alternative views. When radicals launch into heated and polemical diatribes against the Crusaders, Zionists, and apostates and propose violence, most Muslims tune out. But some experience a cognitive opening in which they become more receptive to the possibility of new ideas and worldviews. Radical activists try to foster openings through conversations with friends and other familiars in their social networks and through propagation outreach to strangers. The objective of such activism is to shake certitude in previously held beliefs and generate a sense of crisis and urgency. Activists struggle to convince others that there is dire need for immediate responses to the current crises facing Muslims and that established or mainstream understandings of Islam do not offer effective remedies. The individuals who experience a cognitive opening constitute a broad potential recruitment pool for a group like al-Muhajiroun, which offers its own ideological proscriptions as solutions for the assortment of different crises facing Muslims.

Of course, this pool is quite deep and expansive. In the Middle East, for example, many people have experienced cognitive openings as a result of political repression and socioeconomic discontent. In the West, many Muslims have experienced an identity crisis that makes them question what it means to be a Muslim in a non-Muslim country. Yet very few attend activities sponsored by radical Islamic groups. Even fewer actually go on to join these movements.

The pool is narrowed as a result of religious seeking and movement outreach. Many who experience cognitive openings resolve the underlying crises through previously accepted beliefs. Still others do nothing. But there are some who search for answers through a religious idiom, a process of religious seeking whereby they look for religious answers to address their concerns. Some religious seekers find solace in mainstream and established religious interpretations. Those who are most likely to be drawn to a movement like al-Muhajiroun, however, find these interpretations and their representative institutions wanting: they do not seem to fully or effectively address the concerns of the seekers. In such cases, religious seekers extend their search for meaning to perspectives outside the mainstream.

Al-Muhajiroun and other Islamic groups try to draw these disaffected seekers toward movement activities and events. In this context, the movement operates in a competitive marketplace of ideas. In its struggle to attract disaffected seekers, al-Muhajiroun competes primarily with three movements: (1) Hizb ut-Tahrir; (2) the Tablighi Jama'at (a quiescent missionary movement founded in India in 1927 that emphasizes spiritual purity and avoids politics); and (3) the Salafis (a puritanical movement whose competition with al-Muhajiroun is discussed in chapter 4).[1]

As social movement theory argues, social ties to a movement are critical for the process of joining, particularly in the context of intermovement competition. Disaffected seekers may be predisposed or open to al-Muhajiroun and its message, but they rarely attend activities or events unless they know someone in the movement. Activists consciously try to draw their friends to the movement, and they develop new social relationships with strangers as a vehicle for sparking initial interest. This is particularly the case where activists are involved in facilitating cognitive openings and inspiring religious seeking in the first place. The point of this kind of activism is to "get people in the seats" at movement events. Attendance at movement activities does not ensure recruitment, but it is certainly an important prerequisite.

To enhance its ability to attract potential joiners, the movement has developed an expansive organizational presence in society through the movement structure and various front organizations. The organizational network offers an assortment of different activities, representing a wide diversity of Muslim concerns so that seekers will likely find something of interest. Even more importantly, these activities are strategically designed to directly address the specific interests of disaffected seekers, who feel as though mainstream institutions and religious figures fail to focus on concerns that matter to Muslims like themselves.

IDENTITY CRISIS

One of the most pressing issues facing the British Muslim community today is what it means to be a Muslim in a non-Muslim country.[2] Muslim minorities currently enjoy only limited theological guidance about how to practice Islam in a Western country dominated by secular social, political, economic, and cultural traditions.[3] Religious jurisprudence about Muslim minorities is sparse, despite the fact that an estimated 40 percent of Muslims worldwide live in minority status.[4] This is complicated by the fact that Muslim minorities in Western countries are heterogeneous: they are frequently divided by ethnicity, language, culture, and religious traditions. As Olivier Roy observes, "While old minorities had time to build their own cultures or to share the dominant culture (Tatars, Indians, Hui in China), Muslims in recently settled minorities have to reinvent what makes them Muslim, in the sense that the common defining factor of this population as Muslim is the mere reference to Islam, with no common cultural or linguistic heritage."[5]

Muslims in the West live in countries where secular laws often clash with religious principles over issues like gambling, alcohol, investment, gender, adultery, homosexuality, and blasphemy. Western legal systems permit behaviors barred under most understandings of Islamic law, and Islamic law permits behaviors that are prohibited by Western legal systems (e.g., polygamy). As one reporter put it, "Reconciling these contradictions without compromising their faith and way of life is a central challenge for British Muslims and the society in which they live."[6]

This challenge manifests itself in debates within the Muslim community about what it means to be a Muslim in Britain. Should Muslims fully assimilate and integrate? Is there a hybrid Islam capable of reconciling competing pressures? Should Muslims withdraw from the broader society and live parallel lives? Should they interact and, if so, how? How does one reconcile "being British" with "being Muslim"?

The urgency of this question is partially driven by the widespread perception among Muslims that they are not accepted by British society, despite government programs to support multiculturalism. Their own experiences with "Islamophobia" belie claims of tolerance. This is particularly the case for the sons and daughters of recent migrants, who have grown up in Britain and find themselves trapped between two worlds: the traditional culture of their families and a secular society that does not seem fully accepting. According to a survey in 2002, 69 percent of Muslims feel that the broader society does not consider them an integral part of life in Britain.[7] One-third of respondents indicated that they or another member of their family had experienced personal abuse because of their religion.[8]

Many Muslims feel the situation has grown worse since September 11. In a poll of Asian Muslims shortly after the September 11 attacks, 57 percent indicated that relations with non-Muslims had deteriorated.[9] More than a year later, 37 percent of Muslims felt they had suffered more hostility.[10] Nearly half of Muslims believe that non-Muslims are less sympathetic to Muslims since September 11;[11] and this perception is not an artifact of community sensitivity: 84 percent of non-Muslims have indeed become more suspicious of Muslims since the attacks.[12]

The legal system tends to aggravate this sense of hostility, exclusion, and alienation. Although protection against religious discrimination was considered in debates about the Race Relations Act of 1976, religion was rejected as a voluntary identity and thus fundamentally distinct from ascriptive ethnicity. The law does, however, recognize Gypsies, Sikhs, and Jews as special "ethnic groups" and provides them with racial protection. Muslims view this protection (especially for Jews) as reflecting biased domestic and international policies toward Muslims. Muslims do receive some indirect protection, but plaintiffs must demonstrate that there was *racial* discrimination, which does not always overlap with religious bias. In a case in 1996, for example, two Muslims were fired because they conducted prayers during their break. Since the employer was from the same North African ethnic group, the court ruled that it was not racial discrimination.[13] This indicates that there are a number of scenarios in which indirect protection fails to protect Muslims.

Many Muslims also believe that the law treats them more harshly because of their religion. The Muslim community, for example, cites the prison sentences given to predominantly Muslim Asian participants in the Bradford riots, which erupted in July 2001 after a rumor spread that the National Front (a unit of the British National Party, a racist and anti-Muslim organization) planned to march through the city. The average sentence for forty-six rioters was 4.5 years, longer than terms handed down to rioters in Belfast.[14] The community responded by launching the Fair Justice for All campaign to get sentences reduced.[15] In addition to specific cases such as this, Muslims are more generally concerned that anti-terrorism laws target Muslims in particular.

The sense of exclusion is complicated by the relationship between Islam and ethnicity. In the United Kingdom, as in all Western countries, Islam is the religion of ethnic minorities (see table 2.1). The majority of Muslims are of South Asian descent (65 percent). The largest ethnicities in the Muslim community are Pakistani (43 percent), Bangladeshi (17 percent), and Indian (8 percent). Ninety-two and 93 percent of Pakistanis and Bangladeshis in the United Kingdom, respectively, are Muslim;[16] and these ethnic groups are more likely than other minority groups to see religion as "very important" to how they live their lives. This is consistent across age cohort. For example, two-thirds of Pakistanis and Bangladeshis between sixteen and thirty-four believe religion is important to how they live their lives, as compared with only 5 percent of whites and 18 percent of Caribbeans in the same age category.[17]

Because of the inextricable connection between race and religion, experiences with racial disparities tend to overlap with religious identity.[18] Pakistanis and Bangladeshis are the most disadvantaged ethnic groups in Britain. Men from these groups are 2.5 times more likely to be unemployed than a white man. More than 40 percent of young Bangladeshi men are unemployed, as compared to 12 percent of whites from the same age cohort. On average, those who are employed earn less than whites and other minority groups per week: £150 less than whites; £115 less than Caribbeans; and £116 less than Africans (about $270,

Table 2.1. Muslims in the United Kingdom by Ethnic Minority Group

Ethnic Group	% Muslim*	% all Muslims	% Minority Population
Pakistani	92	43	16.1
Bangladeshi	92	17	6.1
Indian	13	8	22.7
Black Caribbean	1	Less than 1	12.2
Black African	20	6	10.5
Other ethnic group (excluding Chinese)	26	4	5
Mixed	10	6	14.6
Other Asian	37	6	5
Other black	6	Less than 1	2.1

Total Muslim population = 1.59 million (2.7 percent of total population)
*For those who answered religion question (range is 96–99 percent).
Source: 2001 U.K. Census

$207, and $209, respectively, at a 1.8 exchange rate). Sixty-eight percent of Pakistani and Bangladeshi households live below the poverty line (defined as incomes below 60 percent of the median income after considering housing costs). This is contrasted with 23 percent for all households in the country. Even when religion within ethnic groups is controlled for, Muslims are more likely to be disadvantaged. After controlling for education and area of residence, Indian Muslims, for example, are twice as likely to be unemployed as Indian Hindus.[19] Pakistanis and Bangladeshis are two of the worst off ethnic groups in terms of housing,[20] health,[21] and rate of imprisonment.[22]

Although these disparities may not be a direct result of racism, racial discrimination compounds the sense of exclusion and inequity. Forty percent of *all* Britons believe Britain is a racist society. Forty-five percent say that they know someone who is prejudiced. Sixty percent of blacks and Asians say they have experienced verbal racism; 20 percent complain of physical racial abuse.[23] And 33 percent of Asians feel that racial prejudice is worse now than it was five years ago.[24]

This experience is exacerbated by the activities of racist, right-wing groups like the British National Party (BNP). Members of the BNP have been elected as local councilors, particularly in the northern cities, and have launched public campaigns against Muslims. In its Campaign against Islam in October 2001, for example, the BNP distributed leaflets with titles like *Looting, Arson, and Molestation: It's All in the Koran!* This was accompanied by posters that mocked Islam as a disparaging acronym: intolerance, slaughter, looting, arson, molestation of women (ISLAM).[25] Although the BNP hardly represents mainstream British society, its open activities are frequently seen as simply the most extreme example of racism and anti-Muslim discrimination and hostility. One al-Muhajiroun activist went so far as to decry Britain as "the most racist society in the world."[26]

The experience of both racial and religious discrimination has prompted some young Muslims to think about their identity and how they fit into British society. This is particularly the case for young university students who suffer from a sense of blocked social mobility. Anjem Choudary, the leader of the U.K. branch of al-Muhajiroun, explains this phenomenon:

> Maybe thirty, forty years ago in Britain people were coming over here as economic migrants. And they were really trying to find where the next meal was coming from. In the 1970s, it got gradually better. The Race Relations Act came in 1976. In the 80s, you talk about the second generation coming along, and these people have gone to university. They don't have the financial pressures. They have certain laws they can rely upon to make sure they are not discriminated against. And

if you are not thinking about where your meal is coming from, you are thinking about the problems that beset society. You have a chance to reflect and to think about whether this is the kind of society I want to live in and bring up my children in. And despite the fact that you have just as many qualifications as the next man and [have] gone to the same universities, there is still a feeling that you are disadvantaged or people are still discriminating against you. And those kinds of obstacles have pushed people to reevaluate their ideology, their culture, to say that "I am more successful than Mr. Jones, and he still has a job."

Look, say I wanted to be a physician and those doors weren't open to me. I am still being discriminated against. Many of the kinds of problems in society like racism, the breakdown of the social structure of society, the stigmatism attached to your own religion, your own color, and your own nationality, all of those things have pushed many people, youth especially, to reevaluate their own religion and their own ideology and that has led to a massive revival taking place. That new generation has come out from the universities, from the cities, from the professions.[27]

This is the dominant recruitment pool for al-Muhajiroun. Most activists are university students or recent college graduates with aspirations of upward mobility, a finding that is consistent with comparative research on the demographics of Islamic movement activists in the Middle East.[28] Although precise numbers are not available, my own observations at various events indicate that 90–95 percent are of South Asian descent. These young Muslims believe they face a discriminatory system that prevents them from realizing their potential. They grew up in Britain, but they are not considered British by many in society. Omar Bakri notes the problem facing many young Muslims in the United Kingdom:

People are looking for an Islamic identity. You find someone called Muhammad, who grew up in western society, he concedes a lot so people accept him. He changes his name to Mike, he has girlfriend, he drinks alcohol, he dances, he has sex, raves, rock and roll, then they say, "You are a Paki." After everything he gave up to be accepted, they tell him he is a bloody Arab, or a Paki.[29]

The movement leadership recognizes the importance of this identity crisis for attracting potential joiners. "If there is no racism in the west, there is no conflict of identity," observes Omar. "People, when they suffer in the West, it makes them think. If there is no discrimination or racism, I think it would be very difficult for us."[30]

Amid this crisis, the movement tries to offer an identity of empowerment. Omar is explicit about his function in the context of discrimination and alienation: "Here is my role: 'Come on Abu Jafar. You are not *Bobby*. You belong to a very great nation [Islam]. You belong to the history of civilization, 1300 years of a ruling [Islamic] system.'" Activists hope that the cognitive opening prompted by the identity crisis will enhance the prospects that young Muslims looking for a sense of belonging will turn to al-Muhajiroun for their "political identity and din [religion]."[31]

This is not to argue that every cognitive opening is prompted by an identity crisis. One activist, for example, lost his mother at a young age. The shock of the experience was immense. He initially responded by going to the pub, but the emotional pain persisted. After a time, he began exploring religion and the hereafter. What happens after death? Is it part of a plan? At the time, he worked nights and initially delved into his family's faith, Sikhism. He found it lacking, and some Muslim friends who were activists in al-Muhajiroun took him to lessons by Omar. The predominant pattern for most activists, however, revolved around identity-related issues.

FACILITATED COGNITIVE OPENINGS

While some activists experienced a cognitive opening as a result of this identity crisis or personal experiences, many were prompted by movement outreach and activism (and these are not mutually exclusive). Al-Muhajiroun views one of its primary functions as "raising public awareness" about the plight of the Muslim world and the onslaught of a Western Crusade. As a result, it directs individual and organizational energies toward fostering cognitive openings. Activism is used to shake certitude in previously held beliefs and ways of looking at the world.

Two primary methods are used to facilitate cognitive openings. First, public demonstrations, *da'wa* stalls, conferences, and other activities are used to inform the Muslim public about attacks against coreligionists, both at home and abroad. Inflammatory rhetoric, loud and contentious collective action, and disturbing images of injured or dead Muslim children and civilians are used to induce moral shock and outrage. Images, in particular, are intended to prompt questions from bystanders and observers, and there is evidence that this is an effective technique. At one *da'wa* stall, for example, a number of people stopped to look at the pictures and began asking questions like, "Is this true?" "Did this really happen to Muslims?" Most pedestrians either ignore the *da'wa* stalls or keep walking, but there are a few who interact with activists, ask questions, and begin conversations. In one case, a Hindu woman initiated a long conversation with one of the activists about the plight of the Palestinians. She was horrified by the graphic images purportedly of Palestinian children suffering under Israeli aggression and asked the activist at the stall about the conflict, oblivious to the movement's rather anti-Hindu stance. *⟶ Finally!*

One activist recounted a particularly illustrative example of this kind of facilitated cognitive opening. Al-Muhajiroun brought an affiliated scholar from Pakistan to a Southampton mosque to give a lecture about Bosnia, Kashmir, and other "forgotten jihads." This individual attended the talk because one of his fellow students was the imam at the mosque. During the lecture, the speaker had tears in his eyes as he discussed the plight of Muslims. The activist recalls a particular part of the talk and its profound effect: "Then when he mentioned our pregnant sisters over there had their stomachs ripped open and fetus thrown in the fire, I was thinking no human being can do this. They aren't human beings."[32] As a result of the lecture, he started asking questions about Islam. These kinds of events are intended to prompt questions, at which point activists can direct interested Muslims to additional movement events where they can learn more about the atrocities committed against Muslims and possible solutions.

Although the public events attract some interest from strangers, this does not appear to be a dominant trajectory of joining. A few activists thought others in the movement may have initially been exposed to al-Muhajiroun through the public demonstrations and *da'wa* stalls, but there is little empirical evidence to support this supposition.

The second, more common mechanism for facilitating cognitive openings is individual outreach. Al-Muhajiroun's activist ideology and identity demand *da'wa* (propagation) to others. Following classic patterns of social movement recruitment and religious conversion, activists turn to their established social networks. They discuss religion and political issues relevant to the Muslim community with friends, family, and colleagues. In these conversations, activists try to challenge accepted understandings of Islam. The objective is to break down calcified preconceptions about the role of Islam so that individuals become amenable to discussing the possibility of new interpretations and understandings. Since these social networks represent established relationships, activists can discuss things they may not be able to discuss with strangers in the street or mosque. There is preestablished trust that facilitates the conversation.

One former activist described this experience as "hanging out." In the context of hanging out and socializing, friends discuss religion and politics, not atypical for young Muslims, especially those who consider themselves religious. They discuss the situation in Palestine, the conflict in Kashmir, Western bias in international politics, inequities in the distribution of wealth, and other topics of interest. These conversations take place during ordinary interactions at friends' houses, schools, dorms, restaurants, and other ordinary locales. As in many such conversations, there is debate and disagreement, and activists try to get their friends and others in the social network to accept the argument that Muslims face real, immediate problems in the world and that something needs to be done. Furthermore, the typical argument goes, current approaches to problems like discrimination, military conflict in the Muslim world, and poverty have failed. Some other solution or approach is needed.

Because these conversations take place among familiars, there is a certain social pressure from activists: I am doing something about these issues so why aren't you? In addition, for Muslims in the network, there is pressure to be a "real" Muslim. One former al-Muhajiroun activist describes this experience in the context of his early interactions with Hizb ut-Tahrir (HT):

> A lot of people just joined HT because either their roommate was HT or their friend became HT. You are hanging out with this guy for a long time and he is HT and you are not, and all of a sudden you get motivated. I mean you are Muslim after all, and you are getting the guilt trip that you are not a good Muslim. Eventually, you give in or you, as HT says, "see the light."[33]

This indicates that some individuals may initially go to movement events because that is what others in their social network are doing. (They may also remain involved because of these relationships rather than conviction, at least at the level of low-risk activism.)[34]

Because of the personal nature of the relationship, activists can sculpt their conversations to fit the particular interests and concerns of others in the network. An older member of al-Muhajiroun, for example, recalled his earlier life in a rough section of London. He was involved in crime at the time, and some friends of his family, who belonged to al-Muhajiroun, worked to bring him "back to Islam." They focused on addressing his criminal activities and getting him to reexamine his life. Eventually they convinced him to "shape up," and he started attending movement lessons. Today, as an activist in al-Muhajiroun, he repeats the same process for others in his community. He works in his old neighborhood with disadvantaged youth who knew him before he joined the movement, and he uses his transformation as a role model. He argues that the purpose of his interactions is not recruitment per se but to bring them to Islam. Several of these youth have since joined the movement.[35]

There is some evidence indicating that these "self-improvement" appeals resonate with people. When asked about the most important reason for learning about Islam in the control survey for this study, the modal response was related to self-improvement and development (32.3 percent). The second most common response was that people should understand their faith (25.8 percent) (see figure 2.1).

Activists also modify their conversations with Christian friends. In these cases, they try to generate a crisis of belief by debating the tenets of Christianity. One young member, for example, was born into a Catholic family. He believed in a creator but was nonpracticing. "At the time, I did not think about the world too much," he recounts. "I didn't really care." He went to school with a number of friends who were al-Muhajiroun activists, and as a group they would discuss a range of problems besetting society, such as crime, homelessness, drug abuse, rape, and the gap between rich and poor. For this activist, the latter issue seemed to have been of particular interest:

> I did feel that it was unjust that the wealth was not being spread around equally, and you have people complaining about their millions, and you have people working in factories and stuff and they are working hard and they earn much less . . . Today there are people who steal, but that is only because they need to steal, because the system failed to provide for them. This system does not provide for the people . . . The rich get richer, the poor get poorer.[36]

The activists brought religion to bear on these issues and debated the merits of Christianity and Islam. A common approach for activists is to emphasize inconsistencies in Christianity, a tactic that affected this eventual joiner: "I always

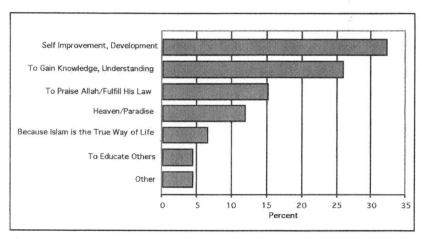

Figure 2.1. Most Important Reasons for Learning about Islam

believed in God, but when it came down to the Bible, there were so many contradictions. And there are so many versions of the Bible, but there is only one Qur'an." He was convinced that Islam could provide solutions to specific problems like crime: "The way I look at it, if you look back in history, the Islamic state, and under the system, there was hardly any crime. There was, I think, only 200 people who lost their hands during that period over theft." The interactions produced a cognitive opening in which this individual voluntarily exposed himself to alternative religious views (in this case, an alternative religion) and eventually converted.

In another example, a white atheist (Christian by birth) debated and deliberated about religion with some Muslim friends from al-Muhajiroun for a year, and the consistency of the debate finally eroded his certitude about the nonexistence of God. This is something his friends were trained to do in movement lessons. A number of lessons deal specifically with the existence of God and arguments directed at atheists. Activists are taught to present very rational lines of reasoning to ensure that their argument is comprehensive, agrees with reality, and is a verifiable fact.[37]

Although established relationships are a common focus of facilitated cognitive openings, activists also propagate to strangers and acquaintances. In these cases, trust has yet to be established. As a result, activists do not immediately leap to challenge beliefs. They instead begin slowly through casual conversations about the individual and his or her life. The objective is to learn about the particular concerns of targeted individuals so that conversations can be shaped to address issues of interest.

Omar Bakri is explicit about this approach, and he identifies the mosque as the typical starting point for creating new social ties: "The relationship in the mosque is the best type of relationship because the people are sitting in the house of Allah. People are there reading the Qur'an."[38] It is a natural religious setting where individuals are already predisposed to discuss issues related to religion. This predisposition does not mean these targets are prepared for discussion about the need for jihad and radical transformation; such rash behavior will likely estrange the average Muslim. Many strangers might also dismiss *da'wa* overtures if they know the propagators are from a radical movement like al-Muhajiroun, so activists limit their ideological discussions and hide their organizational affiliation.

The style of interaction is to take each individual on a case-by-case basis and identify the most relevant concerns and issues. The activists are, in essence, trying to find a comfortable entry into a conversation that can eventually be tied to Islam as a solution. Omar provides an example that is worth quoting at length:

So what is the problem today? The way you open it is you need to address the person. Where do you come from? "Bangladesh." Oh, Bangladesh. How is the situation there in Bangladesh? What do you yourself think is the problem? Why all these bombs here and there? He will say, "Oh, the problem is the increasing of the price on rice, the rice and the sugar [prices] increased." See he makes his own analysis. Oh, but do you think the problem is a shortage of food? "I don't believe so." What about the hospitals? "There is a shortage of doctors and space and places." What about the court? "There are cases that take years." So there is a problem of management as a whole. So you can link it to Islam.

All meetings, when you meet a Muslim or non-Muslim, in your mind three questions: problem, solutions, action. Now you want to let people know the problem. They look to the symptoms. Look to the cause! Make him think about the cause, not the symptoms. Not the effect, the cause—the main problem. After that you start to inspire. "What should we do about that?" Inspire him to think and give him some light. Interact with him, let him see. That is a solution.[39]

↱ manipulative

Rather than forcing a problem as a vehicle for conversation, activists are careful to let the individual come to his or her own conclusion about the issue through conversation and dialogue. As Omar describes it, "Let himself tell me the problem. You just say, 'I don't hear this. What about this?' He starts to figure it out. You don't figure it out for him. You want him to figure out the problem."[40] The objective is to give the individual ownership over his or her decision to look deeper into Islam. Omar continues:

Unless he himself determines the problem, he will never have conviction. That is the fundamental condition of conviction—self-determination. So how can we help him determine that? We come with religious advice, but let him highlight the area [of concern]. You put the spotlight on it for him, and he sees it. [But] someone who has been sitting in prison for fifty years, he never sees the light. You cannot open the door for him and all the light comes. He is so frightened because he is not used to it. He is used to living in the dark. To put the light [on it] straight away you would cause damage to his eyes. So you want him to think about it first. I think that unless he thinks about it and he prepares psychologically for the big issues, he is going to become [scared].[41]

In other words, activists do not immediately jump into a discussion about reestablishing the caliphate. Such a direct approach will likely turn away new contacts. Instead, the technique is to find issues that are personally relevant to the individual to open a discussion about Islam and hopefully foster a cognitive opening. The movement trains its activists in this approach during lessons.

↳ makes the ind. come up wi himself

This technique seems to be quite effective. Take the experience of Islam, now a local leader in the movement. Like most eventual joiners, he was not particularly religious prior to his exposure to the movement. In retrospect, he characterizes his past self as "quite corrupted," a common retrospective biographical narrative for converts to strict religious sects.[42] "I didn't feel like I was getting what I wanted in my life," Islam explains. "Something wasn't right. It wasn't taking me anywhere. I mean I didn't come here to do nothing, there must be a reason for me to be here."[43]

Although born into a Bangladeshi Muslim family, he never practiced and did not go to the mosque. One year during Ramadan, however, his uncle pushed him to go, in one case actually grabbing his arm and forcing him out of the house. Islam relates the story:

> I didn't want to go, because we were supposed to pray. And I sat down, forced there. A young brother, quite young, about fifteen, clever, intellectual, and he started giving me da'wa. I didn't know. The funny thing was, every time I would sit down, and I used to be very ignorant and stubborn, I didn't want to hear what he had to say. And the next day he would come back and sit down in the same place. I was saying, "Listen man, I don't want to hear it." So then what happened is he asked me a few questions about freedom in this country and democracy, and Marxists, and all these different ideologies, and he started to make this comparative analysis of these three ideologies. And after that, it stimulated my brain, and I started asking questions. He gave me some leaflets. At that time I was more emotional than anything else because I inherited my beliefs [a Muslim by birth rather than conviction]. And I was convinced in the heart, but in the mind, I needed to be freed and have it explained.

The fifteen-year-old in this story was a young al-Muhajiroun activist. During the initial conversations, he hid his affiliation with the movement because he wanted Islam to come to his own conclusions.

This approach is not unique to al-Muhajiroun. In Egypt, for example, Islamist pamphlets advise propagators, "Before broaching the sensitive issue at hand, the *da'i* [propagator] must cultivate a relationship with the individual in question or 'addressee.' The *da'i* should demonstrate his empathy and concern for the addressee's problems and, when possible, help resolve them."[44] The objective is to first "awaken his dormant faith"[45] so that "the addressee's heart will become open to knowledge of the Day of Judgment."[46] Then teach him or her about obligations to God. Al-Muhajiroun and other Islamic groups use this approach to facilitate cognitive openings.

EXPERIENCES WITH RELIGIOUS SEEKING

Faced with a sense of alienation and/or crisis (often elicited by the movement), eventual joiners felt as though traditional sources of authority in the family and community failed to provide guidance. Many parents, for example, originally migrated to the United Kingdom for economic reasons. With low levels of education, they took blue-collar jobs in the textile and manufacturing sector in London and the midlands.[47] The relocation was frequently seen as a temporary move prompted by economic necessity rather than as the start of a new life. Many in this generation thought they would eventually return to their country of origin and as a result did not try to integrate or assimilate. Instead, they opted to recreate community structures and practices in ethnic enclaves, limiting interactions with the broader society. They continued *biraderi* (clan) politics and arranged marriages and built traditional South Asian institutions. Some never learned English. The result is that many parents live in Britain but do not understand British society. This leaves them ill equipped to address the complex identity issues and sense of crisis facing young Muslims in the United Kingdom as they struggle to practice Islam in a non-Muslim country and secular society.

To many young Muslims, their parents' version of Islam seems archaic, backward, and ill informed. It is focused on issues of ritual and tradition, devoid of political import. Parents are concerned with creating microcosms of their home country, ethnic enclaves, and parallel societies, rather than political activism. And there is little intellectual discussion about Islam. In contrast, Muslims who grow up in the United Kingdom are better educated and more intellectual about religion. They want to understand the relationship between religion and politics, something their parents typically avoid. Even if parents did support a more politicized understanding of Islam, many would not know how to apply religious principles to the British context. There is a generation gap.[48]

Community religious figures and institutions are seen as little help. Many local imams at the mosques are foreign-trained immigrants from Pakistan and still give sermons in Urdu rather than English (some do not speak English at all). They focus on topics like damnation, Paradise, and living a good life. They avoid politics. As the chairman of the Federation of Muslim Organisations in Leicester notes, "The imams are pivotal in the mosque, but they are not so interested in helping Muslims understand the changing world they live in."[49] A report about religious discrimination concludes, "At the very time that they [young Muslims] become more devout and observant in their own personal Muslim beliefs and in their determination to live according to Muslim principles, they feel that the mosques and imams are often unable to respond to their particular needs and concerns."[50]

As young Muslims become politically conscious and seek to better understand their religion as it applies to social and political issues, some find traditional institutions lacking. "The average mosque, you go there today and it is just a case of read, you pray, nothing is discussed about Islam properly," complains Khalid, an al-Muhajiroun activist in his late twenties from Harlow. "There was nothing motivating . . . We would go to the mosque on Friday, the mosque on Saturday, the mosque on Sunday, and they just read the Qur'an . . . The imams were not good, they didn't have the right culturing. You read the Qur'an but they wouldn't tell you the meaning. And I think that was a failure for a lot of brothers in Harlow."[51] A former activist explains, "When you are talking about Islam, you can't escape the 'mullahism'—the sort of traditional Islamic point of view that has nothing to do with the reality. It's prayer; it's fasting; it's the obligations. But when it comes to public life, political life, social life, they don't really have much to say except, 'Let's implement the *shari'a*.'" The concern that imams focus on rituals rather than politics is shared by radical Islamic activists in other countries as well, who often turned to militant groups because they were the only ones addressing political issues of concern.[52]

The opportunities for continued religious learning at mosques and established Islamic institutions are also limited for those seeking to better understand their religion. In many cases, religious instruction at mosques ends at age fourteen, and it tends to rely on didactic techniques of recitation and rote memorization without providing the kinds of analytic skills that could help young Muslims evaluate their religion and its relationship with the contemporary world. As one study laments, "Muslim children who complete their religious education in the mosque sector are able to recite prayers and read the Qur'an and have a very basic knowledge of Islam. However, they often lack knowledge about the history and traditions of Islam—knowledge that would provide them with the tools to fully engage with their religion."[53] The consequence is that they "complete their education knowing that they are Muslim but with little understanding of Islam."[54] Many Muslims seem to recognize this problem: in the control survey, 93.1 percent indicated that Islamic education in the United Kingdom is an important issue for Muslims to address (70.6 percent consider it "very important").

Because of the diversity in the Muslim community, there is no truly representative institution that can provide authoritative guidance. Even the Muslim Council of Britain (MCB) has its detractors. *Q-News*, a mainstream news source for Muslims, dismissed the MCB as "the government's favourite Muslim umbrella organisation." The magazine's editor complained, "In Britain we have 56 nationalities of Muslims, who speak over 100 languages—it's not fair for anybody to consider anybody to be representative."[55] There is even evidence that, despite a widely shared sense of exclusion and discrimination, differences within the community might be getting worse. In a poll conducted in 2002, for example, 49 percent stated that September 11 and related events created divisions in the British Muslim community.[56]

Within this context, al-Muhajiroun activists offer themselves as "guides" for disappointed religious seekers trying (often for the first time) to navigate the complexities of Islam. Since the seekers are usually members of an activist's social network or represent new social ties generated through propagation, there is a degree of trust. Activists present themselves as neutral guides strictly motivated by a desire to help seekers learn about Islam.

activist = guide.

These guides encourage seekers to sample different religious perspectives and bring them to talks and study circles sponsored by various Islamic groups. This gives seekers a sense of empowerment: they feel as though their conclusions are based on analysis, comparison, and study. A fifteen-year-old activist explains that in the process of sampling, "I had to prove it for myself."[57]

Although one might expect pressure from the guides, activists cite the *absence* of such pressure as one reason they were attracted to al-Muhajiroun's lessons. This is contrasted with groups like Hizb ut-Tahrir, which actively discourages seekers from sitting with other movements and groups. One al-Muhajiroun activist noted that during his process of religious seeking, people from Hizb ut-Tahrir confronted him if he missed a lesson or an event. There was quite a bit of pressure to establish an exclusive relationship of religious learning with the movement. Because of this, some seekers sense that groups like Hizb ut-Tahrir are more concerned with membership numbers than learning about Islam and fulfilling duties to God. By actually encouraging seekers to sample different religious perspectives, al-Muhajiroun and its guides give the impression that they are truly focused on learning and finding religious truth and not on the size of the following.

This process is, of course, still subtly influenced by the movement guides. They are obviously advocates of a particular ideology and as a result debate in a manner intended to persuade and encourage seeking in the direction of al-Muhajiroun activities. And the sampling that takes place under a guide is limited to a particular segment of the Muslim community: fundamentalists. The seekers do not actually explore the entire range of Islamic perspectives. Instead, they are brought to a limited number of groups, all of which adopt similar interpretations with only a few nuanced differences. The most common groups in this sampling are the Salafis, jihadis, Hizb ut-Tahrir, and al-Muhajiroun.

COMPARING NONJOINERS

In comparing eventual participants with nonjoiners in the control survey, one is struck by the similarities. Like those attracted to al-Muhajiroun and the broader Muslim community, respondents in the survey are from ethnic minority groups (only two are white): 62 percent (64) are Pakistani; 10.8 percent Indian (11); 6.9 percent Bangladeshi (7); and the rest from other ethnic groups. Like those who seek through al-Muhajiroun, this sample is well educated: 98 percent have completed some kind of secondary education (36.3 percent are current postsecondary students). And respondents in the control group also believe there are problems with racism in Britain. What, then, distinguishes seekers who turn to al-Muhajiroun from the general population?

Although we must be cautious in making generalizations from the survey, as explained in the introduction, there are several interesting patterns that emerge from the data. First, most al-Muhajiroun activists were irreligious prior to their seeking and involvement in the movement. They describe their prior selves as secular and typically British. In contrast, respondents in the control survey, like many in the general population, see religion as extremely important to their lives. Respondents were asked to rate the importance of religion to the way they live their lives on a scale of 1 to 10, where 1 is "not at all important" and 10 is "most important." The average is 8.65, and 47.6 percent rated its importance a 10.

Just as importantly, respondents believe that religion should be an essential component governing society. The survey asks respondents to place their views on a 1 to 10 scale, where 1 means they "completely agree" that God's law should govern and 10 means they "completely agree" that man-made law should govern. The mean was 2.63, and 48 percent completely agreed that God's law should govern (they selected 1).

While those who were attracted to al-Muhajiroun did not see themselves as religious prior to seeking and therefore were unlikely to have adopted a religious identity, respondents in the control group survey view themselves first and foremost as Muslims. When asked which label describes them best, 68 percent (68) responded "Muslim," 26.2 percent (27) responded "British Muslim," and only one said "British": more than two-thirds of the sample views itself primarily in terms of a religious identity. When asked which label describes them second best, 46.5 percent (46) said "British Muslim," 35.4 percent (35) said "Muslim," and only two responded "British."

At the same time as respondents express strong religious attitudes and affinity for a religious identity, they are not completely closed from alternative religious views. When asked to place their views on a 1 to 10 scale, where 1 means they "completely agree" that they are open to considering religious views other than their own and 10 means they "completely agree" that they are not open to considering religious views other than their own, most responded somewhere in the middle. The mean was 4.68; the mode was 5 (31.6 percent of the sample); the second largest response was 1 (14.9 percent).

 Second, while respondents in the control survey express similar concerns about racism, the intensity seems to be lower than what is found for al-Muhajiroun activists. Respondents were asked to rate the prevalence of racial discrimination in the United Kingdom on a scale of 1 to 10, where 1 is "not at all a problem" and 10 is "a problem in every aspect of British society." The mean was 6.19. The modal response was right in the middle (24.2 percent selected 5). Twenty-three percent indicated that they had suffered racial discrimination at their job, but their attitudes about racial discrimination in British society as a whole did not vary much from those who had not: the former rated racial discrimination a 6.28 while the latter rated it a 6.17 on the 1 to 10 scale. This level of concern seems consistent with the general non-Muslim population which, as we have seen, also believes racism is a problem. It seems to differ, however, from the kind of "suffering" referred to by Omar when discussing racism and identity. It certainly does not rise to the level of sentiment expressed by the activist Islam about Britain as the most racist society in the world.

 Third, respondents in the control survey are more generally satisfied with their lives than those who turned to al-Muhajiroun. For example, while those who were drawn to al-Muhajiroun express strong sentiments about blocked social mobility, as Anjem notes, this does not seem to be the dominant attitude among nonjoiners. Respondents were asked how satisfied they are with the financial situation of their household on a scale of 1 to 10, where 1 is "completely dissatisfied" and 10 is "completely satisfied." The mean response was 6.49. Even when broken down in terms of whether individuals had been unemployed during the last year, there seems to be general satisfaction. Those who had been unemployed (36 percent of the sample) rated their financial satisfaction a 6.1, only slightly lower than the 6.7 rating given by those who had not been unemployed. Interestingly, those who were unemployed over the past year had slightly higher levels of overall satisfaction with their lives, on average rating satisfaction a 6.8 on a 1 to 10 scale, where a 1 means they are "completely dissatisfied" and 10 means "completely satisfied." The average for those who had not been unemployed was 6.5. Overall average life satisfaction was a 6.57. Only 16.5 percent rated their level of satisfaction below a 5.

Ⓤ   Fourth, there is some evidence that nonjoiners have more confidence in the British political system. Though not necessarily the case, the sense of alienation experienced by those who were attracted to al-Muhajiroun most likely includes a sense of political alienation and low levels of confidence in the British political system. Perhaps seekers drawn to the movement simply never thought about politics. But the way it is described by Anjem and several other respondents makes it seem as though seekers attracted to al-Muhajiroun did not feel as though the system could help them. In fact, this was part of the attraction: the movement offered solutions where both the British political system and the mainstream Muslim community had failed. If this assumption is correct, then this is another characteristic that distinguishes the two groups. Most respondents in the control group do not feel represented by established political parties but express some optimism about British politics. Twenty-one percent identify most with the Liberal Democrats, 9 percent identify with Labour, and 63 percent do not identify with any party (the rest of the responses were distributed evenly among other parties). Yet when asked to rate the level of British government support for the Muslim community on a scale of 1 to 10, where 1 is "not at all supportive" and 10 is "completely supportive," the mean response was 4.59, in the middle of the scale. Eighty-seven percent indicated that it was "very" or "somewhat" important to work through the British political system to address issues of concern for the Muslim community. So while Muslims in general may not feel represented in politics, there is evidence that they do feel it is still possible to work through the political system.

Ⓢ   Fifth, there were no indications that respondents in the control group experienced a cognitive opening as a result of movement outreach and activism. Forty-three percent of respondents had some kind of experience or revelation that led them to investigate their religion more deeply. The most common catalyst was the death of a family member (31.7 percent), typically someone in the immediate family. Other catalysts and the distributions are outlined in figure 2.2. In related narrative responses describing the experience or revelation, no one indicated any involvement of an activist from al-Muhajiroun. This, of course, does not preclude the possibility that respondents simply failed to note such involvement, but this seems highly unlikely since most either know nothing about the movement or hold negative attitudes toward it. Only six view the movement in a favorable light; 48 percent view it unfavorably and 25 percent know nothing about it. It seems reasonable to assume that had experiences of cognitive openings resulted from movement outreach, respondents would have viewed the movement positively and have known something about it.

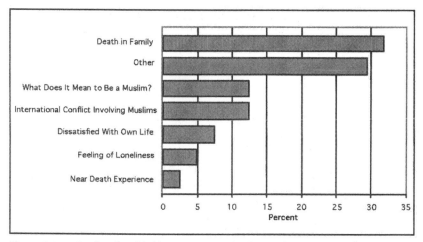

Figure 2.2. Catalyst for Thinking More Deeply about Islam

Finally, there was no evidence that members of the control group had social ties to the movement. Only two respondents noted interaction with the movement, indicating the possibility of social ties. Again, this does not preclude the possibility of relationships with al-Muhajiroun activists, but given the negative views toward the movement, the number of respondents who know nothing about it, and the fact that only a few indicated some level of interaction, this seems unlikely.

This comparison is suggestive, not definitive. Methodological issues and at least a few assumptions preclude drawing firm conclusions and generalizations, but the data intimate some possible distinguishing characteristics that differentiate nonjoiners from eventual activists. As social movement theory suggests, grievances do matter as fodder for revolt. Those attracted to the movement expressed higher levels of dissatisfaction with race relations, their socioeconomic situation, and their lives prior to participation in movement activities. Religion was not a particularly important part of their lives or identity, as compared to both the general population and the control group, and eventual activists felt greater levels of alienation than most Muslims. While an identity crisis catalyzed religious seeking for some, many others were prompted by movement outreach. This increased the prospects that seekers would actually seek through the movement, especially given that many were dissatisfied with mainstream imams and mosques. And as studies of social movement recruitment indicate, social ties are important for channeling grievances and the search for religious meaning toward the movement. Once again, the comparative analysis is limited, but the data do

provide some evidence suggesting that differences in terms of levels of grievances and social networks matter.

FILLING THE GAP

The ability to attract religious seekers and draw them toward participation in
movement events is contingent upon the capacity of the movement to create a
societal presence. Grievances (either self-experienced or created by movement
outreach) are necessary, and networks draw individuals toward the movement.
But the movement must actually offer something to seekers. As resource mobilization theory argues, resources and mobilizing structures are necessary to
translate grievances into collective action, organize contention, and mobilize
like-minded activists.[58] In less open political systems, this kind of organization
is frequently informal, a strategic choice born from necessity in repressive contexts.[59] In more open political systems such as the United Kingdom, however,
formal organizations are an attractive institutional vehicle since they offer greater
visibility and outreach capacity. For radical Islamic groups, an organized
presence creates points of interaction with religious seekers where they can
introduce arguments and possibly initiate the socialization process. The
al-Muhajiroun leadership is conscious of the importance of organization and has
attempted to develop a thick network of institutions. The movement wants its
organizations to be visible and available to serve seekers with a range of concerns
and interests.

The organizational structure of al-Muhajiroun is intended to foster a ubiquitous presence without relinquishing central leadership control. Figure 2.3 depicts the structure of the movement (arrows signify the direction of reporting
and thus authority). Omar Bakri stands at the pinnacle of the hierarchy as the
worldwide *amir* (in this context, religious leader). In each country, there is a national *amir,* an assistant to the *amir (naqeeb[a]),* a national leader *(mu'tamad),*
and an assistant to the national leader. The *amirs* serve as theological guides
while the national leaders administer the movement. In the British context,
Omar is the national *amir.* Anjem Choudary serves as both the assistant to the
amir as well as the U.K. leader. Because of the density of activities in the United
Kingdom, as the worldwide center of al-Muhajiroun, Anjem has multiple assistants to cover the north and south of the country. At the international level, a
leadership committee comprised of the worldwide *amir* and the national *amirs*
and their assistants is responsible for coordinating activities and selecting the
worldwide *amir* of the movement by secret ballot every five years. At the local

level, there is a national committee and local *da'wa* committees. The former is responsible for electing both the national *amir* and the national leader. The latter are composed of formal movement members representing each local branch. There are some twenty to fifty members in each branch. Finally, local branches have local leaders *(masoul)* and individuals *(mushrifs)* responsible for running the various *halaqahs* and activities.

The breadth and reach at the local level in the U.K. provide a visible presence. Each area holds its own public study circles, lectures, lessons, *da'wa* stalls, and other outreach activities. For the most part, an area is defined as a city. London, however, is divided into North, South, West, East, and Central because of its size. The London metropolitan areas are by far the most active, not surprising given the location of the worldwide headquarters in Tottenham (Luton is also quite busy). In total, the movement claims to have branches in as many as forty cities throughout the country. If one only considers areas that hold regular study circles and *da'wa* stalls as indicative of areas that are really active (as opposed to local branches in name only), there are about nineteen local areas in Britain (see list in figure 2.3).

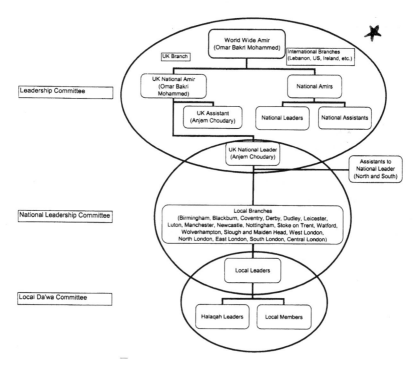

Figure 2.3. Movement Structure

While local imams avoid touchy political issues and generally fail to accommodate the pressing questions posed by many religious seekers, al-Muhajiroun offers a very political and open alternative at the local level to attract interest.[60] Anjem outlines the strategy:

[handwritten margin notes: What amt can other people: addressing their concern for example. + someone who actually listens to them / should make this more obv. ↓ failing or remain in not giving them a voice. is it right to have sympathy for them?]

Addressing the concerns of the people is the most effective way of recruiting. So if you are out there propagating and you take on board the problems that the people are facing, like homelessness, drinking problems, poverty, discrimination, racism, I think that is the classic way of recruiting anyone. If you tap into their problems and you give them a solution, then you have called them. And that is what we are doing . . . People are concerned about their children, and if you are there and talk about their children and say, "Look, we have an alternative. Look at what is happening to your kids in school. Is that the way that you want them to grow up?" And you provide them with an alternative. People will listen, and they will think these people [al-Muhajiroun] are concerned about us. And obviously they will tell others, and this is the way that public awareness is created. And that is the classic way that the Prophet Mohammed created public opinion in his time. He talked about the people who used to bury their daughters alive, people who were cheating in the market, the corruption of the regime. And those very mothers who had their daughters buried alive were on his side. The homeless were on his side, the poor and the meek, the slaves, all. And if you look at any messenger, he got the people on his side because he was concerned about their interests.[61]

Anjem meets regularly with the various local leaders to strategize about which issues to address. As a group, they come up with a list of themes, which the local leaders implement in their respective areas. The headquarters is responsible for providing leaflets and support materials to help organize the relevant activities. Through this arrangement, the movement ensures that all local branches coordinate to address "hot" political topics at *da'wa* stalls, demonstrations, public study circles, and other events. The top-down process means that activities usually emphasize national and international issues likely to attract interest from a broad spectrum of Muslims, rather than narrow subjects that matter only to specific communities.

Although the topics range, a large number address "the oppression" of Muslims. These are the most likely to elicit emotional responses and attract audiences predisposed to sympathize with the general discourse of anger promoted by al-Muhajiroun. In a sample of seventy-eight notices for conferences, debates, demonstrations, seminars, lectures, and rallies between February 1997 and May 2004, 40 percent (31) of activities explicitly focused on the "oppression of Muslims" by non-Muslims. The most common topics were

U.S. aggression (especially toward Iraq) and the Israeli occupation of the Palestinian territories.[62] Public demonstrations were the most common format for "educating" Muslims about oppression: two-thirds of all protests (19 of 29) were about the oppression of Muslims (most others were calls for jihad against various international actors and still included discourse related to "oppression"); and protests constituted 61 percent (19) of all events related to the general topic. The movement uses language, phrasing, and pictures on the advertisements that suggest genocide against Muslims, a technique intended to prompt emotional responses and enhance the prospects that a reader will attend the events. This appeal to concerns about "oppression" likely plays to a broad cross section of the Muslim community. In the control survey, for example, 93.9 percent indicated that the "oppression of Muslims" is a very important issue to address.

The rest of the activities are generally advertised as theological in nature, such as discussions about the relative merits of Islam and Christianity, the need for the caliphate, the "saved sect" in Islam, and foreign policy in Islam. Despite the theological topics, advertisements for these events still include political language and references to oppression (or at least the oppression of the "true" Muslims, such as supporters of al-Qaeda).

The specific topics addressed by the movement are of interest to radicals and moderates alike and thus have broad appeal. The "war on terror" is one important example. After September 11, the British government increased its surveillance of mosques and added mostly Muslim organizations to its list of proscribed terrorist organizations. There was palpable fear among British Muslims that, despite the American and British rhetoric of tolerance, the war on terror would become an indiscriminate war on Islam and Muslims. In fact, a poll conducted for the BBC in December 2002 showed that 70 percent of British Muslims believe that the war on terror is a war on Islam.[63] Al-Muhajiroun plays to this fear by referring to American actions and the more general war on terror as a Christian Crusade against Islam (radicals were overjoyed when President Bush actually used the term "Crusade" in one of his speeches about the war on terror).

The movement also taps into widespread opposition to military actions in the Muslim world as part of the global war against terrorism. Large portions of the Muslim community, for example, opposed the American/British-led invasion of Afghanistan to depose the Taliban and root out al-Qaeda. Fifty percent disapproved of Tony Blair's overall response to September 11. Sixty-four percent opposed taking action against Afghanistan. Fifty-two percent specifically opposed trying to bring down the Taliban. And 35 percent believed the military strikes in Afghanistan were a war against Islam.[64] Compare this with poll results for Britons as a whole conducted around the same time. In the initial months after September 11, polls indicated that 65-74 percent of Britons supported military action against Afghanistan.[65] Among non-Muslim Asians (Hindus and Sikhs), 62 percent supported the attacks.[66]

This kind of mainstream Muslim opposition to U.S.-U.K. military action in the Muslim world was found for Iraq as well. In a sample of seventy-eight Muslim organizations affiliated with the Muslim Council of Britain polled in September 2002, 100 percent said that the United Kingdom should not support a U.S. decision to attack Iraq. Seventy-seven percent said that even if Iraq continued to refuse U.N. inspections and the Security Council passed a resolution authorizing force, an attack was still not justified.[67]

This pattern of concern is consistent with findings in the control group survey. Respondents repeatedly indicated that international conflicts involving Muslims are "very important" issues for Muslims to address. The frequency of those responding that these conflicts are "very important" to address range between 80 percent and 90 percent (see figure 2.4).

Not only does al-Muhajiroun address commonly shared issues and concerns, but elements of its framings are often quite similar to those offered by mainstream Muslim organizations as well. An analysis of public statements related to

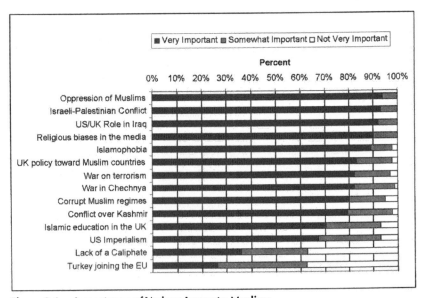

Figure 2.4. Importance of Various Issues to Muslims

the crisis in Iraq prior to the U.S.-led invasion in 2003 indicates stark similarities between the frames used by al-Muhajiroun and its moderate nemesis, the Muslim Council of Britain (MCB). The diagnostic frame for both organizations, in particular, attributed responsibility for the crisis to the United States. The major difference was over whether the pending invasion was part of a "Christian" Crusade or an American drive for global hegemony. The MCB emphasized the latter while al-Muhajiroun focused on the former (the movement would argue that they are really one and the same).[68] As one would expect, their solutions differed starkly (al-Muhajiroun called for a jihad while MCB pleaded for negotiations through the United Nations), but the overlap in the diagnostic frames means that the movement has the potential to attract audience participants outside the radical or fundamentalist community. ⟶ nor only radicali.

A real issue for the movement is that its prognostications will drive away *The movement* potential audience members. The majority of Muslims do not share the *movement* movement's proscribed solutions (see figure 2.5). For example, 81.2 percent *solution* of respondents in the control group survey believe that it is "very important" to use prayer to address the pressing issues of the Muslim community (14.9 percent said this was "somewhat important"), hardly the activism of al-Muhajiroun. Sixty-eight percent believe Muslims should work through the European Union; 87 percent believe it is "very" or "somewhat important" to work through the British political system; and an overwhelming 95 percent

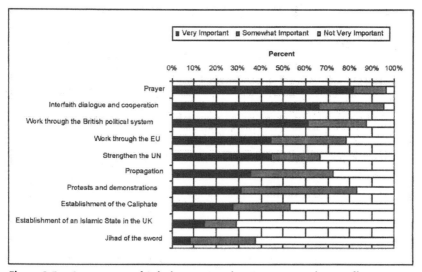

Figure 2.5.   Importance of Solutions to Pressing Concerns Facing Muslims

prognostication: to predict according to present indications/signs

believe that interfaith dialogue and cooperation is an important solution (65.7 percent view this as "very important"). Al-Muhajiroun ardently rejects working through secular organizations, like the E.U. and British political system, and fervidly opposes interfaith cooperation. There was some support in the survey for jihad of the sword (29.4 percent view it as "somewhat important" and 4.9 percent see it as "very important"), but this is a minority opinion and may be related to specific views about the Israeli–Palestinian conflict rather than a more general attitude toward jihad abroad. Seventy-one percent do not view the establishment of an Islamic state in the United Kingdom, in particular, as an important solution, though 53 percent believe it is an important solution in general. This indicates that while al-Muhajiroun's prognostication for problems in Britain (an Islamic state) does not have much support, its more general argument about the need to reestablish the caliphate might.

Recognizing that it could initially alienate seekers with its radical prognostications, the movement issues advertisement captions that usually avoid suggesting a radical agenda, with relatively universal titles like "Global March against Oppressors and Oppression," "Demonstration against U.S. Aggression and Terrorism against Muslims," "Rally for Islam," and "Rally for Iraq." Of course, a handful of leaflets are intended to elicit controversy (and media attention), such as the advertisements for the September 11 commemorative events ("A Towering Day in History" and "The Magnificent 19"), but most seem to focus on generic appeals to the Muslim community. In this manner, the movement taps into widely shared concerns about "the plight of Muslims" in order to draw initial interest without necessarily estranging seekers and other potential audience members by advertising radical solutions.

Although most of its activities focus on international oppression, the movement addresses a handful of national issues specific to the British context that affect large swathes of the Muslim population. Education is perhaps the most prominent example. The Muslim Council of Britain found that access to a quality education was more important to Muslims than all other issues combined.[69] Muslim parents are concerned that state schools do not meet the specific needs of Muslim children, including courses in Arabic and the provision of *halal* (religiously permitted) foods. Many are also concerned with problems of equity and the quality of education.[70] Although Muslims are concerned about Islamic education, they believe in secular educational achievement and want their children to receive quality education in the state school system. In the control survey, 80.4 percent of respondents stated that secular educational achievement is important to them.

While the government provides funding for Church of England, Roman Catholic, and Jewish schools, it has not provided similar levels of support for Muslims. State support for Muslim schools was nonexistent until the election of the Labor Party in 1997 (and there are currently only four sponsored Muslim schools). And there is resistance to expanding this support because opponents believe Muslim schools will promote segregated education and harm multiculturalism.[71] While a majority of Muslims want to expand government sponsorship of religious education, 43 percent of the general population is opposed to "the Government's plan to allow more state funded religious schools such as Muslim, Sikh and Greek Orthodox." The most frequently cited reasons for opposing the expansion are a belief in secular education (34 percent) and concern that religious educational institutions will increase community divisions (29 percent).[72]

Al-Muhajiroun tapped into this broad concern by holding a community "bazaar" in Slough in 2002, where Muslims could purchase Islamic schoolbooks, clothing, and other religious products of interest. Following the bazaar, Anjem Choudary gave a talk on Islamic education in the United Kingdom in which he outlined a design for a parallel Islamic school system (similar to home schooling), including educational goals for each grade. The event was advertised through pamphlets and word of mouth at the local mosque, and attendees came from a wide spectrum of the Muslim population. In the lecture, Anjem embedded elements of the movement's ideology and identity, facilitated by a discussion "moderator" (actually a leader in the movement) who asked strategic questions intended to provide an opportunity for ideological explanations. The talk was just as much about how Muslim parents should educate themselves about Islam as it was about the religious education of children. During the talk, the movement handed out a leaflet titled *What All Muslims Should Know by Necessity* and a protest notice for a demonstration against India scheduled for the following week after Friday prayers.

Another national topic of interest is homosexuality. The Muslim community is fairly unified in its opposition to same-sex relationships. The Muslim Council of Britain, for example, openly voiced opposition to a government proposal to change sex education guidelines to include discussions of marriage and "stable relationships," something the MCB viewed as a backdoor attempt to legitimize gay families and relationships.[73] Despite pressure from the Muslim community, the government eventually implemented the proposal by abolishing a law prohibiting the promotion of homosexuality or "the teaching in any maintained school the acceptability of homosexuality as a pretended family relationship."[74]

Al-Muhajiroun held a number of events condemning homosexuality and issued leaflets with titles like *Homosexuality, Bestiality, Lesbianism, Adultery and
Fornication: The Deadly Diseases,* thus tackling an issue of concern to many
Muslims. In a fatwa against al-Fatiha (a Muslim gay group), the movement issued
the following statement:

> The very existence of al-Fatiha is illegitimate and the members of this organisation
> are apostates. Never will such an organisation be tolerated in Islam and never will
> the disease that it calls for be affiliated with a true Islamic society or individual.
> The Islamic ruling for such acts is death. It is a duty of the Muslims to prevent
> such evil conceptions being voiced in the public or private arena.[75]

At events, homosexuality is framed as the result of a secular system where individual freedom supersedes morality and divine edicts.[76]

In addition to these highly political events, the movement offers an assortment of weekly religious lessons and study circles through local branches. The
stated purpose of these activities is to: "1) Create a profile for the movement;
2) create public awareness about the vital issues; and 3) make new contacts."[77]
Activists are encouraged to bring their "contacts" (i.e., friends and acquaintances) to the sessions, which are held in the evenings for about two hours. Each
local branch is responsible for holding at least one open session per week; the
more active branches usually hold additional lessons. In any given week, the
movement claims to hold about seventy circles and lessons throughout the
country. Specialized seminars and conferences are also offered intermittently.

Many of these circles and lessons address very specific issues about living as
a Muslim in a non-Muslim country. In contrast to local imams at mosques, the
movement delves into details about what Islam permits and forbids in the British
context. It provides succinct guidance about how to live as a Muslim. Take economic issues, for example. Islam explicitly prohibits certain economic transac-
tions, such as *riba* (usury or interest), that are widely practiced in many countries, particularly in the West. Al-Muhajiroun held a series of circles to directly
address related questions. Muslims need to engage in economic activity, but how
do they do this if most established economic institutions violate Islamic mores?
Do they open a savings account if a bank uses interest for the account? Can they
purchase stocks? What if their pension invests in speculative activities? Whereas
many imams focus on rituals, al-Muhajiroun offers to answer practical questions
for religious seekers interested in living according to Islam. This is typical of its
study circles and lessons, and seekers find guidance where mainstream institutions seem silent.

Ostensibly, the focus at the lessons and study circles is learning about Islam, but politics are invariably injected into the lectures and discussions. In fact, the leadership recognizes that many of these lessons are more about motivation than education. At a lesson at the William Morris Community Center in London, for example, Omar gave a motivational lecture on Kashmir and the modern-day Western Crusade to an audience of mostly teenage South Asians. He whipped the audience into an emotive frenzy as he outlined the Western Crusader conspiracy and its connections to the conflict in Kashmir. The purpose was not to delve into the complexities of religious jurisprudence or disseminate the movement's ideology in its entirety but rather to pique emotions and interest, as Anjem acknowledged in our conversation prior to this particular talk.

The density of this societal presence situates al-Muhajiroun as a resource for religious seekers. In a few cases, seekers simply stumbled on Omar at one of the many events. This was the case for Anjem Choudary, who was sampling the Muslim community and came to a local mosque where Omar gave a *tafsir* (an explanation of Qur'anic verses). Most eventual joiners, however, were drawn to these activities and events through friendship networks and new social ties to al-Muhajiroun. Regardless of whether individuals randomly show up at events or are drawn through networks, the point is to offer activities as a starting point for possible socialization.

OPPORTUNITIES FOR WOMEN

Unlike many Islamic fundamentalist movements, al-Muhajiroun encourages female activists. In fact, relative to other radicals, the movement is quite liberal in its views toward women. Activists believe that men and women have many of the same duties toward God, including *da'wa* and learning about Islam, since the relevant verses of the Qur'an are general and do not specify a gender. As a result, the movement encourages women to participate in an assortment of activities and offers itself as a unique resource for female religious seekers.

Women were initially recruited into the movement through their husbands. Not every activist's wife became a member, but there are a number of such cases. Omar argues that it is obligatory for a man to encourage his wife's participation, and activists often bring their wives to lectures and events.[78] Once the movement established a critical mass of female activists, recruitment generally followed the same pattern as men: women used their social networks or established new relationships to encourage religious seeking through al-Muhajiroun events and activities.

To foster female participation, the movement provides a number of women-only study circles and lessons. At one point, for example, it offered weekly religious circles for women at the CYCD Community Centre in Luton. Most women-only lessons these are taught by female activists, though Omar and other male leaders in al-Muhajiroun do teach women-only groups on occasion (usually specialized lessons or circles for female activists in the movement, who need to be properly trained as representatives of al-Muhajiroun). There are also special women-only circles offered at a number of universities throughout the country.[79]

Women at these events frequently bring their children, thereby reducing the possible cost for participation.[80] Since conservative Muslims typically argue that a woman's first priority is the home (including her children), a permissive educational environment where children are welcome helps overcome a limitation to biographical availability.

In addition to women-only lessons, the movement holds a number of open activities that include both men and women, a practice that is generally taboo in the fundamentalist community because of norms against "mixing" with the opposite sex (unless they are close relatives). When both genders are involved, the movement tries to adhere to standards of gender segregation by keeping some physical distance between female and male attendees. At mixed lectures and study sessions, for example, men are required to sit at the front of the room while women are seated in the back. This is intended to ensure that men watch the speaker and do not gaze at women in the audience. At these events, women actively participate, though some choose to write down questions and pass them to the speaker.

At these activities, women frequently ask questions related to whether or not they can be activists and work outside the home. A typical phrasing is something like the following: "My husband says Islam does not allow women to do [a certain activity]. Is that true?" The consistent response is that the male instinct to restrict the participation of women (whether wives or daughters) is emotional and not based on religious evidence in the Qur'an or Sunna.[81] Men, for example, may be motivated by jealousy. At one lesson, the speaker argued that this knee-jerk reaction is a backlash against feminism, which allows women to do whatever they want. It is not, he argued, rooted in Islam. He and other activists highlight the important role played by historical female activists, including the Prophet's wife Aisha.

Women also participate in the more volatile activities. At one protest, about fifteen women (out of a total of fifty demonstrators) held up signs calling for jihad outside the Pakistani embassy. To again maintain some gender segregation, the men congregated about ten feet away from the women. Female members are expected to adhere to the same duties and responsibilities as their male counterparts, including *halaqahs, da'wa* stalls, and demonstrations.

The movement recognizes that it faces opposition from other conservative Muslims, who often complain about al-Muhajiroun's loose interpretation of gender segregation. At one event, a movement activist got into a heated exchange with another participant over the presence of women. He repeated the movement's argument that women and men must follow the same divine edicts expressed in the sources of Islam, unless there is an explicit reference to some restriction. In addition, he argued, since women are responsible for teaching their children about Islam, it is critical that they participate in lessons and other educational activities to ensure that they pass on proper religious understandings.

There are some limitations to female participation, but they generally come from husbands and fathers rather than al-Muhajiroun itself. Ultimately, according to activists, a woman can only leave the home with the permission of a male guardian, who holds final authority in the family. As "honor that needs to be protected," a woman must obey her guardian to protect her virtue and the reputation of the family. But so long as she receives permission, she can attend the activities.[82]

Although numbers are not available, it appears that this stance on women encourages relatively high levels of female participation when compared to other radical Islamic groups. Even when Omar launched the first incarnation of al-Muhajiroun in Saudi Arabia, women were involved (about nine of the seventy members).[83] Women have their own events and maintain a strong presence at public activities in the United Kingdom. There is even a leadership structure for women. While the *amirs* and national leaders are all men, each national leader has a male and a female assistant. Each assistant, in turn, is responsible for overseeing local branches run by gender.[84] According to the former head of the women's branch, "Right from the beginning it was the sisters who were very proactive, organized, creative and very well versed in many subjects (it is usually the opposite [in] most Islamic groups)."[85] Though men still dominate the upper echelons of the leadership, female seekers find ample opportunities for activism and involvement.

PLATFORMS AND FRONTS

Al-Muhajiroun relies on public outreach to build supporters and recruit new activists, and the movement has openly booked a number of public venues to hold

[handwritten margin notes: "working for the / politicisation or / space → community centre → can become something else."]

[handwritten margin note: "Public space which bear event."]

talks, meetings, and religious lessons. Prior to September 11, it encountered relatively little resistance to using public spaces like community centers and public libraries, which represent low-cost venues with established ties to local communities. For the most part, those in charge of the spaces were unaware of al-Muhajiroun's radical agenda and gave the movement free access. Ironically, given the movement's views toward violence, one event was even scheduled to be held at the Quakers' Friends House (it was canceled once administrators became aware of al-Muhajiroun's activities).

An analysis of sixty-one movement announcements for activities and events held between January 1999 and March 2004 (three of these were eventually canceled) gives a sense of this access (the sample does not include demonstrations and *da'wa* stalls, since these are held on sidewalks and outdoor public squares). Nearly 60 percent of these events were held at community centers, libraries, and local Muslim centers (35) (see figure 2.6). Another 16 percent (10) were held at local mosques. Twenty percent (12) did not list a venue. Interestingly, none of the announcements listed al-Muhajiroun's offices as a venue location, even though many movement-only activities are held at the headquarters and the facilities can certainly accommodate large crowds.

As the movement's notoriety grew, this access became increasingly limited. Authorities have become more aware of al-Muhajiroun's radicalism; and despite the movement's best efforts at image management in the media, the general pub-

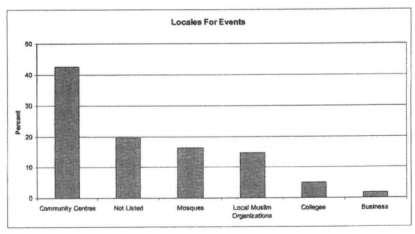

Figure 2.6. Locales for Events

lic perception (where there is awareness) is that it is part of a radical fringe that supports terrorism. Whereas in the past officials and those in charge of public spaces might have been unaware of the movement or willing to tolerate its antics, this is no longer the case. In 2000, for example, police advised officials at the Platfield Park in Manchester to cancel al-Muhajiroun's access to the park for an event on August 13, forcing the movement to relocate to another venue without sufficient advertisement.

The movement has faced particular pressure on university campuses, which *University* were previously considered an important locale for recruitment and activism. At campus events, such as "freshers," the movement set up booths with controversial pictures and statements in the tradition of the *da'wa* stalls. Like Hizb ut-Tahrir before it, al-Muhajiroun distributed anti-Semitic leaflets, and its aggressive posture (both verbal and physical) toward other students raised increasing concern from student unions and Jewish organizations. In response to a rash of complaints, the National Union of Students (NUS) banned al-Muhajiroun from campuses as part of a broader antiracism campaign. In February 2001, the NUS passed a motion stating that "extremist views of any kind intimidate and threaten students on campus and prohibit the building of an active Student Union." The following NUS motion was passed in response to al-Muhajiroun activities:

1. That recent events have shown us that extremism is still a threat in all its forms.
2. That Al-Muhajiroun employ tactics of intimidation through distributing inflammatory and hate-filled literature in student unions stopping students being involved in building an active Student Union.
3. That religious extremist groups continue to incite hatred on our campuses, one example being the posters recently put up around Birmingham by Al-Muhajiroun stating that "the final hour will not come until the Muslims have killed the Jews."
4. That Al-Muhajiroun have explained the Middle East conflict to achieve their own ends. Their literature has also consistently called for the destruction of Sikhs, Hindus, moderate Muslims, women and homosexuals.
5. Both Muslim students and Jewish students feel intimidated by Al-Muhajiroun's tactics and actions over the situation in the Middle East.
6. That Al-Muhajiroun and other extremist organisations have no place in the student movement.[86]

Since the movement depended in part on access to universities to tap into its student base, the ban directly threatened recruitment.

*Difficulty
in access
to public
space.*

Restrictions to public space have become common since September 11. As Anjem notes, "It is very difficult to book venues now, community centers, mosques, local authority venues. They know that you are from al-Muhajiroun coming to book a venue. They are not going to have you there. And one of the things that happened to us after the eleventh of September was that many of our venues were in fact canceled. All the ones in London were canceled, many of them in the north as well."[87] Almost immediately after September 11, for example, al-Muhajiroun organized a meeting titled "World War III against Islam. As America declares war on 1.5 billion Muslims worldwide . . . What is your duty?" It was scheduled to be held at the Bangladesh Centre in Riverside, but the center's administrators canceled the meeting once they became aware of the controversy surrounding al-Muhajiroun and the radical nature of its message.[88]

In another example, the movement tried to hold an event called The Magnificent 19 on the second anniversary of September 11. It was intended to commemorate the "bravery" of the hijackers, and advertisements used pictures of the hijackers and an angelic image of bin Laden superimposed on the World Trade Center towers as they smoldered. According to the movement, venues in London, Manchester, Birmingham, and Leicester were canceled. The movement instead held a press conference at its headquarters.[89]

In the sample of sixty-one movement announcements, ten out of the twelve events that did not list a venue were scheduled after September 11, providing further evidence of diminishing access to public space. In these cases, leaflets and advertising included a request that interested individuals call a contact number the day of the event for information about the location.

*Platforms
developed*

Although the movement has found it increasingly difficult to hold events and activities under the "al-Muhajiroun" label, it has developed an extensive network of platforms and front organizations over the years and uses these to continue public outreach efforts. These organizations use innocuous names like Society of Muslim Parents, Global Truth, and Peaceful Society and are intended to facilitate movement access to public spaces (see table 2.2).

The platforms are not administratively tied to al-Muhajiroun, in the sense of shared bylaws and bureaucratic structure, but they are connected at the level of individual activists. The founders and leaders of the platforms are what Omar terms the "A-team" of al-Muhajiroun—the top elite of the movement. Members of the A-team have undergone substantial ideological training and are personally certified by Omar as knowledgeable enough to give religious lessons and public talks. These are considered the emerging *ulama* (scholars) of the movement, capable of accurately representing and teaching the ideological precepts of al-Muhajiroun. The majority are highly educated professionals from fields like

Table 2.2. Al-Muhajiroun Platforms and Fronts (Past and Current)

Al-Khilafah Movement	Islamic World League	Shari'ah Court of the
Al-Maddad Society	Society of Muslim	UK
Society of Muslim	Doctors	Muslim Cultural Society
Lawyers	Society of Muslim	Party of the Future
Society of Muslim	Teachers	Society of Muslim Youth
Parents	London School of Shari'ah	International Islamic
Society of Converts to	Luton Islamic Education	Front
Islam	Centre	One-to-One Society
Society of Muslim	Derby School of	Peaceful Society
Women	Shari'ah	ALM Publications
Society of Muslim	Manchester School of	Mujahid Distribution
Students	Shari'ah	Network
Defenders of the Faith	Sheffield School of Shari'ah	Islamic Council of
Islamic Tahreek for	Society of Juristic Scholars	Britain
Pakistan	Hizb ut Tawhid	Info 2000 Software Ltd.
Kosovo Support Council	Muslim Committee	Human Society
Islamic Cultural Society	Chechnya Support Council	Muslim Media Forum
Global Truth	West London Islamic	Muslim Youth Forum
Action Committee against	Cultural Society	Muslims in the UK
British Terrorism	Concerned Muslim	Slough Islamic Forum
N17 Studios	Citizens for Justice	Intellectual Thinkers
Association of London	Jamaat al-Nusra	Jihad in Manchester
Muslims		
The Way for Unity		
Society of Converts to		
Islamic Freemasons		

Sources: Al-Muhajiroun constitution; interviews with al-Muhajiroun leadership; various movement publications; newspaper reports.

medicine, law, and engineering; and these leaders use their educational background and work experience to form functionally differentiated platforms that address particular issues related to their professional skills. Not everyone who participates in a platform is an al-Muhajiroun activist, but the majority are from the movement.

At least from the movement's perspective, the use of platforms has secured continued access to public spaces for activities. For example, despite the NUS ban, al-Muhajiroun continues to operate on university campuses through a variety of alternative organizations. Anjem argues that "the whole university campus issue was blown out of proportion because we were never there solely under the platform of al-Muhajiroun . . . We were using so many different platforms and names. There are a whole host of organizations and titles and they just continued, because most of the time the idiot [NUS] doesn't have a clue.

The National Union of Students didn't have a clue that they were associated or affiliated with us."[90]

The platform names are frequently used to obfuscate the movement's identity on leaflets and advertisements. Because the movement wants to maintain a public presence and claim importance, it uses its own name in certain instances. But where notoriety could cause trouble, it turns to platforms. In addition, it will list "al-Muhajiroun" and a series of platform names on advertisements to give the impression that an event is sponsored and/or supported by a coalition of Islamic organizations. In a small sample of forty-seven advertisements for events and weekly study circles produced only in leaflets and flyers between January 1999 and May 2004 (again not including demonstrations and *da'wa* stalls), about half use the "al-Muhajiroun" label alone (25); 25 percent list only a platform name (12); 8 percent include both "al-Muhajiroun" and at least one platform (4); and 13 percent do not list a sponsor (6) (see figure 2.7).

Not only do platforms facilitate access to community space and thus enhance the movement's presence in society, but the resulting functional differentiation allows the movement to offer services and programs specifically tailored to different Muslim interests as well. For example, Muslims interested in learning about how to raise children in a predominantly secular society might be drawn to the movement's Society of Muslim Parents.[91] Recent converts to Islam might be attracted to the movement's Society of Converts to Islam. And children and

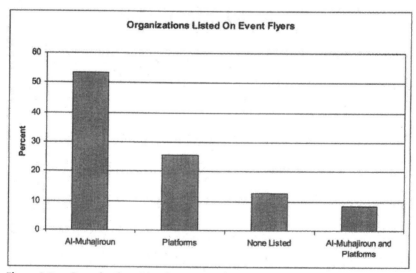

Figure 2.7. Organizations Listed on Event Flyers

university students might find the Society of Muslim Youth interesting. The idea is to create a number of alternative focuses to tap into the diverse and specific interests of the Muslim community. The greater the number of platform options, the greater the likelihood that the movement can tap into community interests and draw individuals to movement activities.

Typically, those who initially express interest in the platforms are unaware of the al-Muhajiroun affiliation. Activists recognize that potential joiners might a priori reject the organizations and their messages if they know that they are linked to the notorious al-Muhajiroun. Most Muslims view al-Muhajiroun negatively. In the control survey, as noted earlier, 48.9 percent viewed the movement very unfavorably, 6.1 percent favorably, and 25.5 percent didn't know about the movement. This means many might avoid an event if they are aware that al-Muhajiroun is involved. To limit this, the leaders of the platforms attempt to obfuscate the relationship while passing on the movement ideology through religious lessons, talks, and discussions. In this manner, "he [a platform leader] can pass to them [platform participants] whatever we [the movement] want without them knowing."[92] The leaders give *halaqahs* and still hold *da'wa* stalls but focus more narrowly on the specific topics of the platforms. As it becomes clear that an individual has adopted many of al-Muhajiroun's ideas and is no longer prone to rejecting the message based on the movement's negative reputation, the connection is revealed. In short, the movement believes that, in some circumstances, it needs to persuade individuals to accept the ideological message before telling them about the platform's al-Muhajiroun connection. Anjem explains:

> What this means is that when we actually go to these people, we adopt different things, like "Muslims in the UK," "Muslims in Britain," or something like that. And people come to us and they realize that we are also al-Muhajiroun. Then I think they appreciate that what they heard hitherto was not really accurate . . . when they actually listen to us, and they speak to people like sheikh Omar, and they listen to the interpretation of the Qur'an, and what we are actually saying about these issues, they find that things are very different from what they seem [in the press].[93]

Omar Bakri echoes the same rationale for the obfuscation:

> What happens is he [a religious seeker] just comes and he participates and later on he starts to argue, he adopts the ideas, he starts to embrace them, he starts to go forward. And then he finds out "Oh, al-Muhajiroun has the same ideas." Why? Because they invite sheikh Bakri, they invite Anjem, they invite Abdur-Rahman, they invite this and that. This is when the situation becomes, "Oh, now I know

them closely, I don't need to listen to the media. I can listen to them directly." So all the media brainwashing is gone.[94]

The obfuscation is also a strategic design to enhance organizational redundancy in case of a government crackdown on the movement and its leadership. The A-team and the network of platforms represent the successors to the movement mantle should the government ban al-Muhajiroun and/or arrest its leadership. It is for this reason that Omar calls the platform leaders "the hidden members." In the event of a crackdown, they would deny affiliation with al-Muhajiroun and fill the void through their network of differentiated organizations. For Omar, the platform network is "Plan B": "If all of us are arrested, they will rise and start to publish leaflets" and continue the activism of al-Muhajiroun.[95]

In the past, several of the platforms were registered as charities, which provided financial benefits to the movement. Charities receive tax breaks on renting space, purchases, and cars and can be used to raise tax-exempt donations. At least until sometime in 2002, al-Muhajiroun, as an organization, (illegally) used platform charity registration numbers, which significantly reduced overhead costs.

The government eventually caught on to the scheme. In one case, The Muslim Cultural Society of Enfield and Haringey, founded by a former member of Hizb ut-Tahrir, released its charity number to Anjem and a few other organizations.[96] The connection became public after the *Sunday Telegraph* reported that the platform was publishing material supporting jihad and producing fatwas by the al-Muhajiroun–affiliated Shari'ah Court against Salman Rushdie and Terrance McNally.[97] In November 1999, the Charity Commission launched an investigation and eventually removed the charity from the registry because of potential involvement in illegal activities and "on the grounds that it did not operate and had ceased to exist under its constitution."[98]

In 2001, the Charity Commission initiated another investigation against the South London Middle Eastern and South East Asian Women's Issues organization, registered in December 2000 as an organization to help women of Middle Eastern or Southeast Asian descent through education, advice and information, and recreation and leisure. The charity listed Abdul Rehman Saleem, one of the senior leaders of al-Muhajiroun, as the chairman of the organization. Not only did al-Muhajiroun use the charity's registration number, but it also transferred occupancy of the movement's headquarters at the Tottenham Technopark from a dissolved front company called Info 2000 Ltd. to the charity. This provided tax breaks and reduced the cost of renting office space.

Several issues raised concerns from the Charity Commission. First, in September 2001, someone sent the commission business cards listing al-Muhajiroun, the Shari'ah Court of the UK, and the Society of Muslim Lawyers with the women's organization's charity number. The business cards included the following statement at the bottom: "Registered Charity No. 1083972 [the number used by the women's organization] in Co-operation with the London School of Shari'ah & The Society of Muslim Lawyers."[99] The number was also used on statements and documents produced by several other movement platforms.

Second, concerns about a possible connection between the charity and illegal activities were raised when Abdul Rehman, acting as a spokesperson for al-Muhajiroun in Pakistan, gave his infamous interview condoning attacks against the British government and Tony Blair. When questioned about connections between the charity, al-Muhajiroun, and several affiliates, both Abdul Rehman and Anjem Choudary disputed an insidious relationship. Anjem argued that he had provided legal advice to the charity through the Society of Muslim Lawyers and that the printer had included the registry number on the business cards by accident. When questioned by the commission, Abdul Rehman would not provide the printer's details or copies of business cards for other suspected organizations (including a card from the South London Middle Eastern and South East Asian Women's Issues organization). He claimed that the business cards for the organizations were all printed at the same time, implying that this was the source of the error. When pressed for specific documents and information, including the names of trustees, finances, membership, and minutes, he claimed to have destroyed them.[100] Aside from bank records, he produced no documentation and admitted that the charity had no income or members.

Abdul Rehman also told the Charity Commission that he was not the "Abdul Rehman Saleem" referenced in press reports about the outrageous statement condoning attacks against Britain and Tony Blair.[101] This claim, however, is dubious. Not only did Abdul Rehman and Omar later argue that the statement was only an Islamic jurisprudential perspective rather than a call to arms (indicating that he did indeed make the statement), but Abdul Rehman also admitted that the telephone number used by the press to contact "Abdul Rehman Saleem" in Lahore was indeed his mobile telephone number. In addition, Omar Bakri's description of the "Abdul Rehman Saleem" from the media reports (married with two children, educated at Queen Mary College and the London School of Shari'ah) is consistent with what I was told about Abdul Rehman during fieldwork.[102]

The commission rejected Abdul Rehman's arguments, and the registration number was revoked. The charity was dissolved on October 19, 2001, and the Charity Commission launched an additional investigation into the activities of al-Muhajiroun, the Shari'ah Court, and the Society of Muslim Lawyers for misuse of charity registration numbers.[103]

The government continued to crack down on some of the platforms and closed additional organizations, but the affiliates are difficult to fully monitor. Members of al-Muhajiroun continue to form new organizations and apply for charitable status, and unless officials at the Charity Commission are aware that particular individual applicants are affiliated with al-Muhajiroun, it is difficult to prevent the movement from forming new platforms. After the government shut down four affiliated organizations, for example, one of these was successfully reestablished under a different name. Even Jamaat al-Nusra, an organization devoted to contacting members of the military who could establish an Islamic state through a coup, applied for charitable status.[104]

Despite this, the loss of the charity registration number has significantly increased the overhead costs for al-Muhajiroun and affected the movement. Without its charity number, the movement pays a £5,000 per month business presence rate in addition to the £1,150 rent plus utilities for its headquarter offices. The increases forced the movement to close a number of branch offices. Omar still believes he can continue to find other organizational vehicles, but he recognizes the impact: "You need to find a mechanism. They close one door you open ten. But they become tighter, and tighter, and tighter."[105]

One new technique is to gain access to venues through nonaffiliated organizations. In at least a few instances, nonmovement organizations have invited al-Muhajiroun activists to appear at events. In one case, the Secular Societies wrote a series of articles critical of the movement, and Omar Bakri responded by challenging the organization to a debate. The challenge was accepted, and the Secular Societies booked a public venue under its own name. The movement, in effect, piggybacks off other organizations to avoid scrutiny. Omar explains the advantage: "They have a platform now, and they invite us on that platform. This way we don't need to book a place and have a cancellation. Now they book the place."[106]

All of these affiliated organizations provide an institutional presence in society. And the range of issues covered by the various platforms offers something for everyone: a seeker is likely to find at least one al-Muhajiroun platform that addresses his or her specific interest. The coverage of the platforms also means that the movement's organizational breadth and strength cannot be measured by the reach of the formal "al-Muhajiroun" structure. As the British government continues to crack down on radical Islamic groups, one could expect these platforms to become increasingly important for movement outreach and survival.

CONCLUSION

There are numerous possible catalysts for the cognitive openings that spark religious seeking. In the British context, many eventual al-Muhajiroun activists experienced an identity crisis. They felt as though the secular society that preached multiculturalism and tolerance in reality delivered both racial and religious discrimination. Others experienced a facilitated cognitive opening as a result of movement activism designed to challenge established beliefs and ways of looking at the world. In both cases, eventual activists engaged in a process of religious seeking in which they sought a religious identity, meaning, and solutions to concerns. Activists use their established social networks and new social ties created by propagation to draw these seekers to movement activities. Whereas local imams and mosques often avoid political issues and robust discussions about how a Muslim lives according to Islam in a Western country, al-Muhajiroun specifically focuses on politics and religious guidance for Muslim minorities. Its organizational presence in society creates points of interaction and opportunities to expose seekers to the movement and its message.

But religious seekers who are drawn to al-Muhajiroun activities are not in a position to objectively evaluate whether al-Muhajiroun represents an accurate understanding of Islam. Most are religious novices, exploring their faith in depth for the first time. During the early stages of seeking, they may find traditional and mainstream religious institutions lacking, but this does not explain why they choose to follow al-Muhajiroun rather than another group. "At one time, I could not tell the difference between HT [Hizb ut-Tahrir] and al-Muhajiroun because they had the same concept," recounts one activist reflecting on his initial seekership. "They were very close, and I could not tell the difference at all."[107] So why choose al-Muhajiroun?

Almost universally, respondents in this study cited Omar's authority as an Islamic scholar as a critical element in their decision to learn about Islam through al-Muhajiroun rather than other Islamic groups. They were impressed with his religious knowledge, awareness of current affairs, character, and personality. Put quite simply, Omar is extremely charismatic and comes across as very knowledgeable. Seekers came to their conclusions about him through comparison in the process of religious seeking: they viewed him as the best alternative, especially compared to local imams and moderate religious figures.

Sacred authority, or the right to interpret Islam for others, is thus critical for translating exposure to movement activities into serious learning through al-Muhajiroun lessons.

NOTES

1. For a detailed discussion of these kinds of movements in Europe and the United Kingdom, see Peter Mandaville, *Transnational Muslim Politics: Reimagining the Ummah* (London: Routledge, 2004); and Olivier Roy, *Globalised Islam: The Search for a New Ummah* (London: Hurst, 2004).

2. For discussions about the issue of identity and Islam in the United Kingdom, see *Islamophobia: A Challenge for Us All* (London: Runnymede Trust, 1997); Claire Dwyer, "Negotiating Diasporic Identities: Young British South Asian Muslim Women," *Women's Studies International Forum,* July-August 1999, 475-86; Kafar Khan, "Muslim Presence in Europe: The British Dimension: Identity, Integration, and Community Activism," *Current Sociology,* October 2000, 29-43; Vered Kahani-Hopkins and Nick Hopkins, "'Representing' British Muslims: The Strategic Dimension to Identity Construction," *Ethnic and Racial Studies,* March 2002, 288-309; Peter Mandaville, "Europe's Muslim Youth: Dynamics of Alienation and Integration," in Shireen Hunter and Huma Malik, eds., *Islam in Europe and the United States: A Comparative Perspective* (Washington, D.C.: Center for Strategic and International Studies, 2002), 22-27; Iftikhar Malik, *Islam and Modernity: Muslims in Europe and the United States* (London: Pluto, 2004), chap. 5.

3. For historical debates about Muslim minorities, see Khaled Abou El Fadl, "Legal Debates on Muslim Minorities: Between Rejection and Accommodation," *Journal of Religious Ethics,* Spring 1994, 127-62; Khaled Abou El Fadl, "Islamic Law and Muslim Minorities: The Juristic Discourse on Muslim Minorities from the Second/Eighth to the Eleventh/Seventeenth Centuries," *Islamic Law and Society* 1, no. 2 (1994b): 141-87; Khaled Abou El Fadl, "Striking a Balance: Islamic Legal Discourse on Muslim Minorities," in Yvonne Yazbeck Haddad and John L. Esposito, eds., *Muslims on the Americanization Path?* (New York: Oxford University Press, 2000), 47-64.

4. Omar Khaldi, page 425, as cited in Peter Mandaville, *Transnational Muslim Politics: Reimagining the Umma,* 2d ed. (London: Routledge, 2004), 115 n. 28. For the connection between identity and Islamic activism in the Muslim world, see François Burgat, *Face to Face with Political Islam* (London: Tauris, 2003).

5. Olivier Roy, *Globalised Islam: The Search for a New Ummah* (London: Hurst, 2004), 18.

6. Paul Kelso, "Believers Try to Live with a Free and Easy Culture," *Guardian,* June 18, 2002.

7. Paul Kelso and Jeevan Vasagar, "Muslims Reject Image of Separate Society," *Guardian,* June 17, 2002.

8. Kelso and Vasagar, "Muslims Reject."

9. www.mori.com/polls/2001/easterneye-topline.shtml

10. BBC, "War on Terror 'Threatens' UK Muslims," December 23, 2002.

11. *Independent,* December 24, 2002. Survey carried out by ICM for BBC that included 500 people.

12. *Attitudes Towards British Muslims,* survey commissioned by the Islamic Society of Britain and conducted by YouGov, November 4, 2002. Report available at www.isb.org.uk/iaw/docs/SurveyIAW2002.pdf.

13. Bob Hepple and Tufyal Choudhury, *Tackling Religious Discrimination: Practical Implications for Policy-Makers and Legislators,* Home Office Research Study 221, Home Office Research, Research and Statistics Directorate, February 2001, 4–5.

14. Open Society Institute, "The Situation of Muslims in the UK," in *Monitoring the EU Process: Minority Protection,* 2002, 405, www.eumap.org/reports/2002/eu/international/sections/uk/2002_m_uk.pdf.

15. Open Society Institute, "Situation of Muslims in the UK," 379.

16. U.K. Census 2001.

17. Tariq Modood and Pnina Werbner, eds., *The Politics of Multiculturalism in the New Europe: Racism, Identity, and Community* (London: Zed, 1997), 306–8.

18. See Tariq Modood, "British Asian Muslims and the Rushdie Affair," *Political Quarterly,* April 1990, 143–60; Modood and Werbner, eds., *Politics of Multiculturalism.*

19. Open Society Institute, "Situation of Muslims," 396. See also Tariq Modood, Richard Berthoud, Jane Lakey, James Nazroo, Patten Smith, Satnam Virdee, and Sharon Beishon, *Ethnic Minorities in Britain* (London: Policy Studies Institute, 1997); David Blackaby, Derek Leslie, Philip Murphy, and Nigel O'Leary, "Unemployment among Britain's Ethnic Minorities," *Manchester School,* January 1999, 1–20.

20. Open Society Institute, "Situation of Muslims," 397.

21. Open Society Institute, "Situation of Muslims," 397.

22. Open Society Institute, "Situation of Muslims," 406.

23. Open Society Institute, "Situation of Muslims," 372.

24. BBC News, October 28, 2002, "British Asians Uneasy over Iraq: Poll."

25. See Arzu Merali and Massoud Shadjareh, "Islamophobia: The New Crusade," Islamic Human Rights Commission, May 2002, www.ihrc.org.uk/file/ISLAMOPHO BIAthenewcrusade.pdf.

26. Interview by author, London, June 2002.

27. Interview by author, London, March 2002.

28. Saad Eddin Ibrahim, "Anatomy of Egypt's Militant Islamic Groups: Methodological Notes and Preliminary Findings," *International Journal of Middle East Studies,* December 1980, 423–53; Hamied N. Ansari, "The Islamic Militants in Egyptian Politics," *International Journal of Middle East Studies,* March 1984, 123–44; Henry Munson Jr., "The Social Base of Islamic Militancy in Morocco," *Middle East Journal,* Spring

1986, 267–84; Susan Waltz, "Islamist Appeal in Tunisia," *Middle East Journal,* Autumn 1986, 651–70; Valerie J. Hoffman, "Muslim Fundamentalists: Psychosocial Profiles," in Martin E. Marty and R. Scott Appleby, eds., *Fundamentalisms Comprehended* (Chicago: University of Chicago Press, 1995); Carrie Rosefsky Wickham, *Mobilizing Islam: Religion, Activism, and Political Change in Egypt* (New York: Columbia University Press, 2002), chap. 3.

29. As quoted in Adam Lebor, *A Heart Turned East: Among the Muslims of Europe and America* (New York: St. Martin's, 1997), 129.

30. Interview by author, London, June 2002.

31. Omar Bakri Mohammed, interview by author, London, June 2002.

32. Khalid, interview by author, London, June 2002.

33. Kamran Bokhari, telephone interview by author, April 2003.

34. I would like to thank Mohammed Hafez for this observation about remaining in movements because of friends.

35. Interview by author, London, June 2002.

36. Interview by author, London, June 2002.

37. "Mankind's Greatest Question? Where Did I Come From?" (n.d.).

38. Omar Bakri Mohammed, interview by author, June 2002.

39. Omar Bakri Mohammed, interview by author, December 2002.

40. Omar Bakri Mohammed, interview by author, December 2002.

41. Omar Bakri Mohammed, interview by author, December 2002.

42. David A. Snow and Richard Machalek, "The Convert as a Social Type," *Sociological Theory* 1 (1983): 267. Also see discussion in Snow and Machalek, "The Sociology of Conversion," *Annual Review of Sociology* 10 (1984): 175–78.

43. Islam, interview by author, June 2002.

44. Wickham, *Mobilizing Islam,* 144.

45. Wickham, *Mobilizing Islam,* 144.

46. Wickham, *Mobilizing Islam,* 145.

47. See the same observation in Suha Taji-Farouki, *A Fundamental Quest: Hizb al-Tahrir and the Search for the Islamic Caliphate* (London: Grey Seal, 1996): 177–78.

48. See Peter Mandaville, *Transnational Muslim Politics: Reimagining the Umma,* 2d ed. (London: Routledge, 2004), 121–32.

49. Gerard Seenan, "Making Do without the Mainstream," *Guardian,* June 20, 2002.

50. Paper based on *Islamophobia,* Runnymede Trust, runnymedetrust.org/meb/islamophobia/Islam_in_Britain.html.

51. Interview by author, June 10, 2002.

52. Quintan Wiktorowicz, *The Management of Islamic Activism: Salafis, the Muslim Brotherhood, and State Power in Jordan* (Albany: State University of New York Press, 2001).

53. Open Society Institute, "Situation of Muslims," 419–20.

54. Open Society Institute, "Situation of Muslims," 419–20.

55. Jeevan Vasagar, "Dilemma of the Moderates," *Guardian*, June 19, 2002.

56. "Anglo-Muslim Attitudes," *Telegraph*, December 6, 2002.

57. Interview by author, London, June 2002.

58. Mayer N. Zald and John D. McCarthy, eds., *Social Movements in an Organizational Society* (New Brunswick, N.J.: Transaction, 1987).

59. See, for example, James Scott, *Weapons of the Weak: Everyday Forms of Peasant Resistance* (New Haven: Yale University Press, 1986); Scott, *Domination and the Arts of Resistance: Hidden Transcripts* (New Haven: Yale University Press, 1990); Karl-Dieter Opp and Christiane Gern, "Dissident Groups, Personal Networks, and Spontaneous Cooperation: The East German Revolution of 1989," *American Sociological Review* 58 (1993): 659–80; Cathy Lisa Schneider, *Shantytown Protest in Pinochet's Chile* (Philadelphia: Temple University Press, 1995); Steven Pfaff, "Collective Identity and Informal Groups in Revolutionary Mobilization: East Germany in 1989," *Social Forces,* September 1996, 91–118; Wiktorowicz, *Management of Islamic Activism*; Diane Singerman, "The Networked World of Islamist Social Movements," in Quintan Wiktorowicz, ed., *Islamic Activism: A Social Movement Theory Approach* (Bloomington: Indiana University Press, 2004).

60. See also Lebor, *A Heart Turned East,* chap. 5.

61. Anjem Choudary, telephone interview by author, June 2002.

62. For this analysis, I gathered all written notices available from the movement.

63. The question was, "President Bush and Tony Blair say the war on terrorism is not a war on Islam. Do you agree or disagree?" Twenty percent agreed; 70 percent disagreed; and 10 percent did not know. *Independent*, December 24, 2002.

64. www.mori.com/polls/2001/easterneye-topline.shtml

65. www.mori.com/polls/2001/ms011104.shtml

66. www.mori.com/polls/2001/easterneye-topline.shtml

67. Muslim Council of Britain, *National Survey of Muslim Council of Britain Affiliate Organizations on Proposed Military Action against Iraq* (London: Muslim Council of Britain, September 2002).

68. This comparative analysis is based on an examination of all major press statements on the topic issued by the Muslim Council of Britain and al-Muhajiroun's written response to the pending invasion, titled "Fight the Invaders vs. Stop the War" (March 20, 2003). The latter was the only available press release on the issue, but it is consistent with the movement's views toward other conflicts in Muslim countries involving the United States. In the analysis, I approximated the method of microdiscourse analysis advocated by Hank Johnston (1995; 2002).

69. Open Society Institute, "Situation of Muslims," 413–14.

70. Open Society Institute, "Situation of Muslims," 392.

71. Open Society Institute, "Situation of Muslims," 392.

72. www.mori.com/polls/2001/tes.shtml

73. Muslim Council of Britain, "Keep Clause 28: Weak Guidelines Are Not Enough for Muslim Parents," press release, March 15, 2000.

74. Section 28 of Local Government Act 1988.

75. Issued July 16, 2001.

76. Omar argues that he opposes homosexuality as an act and not the person (so long as it is private), but the movement's open activities have raised concerns among gay activists in London. At one point, gay activists issued a "queer fatwa" condemning Omar Bakri Mohammed to 1,000 years of "relentless sodomitical torture" for his "crimes against queer humanity."

77. Al-Muhajiroun, *Administration*, n.d.

78. Omar Bakri Mohammed, interview by author, London, June 2002.

79. Omar Bakri Mohammed, interview by author, London, June 2002.

80. This was observed by the author at several public and private movement events.

81. Anjem Choudary, interview by author, London, March 2002; Mohammed, interview by author, London, June 2002.

82. Anjem Choudary, interview by author, London, June 2002.

83. Omar Bakri Mohammed, interview by author, London, June 2002.

84. Anjem Choudary, interview by author, London, March 2002.

85. E-mail sent by former head of the U.K. women's section, October 7, 2003. Name withheld to protect the identity of the former activist.

86. Union Council Minutes, February 5, 2001, www.ucl.ac.uk/ucl-union/minutes_2000_2001/unioncouncil/Uc0006_050201.doc.

87. Anjem Choudary, interview by author, London, March 2002.

88. London Press Association, September 21, 2001, in FBIS-WEU-2001-0921.

89. UPI, September 13, 2001; *Al-Sharq Al-Awsat*, September 12, 2001; Press Association, September 11, 2001.

90. Anjem Choudary, telephone interview by author, June 2002.

91. In an innocuous leaflet, the organization advertised a "parent's evening" to review schooling and an alternative Islamic education system.

92. Omar Bakri Mohammed, interview by author, London, December 2002.

93. Anjem Choudary, interview by author, London, March 2002.

94. Omar Bakri Mohammed, interview by author, London, December 2002.

95. Omar Bakri Mohammed, interview by author, London, December 2002.

96. Siraj, posting to al-Muhajiroun message board, January 2000.

97. *Daily Telegraph*, October 30, 1999.

98. Charity Commission for England and Wales, report on investigation into charity, www.charity-commission.gov.uk/investigations/inquiryreports/enfield.asp.

99. From business cards provided by Omar Bakri and Anjem Choudary. Because the commission eventually decided to shut down the charity, Anjem scratched out the registration number (Omar did not).

100. Charity Commission for England and Wales, *Report on Investigation,* www.charity-commission.gov.uk/investigations/inquiryreports/mesea.asp.

101. Charity Commission for England and Wales, *Report on Investigation,* www.charity-commission.gov.uk/investigations/inquiryreports/mesea.asp.

102. *The Times,* October 10, 2001.

103. Charity Commission for England and Wales, *Report on Investigation,* www.charity-commission.gov.uk/investigations/inquiryreports/mesea.asp.

104. Omar Bakri Mohammed, interview by author, London, December 2002.

105. Omar Bakri Mohammed, interview by author, London, December 2002.

106. Omar Bakri Mohammed, interview by author, London, December 2002.

107. Interview by author, London, June 2002.

3

CREDIBILITY AND SACRED AUTHORITY

Radical Islamic movements are collective endeavors to establish networks of shared meaning and religious interpretation—efforts to persuade others to accept a particular understanding of Islam and its role for individuals, society, the polity, and the global community. Religious meaning, however, is contested by an assortment of competitors, including mainstream moderates, nonviolent fundamentalists, government religious institutions, and other radical groups. For religious seekers, the possible choices are almost overwhelming. This is particularly the case for the religious novice, who has little religious training and therefore a limited knowledge base from which to evaluate the competing perspectives.

Studies of persuasion have consistently demonstrated the importance of reputation in making these kinds of evaluations. Successful persuasion is not just the result of well-formulated and articulated arguments and presentations; it is also influenced by the reputation of the message source.[1] Whether attempts at persuasion have their desired effect is contingent on perceptions about the individual or group making the arguments, including characteristics like expertise, credibility, and even attractiveness.[2] Seemingly knowledgeable and likeable information sources are more effective at swaying audience targets than those perceived as amateurs with negative characteristics.[3] This is particularly the case where audience members have low levels of information and a limited ability to ascertain the validity of competing arguments: they must rely on those who seem informed and well intentioned. The importance of reputation for persuasion has been empirically demonstrated for a wide variety of topics, including advertising, communication in international disputes, policy debates, political campaigns, and education.[4]

In social movement research, the centrality of reputation for persuasion has been mostly emphasized in studies of framing, though empirical support remains limited.[5] Robert Benford and David Snow argue that "hypothetically, the greater the status and/or perceived expertise of the frame articulator and/or the organization they represent from the vantage point of potential adherents and constituents, the more plausible and resonant the framings of claims."[6] In other words, those who speak on behalf of the movement should seem to know what they are talking about. Credible sources elicit trust and enhance prospects for frame alignment and successful message dissemination. Conversely, a messenger of disrepute will undermine the potential frame resonance of a message by leading audiences to question the source of information and argument.

Reputation is of particular importance for complex issues. As Robert Furtell argues, where social movement issues are of a technical nature (as in religious debates over violence), "expert authority may powerfully shape the contours of framing activities. The language of science and expertise can stall efforts of non-experts to understand what is going on. Lay citizens have to place a great deal of faith in the authority and judgments of experts."[7] This faith in experts is, in turn, contingent on the reputation of the vying authorities. In Madison County, Kentucky, for example, the "not in my backyard movement" (NIMBY) tried to block a U.S. Army plan to incinerate chemical weapons at a local site. The movement's framing efforts initially succeeded in mobilizing local opposition in part because army experts made errors in presenting their case, thereby compromising the credibility of the government's technical information and interpretation.[8]

"Experts" are important for Islamic understanding since Islam itself is a complex, technical area of study. There are hundreds of "Islamic sciences," each offering a systematic approach to a particular element of the religion, including such things as jurisprudence *(usul al-fiqh)*, ethics, philosophy, mysticism, epistemology, theology, exegesis, and cosmology, to name only a few. And within each area there are different methodological approaches. Truly mastering even part of the sciences would require impossible amounts of time, acumen, and expertise. As a result, Islamic scholars usually specialize in only a few areas. Those without training, including typical religious seekers, are obviously not well equipped to determine whether a given Islamic interpretation or approach represents "real Islam." As a result, they must rely on the expertise and opinions of Islamic scholars.

For seekers, the process of religious understanding is further complicated by the decentralization of sacred authority in the Muslim world. There is no universally accepted interpretation of Islam. Nor is there a universally accepted religious hierarchy capable of establishing a clerical caste akin to the Catholic

Church (with the exception of the Shiite community, which constitutes about 10–15 percent of Muslims worldwide). Scholars disagree over methodological approaches to the Islamic sciences, proper sources of religious opinions, and conclusions about religious meaning. As a result, although seekers must rely on religious experts, there are a number of alternatives.

Like most Muslims, the choice for seekers is heavily influenced by the reputation of the individual(s) offering a religious interpretation. Those who decided to learn about Islam through al-Muhajiroun were primarily motivated by assessments of Omar Bakri's ability to accurately interpret Islam. Two criteria are paramount in evaluating scholars. First, scholars must be knowledgeable. Obviously, to issue reliable religious rulings a scholar must demonstrate a deep understanding of Islam and its sources, the Qur'an and Sunna. For many Muslims, especially Islamic activists, individuals must additionally demonstrate command of context: does a scholar grasp the surrounding world so that he or she can accurately apply the immutable religious sources to dynamic contemporary conditions?[9] An individual might have a strong command of the Qur'an and Sunna but understand little about contemporary society or politics. Under these conditions, he or she would be unable to explain how the Prophet Mohammed would respond to current social or political challenges. Reliable advice, in contrast, guides the faithful on how to be a Muslim in the modern world by explaining religious edicts and the context of implementation.

Second, a scholar must have a good character. Charges of corruption or deviance undermine the reputation and status of a scholar by calling into question his or her moral certitude. Is the scholar working in the best interests of the Muslim community? Or are there ulterior motives that result in warped interpretations? Is the scholar issuing religious opinions according to what he or she believes is an accurate reading of Islamic sources? Or are outside forces (e.g., an enemy) pressuring or directing the scholar to take particular religious positions? If audiences distrust the character of a scholar, they will likely question whether his or her religious interpretation is motivated by an honest devotion to God or self-interest that could corrupt religious rulings. Scurrilous or unscrupulous scholars invite questions about intentions.

Scholarly reputation is generally weighed in relative, not absolute, terms. It is not simply a matter of whether an individual is knowledgeable or not, but whether he or she is *more* knowledgeable than others. Muslims seeking religious advice, for example, will often initially turn to the person they think is most knowledgeable in their social circles, neighborhoods, communities, or broader networks. Although globalization and information technology have enhanced the accessibility of well-known, international scholars, the tendency is still to seek out religious figures in the local context. This allows direct contact and enhances the prospects that a scholar will understand the concerns of the seeker. As a result, the most important comparison is typically among potential choices in the local environment: who seems *most* worthy of following? Of course, most people will not examine all possible alternatives or gather all the relevant information for making an informed decision; but where they are aware of differences, they will usually choose to follow the advice of religious figures with high levels of knowledge and strong character.

Because evaluations based on these criteria are, to some extent, subjectively derived, reputation is influenced by personal traits, such as charisma and oratory skills. Gregarious scholars can garner large followings not only because they are knowledgeable and Muslims of good repute, but also as a result of their personality and interpersonal skills. Fiery or inspirational lessons, speeches, and sermons facilitate message receptivity and can generate powerful emotive connections between scholars and their followers.

For al-Muhajiroun activists, Omar Bakri Mohammed's reputation, stature as a scholar, and personality were the principle reasons they attended religious lessons with al-Muhajiroun after their initial exposure to the movement. In detailing why they were drawn to al-Muhajiroun rather than other Islamic groups or movements, respondents consistently emphasized their first encounters with Omar, which were both intellectual and emotional. To them, he epitomized what a scholar should be: a knowledgeable, independent-minded truth seeker who spoke out regardless of the consequences. Although most Muslims in the United Kingdom dismiss Omar Bakri as a "loony" or "clown," movement activists recall an entirely different impression during their first interactions with the movement. They believed they had found a "rare gem"—a true Islamic scholar in the midst of a Christian country.

This evaluation was not produced in a vacuum; it represented the product of religious seeking. Seekers who later became activists sought expert insights about issues such as the struggle in Kashmir, the Israeli–Palestinian conflict, and September 11. They yearned for guidance about how to be a Muslim in a predominantly Christian country in the West where the concerns of the *umma* are tangential to the priorities of society and government. As a result, part of the process of religious seeking included a search for scholars who actually addressed controversial political and social issues and could speak with authority to the pressing concerns of young British Muslims. They wanted someone who was knowledgeable and seemed to understand their plight and worries.

KNOWLEDGE

By far, Omar Bakri's knowledge of Islam was the most cited explanation for initially joining al-Muhajiroun religious study circles. Seekers who became activists believed that Omar's level of religious knowledge far exceeded that of other teachers with whom they sat or whose activities they attended. In a Syrian family of twenty-eight siblings, he was selected by his father for religious training at the age of four and sent to study with a religious scholar in an apprenticeship system of religious training based on *ijaz* (certification by a scholar) rather than formal degrees. His education was encapsulated in religious lessons, and he never attended secular schooling. Though Omar considers himself a specialist in *usul al-fiqh* (Islamic jurisprudence), he claims to have studied 134 (out of 256) of the Islamic sciences related to *shari'a*.[10] Currently forty-six years old (in 2004) and a perpetual student of Islam, Omar can boast a long history of religious training. He claims to have a bachelor's degree in Usul al-Fiqh (the foundations of jurisprudence) from Shari'a University in Damascus and a master's in the four schools of Islamic jurisprudence from Shaykh Awzaie University in Beirut. Omar also claims that he finished all the work for a Ph.D. at Oxford University, including a dissertation on Islamic jurisprudence, but that he did not have the money to pay the tuition and fees to receive his degree.[11]

Activists vividly recall specific incidents to illustrate their initial perceptions about Omar's expertise. Anjem, for example, recounted a story in which imams came to a local conference at the Birmingham mosque to ask Omar about the Islamic perspective on voting in U.K. elections. He responded with a long impromptu lecture that made comparisons among the four *madhhabs* (schools of Islamic jurisprudence), demonstrating an enormous breadth of knowledge about different legal perspectives. At that same conference, another scholar approached Omar with a long list of questions that no one else could answer. This led Anjem to conclude that "even among the scholars and the imams, the so-called leaders here, he is a reference point within the community."[12]

Referring to his own experience of religious seeking, Anjem describes his first encounter with Omar as transcendent: "I had never seen anything like what he used to talk about. The science of foundation, the science of Islamic jurisprudence, the science of Qur'an, of hadith. He was like a bottomless treasure. No matter what we asked him he always had a solution, an answer. That was something unique."[13]

While activists complain that traditional imams give rulings without explaining the rationale or religious evidence, Omar is noted for his willingness to delve into details and discuss his reasoning with audiences and students, something that enhances perceptions about his level of knowledge. In explaining an Islamic perspective, he always quotes the religious evidence from the Qur'an and Sunna, first in Arabic and then in English, creating the impression that he is indeed translating the word of God for guidance. And activists argue that his quotes are extremely accurate. Anjem, for example, cites a particular story about Omar when he was still the leader of Hizb ut-Tahrir. At a movement event, he quoted an enormous number of hadiths, each with relevant references, and someone in the audience wrote them down to check for accuracy. The skeptic suspected that Omar was guessing or had made mistakes because it seemed impossible for a single person to recall so many passages and sources. As the story is told, everything Omar had said was accurate, including the citations and referenced *isnads*, or chains of transmission used to determine whether a story about the Prophet is accurate.[14]

This is contrasted with moderates and local imams:

> People will answer your questions, but they won't give you evidence. They will say this is the situation—it is lawful or unlawful. It is *haram* [religiously forbidden] [or] it is allowed. They will never give evidences. They won't give verse numbers. They will never give an explanation of the circumstances of the revelation and what the classical scholars used to say. People aren't bothered with that. They say, "Take it and act upon it. Why are you bothering me?" He is unique like that, he will actually sit down with you and give references and explain. He gives everyone the time of day, which is very good.[15]

For activists, it is not just that local leaders refuse to go into the religious evidence; they do not have the knowledge and skills and therefore *cannot*. A local movement leader explains, "There are people out there that are not at the level of scholar. And they cannot go into the scriptures and say that this hadith is authentic without doubt, or this hadith is verified. All they know is what the previous scholars have told them. It is *taqlid* [blind imitation]."[16]

Perceptions about Omar's knowledge are enhanced by his confidence, which is inspiring and reassuring to seekers. He challenges other scholars to debate, claiming that the best ideas will win. For seekers, this signals confidence in the certitude of his beliefs and conclusions. Many activists have actually tried to persuade Omar not to debate because opponents are not at the same level of knowledge. The fact that he insists is seen as a signal of his willingness and openness as well as humility. Anjem explains that "the sheikh has often said come together and let us bring our evidences and we will see who speaks the truth and who doesn't speak the truth. But they won't come and they won't debate, because they have nothing to debate with. I think it is fear as well of being exposed and being wrong."[17]

Omar is evaluated relative to other scholars, particularly those within the fundamentalist community. Although activists signal respect, they believe these other scholars fall short of Omar's level of knowledge. Anjem argues, "The Muslim community around here is not rich with Islamic jurists. When you come across someone who knows what they are talking about and has the answers to the searching questions you have about religion, about life, about economics and social problems, they stick out. I came across many people in the Muslim community and used to subscribe to all of the different magazines and newsletters and publications, but he is unique."[18] Asked what distinguishes Omar from other scholars, Anjem responds,

> There are a lot of passionate speakers, but there are not that many that can convince you that what they are saying is *the* truth. And his depth of knowledge and understanding of reality and details of the text. Someone who studies Islam now for over forty years puts him in a unique position. There are people in this community who have come across Islam and who have gone to study for a few years at university, and they have a couple of degrees and they have studied five or ten years, and we say they are knowledgeable. But you cannot put someone like that in the same category as someone who has been training his whole life. There is no comparison.
>
> There is the problem that in a town of blind people, the one-eyed man is king. A lot of people are one-eyed in England, and it is just amazing when you find someone who has dual vision . . . And these guys can see, but not really well. They cannot really explain what Islam is about. And he [Omar] is verifiable [in terms of the accuracy of his knowledge].[19]

Activists make explicit and direct comparisons with other leaders in the fundamentalist community, often informed comparisons since as religious seekers they experimented with other leaders and groups. This is particularly the case with Abu Hamza al-Masri, a competitor within the radical fundamentalist community. Activists still respect him. Many continued to attend his sermons and lessons after committing to al-Muhajiroun (although opportunities have recently diminished) because they were inspirational and "hot." But activists still see Omar as much more knowledgeable. A Somali activist states, "Today in this country obviously, the only 'alim [religious scholar] I can see is sheikh Omar. Abu Hamza is a good brother, but he is not like sheikh Omar knowledge-wise. But he is a good brother. So if there is another 'alim, I would consider going and looking him up and seeing how he is. But unfortunately in this country he is the only one that I see. I haven't met anyone like him."[20]

Even Mohammed al-Massari, the radical Islamic activist and leader of the Committee for the Defense of Legitimate Rights (CDLR), describes Abu Hamza in similar terms. He is seen as a well-intentioned Muslim but not a senior scholar:

> Abu Hamza started his scholarly development quite late in age and started [pause], he will not be happy with the way I say this, but on the wrong foot, started by studying, noncritically, classical *fiqh* books . . . Abu Hamza cannot overcome. He gets stuck in the scholarly opinions of the past and you have for a certain issue four or five points of view . . . It does not mean he cannot balance them and find the one that is more convincing on various grounds, but it is still not the critical approach in which you fully digest, assimilate, and produce something new.[21]

Abu Hamza is more famous for fiery sermons than religious lessons, which are less extensive than those of groups like al-Muhajiroun and Hizb ut-Tahrir. Though interesting, many of these sermons do not address the particular concerns of British Muslims. For some seekers, there is a sense that Abu Hamza is a good Muslim but out of touch with the real everyday concerns of Muslims in the United Kingdom. This perception has been reinforced over the years because of his connection with jihadi groups abroad, particularly in the late 1990s when his interest focused primarily on the conflict in Algeria. As a result of this focus, many of his followers are Algerians who do not speak proficient English, something that discouraged at least a few al-Muhajiroun activists from coming to his lessons during their religious seeking.

Omar Bakri's perceived knowledge is coupled with a concern for real life and the local context. Not only does he discuss controversial topics that local imams avoid, but he also moves beyond rituals and provides discussion and answers about difficult issues currently facing British Muslims. Recounting his experience in religious seeking, one activist explains, "And what happened you see was that sheikh Omar, his talks were more linked to the relevant than other talks. He used to talk about the Muslims' affairs and everything. In terms of the other ones, they were restricted [to rituals]. And I used to remember that Kishk [an Egyptian preacher] was a good man and he used to talk about the Muslims' affairs and everything, so when I realized sheikh Omar was like that I said OK, and I started learning from sheikh Omar."[22] Anjem notes that Omar's understanding of the local context and concern for the "affairs" of British Muslims make the religion seem relevant: "He made the Qur'an come alive. This was the thing really. If you read the Bible, someone might make you feel as if you were there at the time, the messenger Jesus or messenger Mohammed, and you think,

142

[handwritten note:] Brings the religion into modern-day life. Provides solutions = make it much more appealing.

'Wow this is what happened at that time.' He explains Islam from the heart, and he touches your emotions and your heart."[23]

Compare this to views expressed in the control group survey. Out of ninety-seven respondents, about half (49) stated that they did not know about Omar's level of knowledge about Islam. Of the 48 respondents who felt they could render an opinion, 62.5 percent (30) stated that Omar knows very little, 33.3 percent (16) believed he knows a moderate amount, and only two believed he knows a great deal. This is contrasted with responses for Zaki Badawi, founder of the Muslim Council of Britain: 43.3 percent (42) believed he knows a great deal; 16.5 percent (16) believed he knows a moderate amount; only 4.1 percent (4) stated he knows very little; and 36.1 percent (35) didn't know.

% companson

↳ *all about perception*

CHARACTER

Omar's character is also seen as an important credential for a scholar. In his purity of intent in particular, he is often contrasted with other scholars in the United Kingdom and abroad who might be influenced by outside forces and nonreligious interests.

A potentially corrupting influence frequently cited by radicals is financial interest. *financial interest* One of the strongest criticisms leveled against nonviolent fundamentalists, for example, is that they are influenced by Saudi government money. Many leading fundamentalist scholars who oppose al-Qaeda are government employees in the Ministry of Awqaf in Saudi Arabia. Osama bin Laden muses that "the offices of the Clerics Authority [in Saudi Arabia] are adjacent to the royal palace . . . In such a situation [when even the offices are linked], is it reasonable to ask a civil servant [for a fatwa], who receives his salary from the king? What is the ruling regarding the king, and should the king be regarded as supporting infidels?"[24]

As Laurence Iannoccone argues, "The clergy . . . are more persuasive when they do not benefit materially from their followers' faith."[25] Independence from financial interests helps create the perception that a scholar is motivated by a spiritual concern in the purity of Islam rather than material gain. In recounting his earlier experience in building activists in Saudi Arabia, Omar is quick to point out the impact financial independence has on perceptions of credibility. His father passed away in the late 1970s, leaving him a substantial inheritance that provided economic security and a degree of credibility:

> When you have money, I think money will facilitate a lot of things, especially if you are *da'i* [propagator] or activist, you will be trusted because you don't take

anything in return, you give. The one who believes in [the] cause, they give, they don't take. I believe that taking from the cause is like committing fornication. It is not allowed.[26]

Omar used his financial independence to support his credibility when he first arrived in the United Kingdom. Before he relocated to London in 1986, Omar had already donated funds to establish a small mosque in Finsbury Park located among stores (not the better known Finsbury Park Mosque). Because of his donations, he was a trustee at the mosque, and Muslims in the community knew him as a generous businessman. When he moved to London, his brothers sent him money from the sale of family land in Syria, which allowed him to focus on developing a movement without financial burdens. The money from his brothers was particularly important, since the Saudi government had seized all of his money in the kingdom (he had approximately £150,000 in the bank at that time). He used his financial resources to build relationships and a reputation through activities at mosques and other Islamic institutions. He argues that this financial security and his work for the Muslim community were "enough for them to respect me. If not agreeing about my ideas, at least they saw me as a devoted Muslim."[27]

His financial independence and credibility were threatened in 1996 when the press discovered that he was receiving the dole, child benefits, income support, a disability allowance, and housing benefits. The public was outraged. How could a man who routinely condemned the British system turn around and benefit financially? Some of Omar's students started raising questions about his decision to take money from the British government. Sensing that his reputation was under assault, Omar argued that there is nothing contradictory in taking money from a non-Islamic government—he had paid taxes through his businesses and was therefore entitled to unemployment compensation.[28] He also argued that a leg injury and negative publicity made it nearly impossible for him to get a job. Regardless of the reason, Omar had to spend some time showing that his actions were permitted by Islamic law.[29]

Beyond financial issues, character is assessed in terms of independence from outside influences in general. The concern is whether a scholar is free from coercion or inducements and can issue accurate religious rulings that reflect the Qur'an and Sunna. Consistently, respondents were impressed that Omar spoke out on controversial topics regardless of the consequences. This was seen as evidence that he truly believed what he said and was willing to countenance arrest and even deportation. Suleyman, a white convert, notes that Omar "dares to say things that no one else does. Other religious leaders don't do that. They don't have the guts."[30] When asked what most impressed him about Omar, another respondent immediately cited "the sincerity of the man."[31]

This is contrasted with moderates who do not support violence. Omar, for example, calls Zaki Badawi "the Queen's mufti," implying that he is influenced by his political connections to the British government. An assortment of other terms are used to connote this lack of independence among moderates as well, including "chocolate Muslims": Uncle Tom Muslims who melt down under pressure.

Similar charges are made against nonviolent fundamentalists, both at home and abroad. The most consistent argument is that they are tied to the Saudi government and therefore incapable of rendering independent judgments. The potency of this criticism derives from increased government usurpation of institutions responsible for producing religious interpretations. Concerned about legitimacy and religious opposition, regimes throughout the Muslim world have attempted to centralize religious authority under state control. Mosques, religious institutes of higher learning, committees responsible for issuing fatwas, and other vehicles of religious meaning have been bureaucratized and linked to the state. Religious functionaries, including many of the *ulama,* are now dependent on the state for their salaries and positions.[32] Serious divergences from government interpretations of Islam can incur reprimands, dismissal (and thus loss of income), and even imprisonment. James Piscatori has gone so far as to argue that the *ulama* in Saudi Arabia are "agents of the state."[33]

While this may prevent broad dissemination of radical ideologies, it concurrently undermines the legitimacy of the *ulama* themselves. Even supporters of the reformist vision admit that state controls create at least the appearance that the reformist scholars are no more than civil servants charged with protecting regime interests. Al-Muhajiroun, al-Qaeda, and other radical groups refer to these scholars as *ulama al-sulta* ("scholars of power")—a term implying an insidious relationship with regimes and authority structures that undermines the independence and legitimacy of Islamic interpretation. It is typically used with other disparaging terms, such as "palace lackeys," "the corrupt *ulama,*" and "the *ulama* who flatter [those in power]."

Since many nonviolent fundamentalists hold Ph.D.s in the Islamic sciences from established Islamic universities, particularly in Saudi Arabia, and are religious luminaries with solid international reputations for knowledge, al-Muhajiroun and other radical groups choose to emphasize the insidiousness of government connections to undermine the credibility of scholarly opponents. Radicals argue that these sheikhs of authority propagate their soporific, depoliticized version of Islam devoid of activism to lull Muslims into a state of apathy. Omar argues:

> They overload the Ummah with thoughts and rules (or rather juristic fabrications), with excuses of being more practical and beneficial, making thereby the divine rules merely theoretical and imaginary since they claim these are not practical. All this instead of trying to find the cause which prevents the Islamic laws being practical and to remove such causes i.e. Kufr law and order dominating the world.[34]

For Omar and other radicals, this is tantamount to hiding the truth, a particularly odious offense to Islam, since scholars have a responsibility to pass on the entirety of the religion.[35] In effect, scholars who propagate a nonviolent, apolitical Islam are complicit in the attacks against Islam promoted by the West and corrupt governments in Muslim countries. They are framed as traitors to Islam who pacify the community with their talk of ritual and individual purification. Omar supports his argument with the following:

> As for those people who hide the truth and conceal the Haq [Truth], Allah (swt) also warns us of them in the Quran: "Surely those who conceal the clear proofs and the guidance that We revealed after We made it clear in the Book for men, these it is whom Allah shall curse, and those who curse shall curse them too. Except those who repent and amend and make manifest the truth, these it is to whom I turn mercifully." (EMQ 2:159–60)[36]

These are the hypocrites who undermine the strength of the Muslim community, purposefully misleading the Muslims and obfuscating the divine duties of real Islam.

> O' Moderates: don't think that the enemy of Islam will honour you rather you will be humiliated by them and by the believers in this life and you will be punished severely in the Hereafter for Allah (SWT) says: "To the Hypocrites give glad tidings that there is for them (but) a grievous punishment. Those who take for friends unbelievers: is it honour they seek among them? Nay, all honour is with Allah [Quran 4:138–39]."[37]

This is contrasted with scholars like Omar Bakri, who are portrayed as self-sacrificing. Since their interpretations and behaviors entail high risk and high cost, they seem to be sacrificing themselves for something greater. Research on social cognition has shown that when sources of information take positions that seem to undermine their self-interest, audiences consider them more trustworthy and credible.[38] Omar recognizes the importance of this perception for drawing in religious seekers: "He [the seeker] does not think he is following someone who just wants to become famous. He wants the thought of Islam to become famous. That is very effective. And I succeed to bring people like this."[39] For those who decided to participate in lessons with al-Muhajiroun, Omar is self-sacrificial, independent, and therefore better situated than moderates and non-violent fundamentalists to provide guidance based on a pure understanding of Islam alone.

PERSONALITY

Omar certainly comes across as knowledgeable and sincere, but religious seekers are hardly in a position to assess this objectively. As a result, his personal characteristics also play a role in seeker evaluations about authenticity and reputation.

Of utmost importance to seekers is that he seems down-to-earth and accessible, especially compared to imams who, many seekers argue, suffer from the "mullah mentality"—they just want Muslims to follow their religious rulings without pestering them for explanations and justifications. Peter Mandaville recounts the experience of Dilwar Hussain, a former member of the Young Muslims U.K. executive board, "who explained that by asking questions in the mosque he seemed only to inflame the tempers of impatient, doctrinally rigid imams."[40] The resulting frustration was shared by religious seekers who were attracted to al-Muhajiroun. Constant comparisons are drawn between the personable and open style and personality of Omar and the closed, remote approach of the imams. An Algerian movement activist describes his experience with imams:

I used to go to the Baker Street mosque, and I talked to some imams over there, and I never heard these intimate feelings with those people. There was no connection at all. I went there sometimes, and I asked them about the issues concerning *talib* [student] and all of issues related to our din [religion]. And the way they speak to you is something that is snobby. Because they come from al-Azhar. I remember the sheikh [Omar Bakri] was telling us a story about being in al-Azhar because he was there for a while, and they were teaching them "The Great Sheikh": how to present themselves in front of people and how to talk and how to give speeches and all that. And the sheikh [Omar] was saying the [professor] [took] a glass of water, and he gargled it and cleared his throat, and all that presentation. They were showing them how to present! And he was disgusted about this—just showmanship. That is one of the things he did not like about Azhar.[41]

Omar's contrasting charisma and personable nature are reflected in his in-teractions with students and even strangers. He describes himself as a "man of the street and masses" and gives the impression that he does not see himself as superior to others. He goes to great pains to show that he cares about his fol-lowers. At various lessons throughout the country, Omar demonstrates a ca-pacity to remember names, faces, and personal details, working his way around audiences and asking personal questions about participants, shaking hands, and exuding warmth and sincerity. He is gregarious and plainly likeable. Prior to a lesson in Luton attended by about thirty young men, he made sure to shake everyone's hand, asking people about their lives and cracking jokes. In other words, Omar maintains a very personal touch with others, and he recognizes this importance. Comparative research indicates that this kind of teacher im-mediacy, such as remembering names and showing an interest in each individ-ual, enhances learning because the teacher seems more approachable, likeable, and credible.[42]

He is also extremely accessible, in contrast to local imams. He constantly gives out his cell, business, and home phone numbers to anyone who would like to discuss Islam or debate. His cell number is listed on pamphlets, notices, and other movement publications. The sheer volume of calls is testimony to the fact that people take advantage of his openness. During our interviews, Omar had to turn off his cell phone because of the number of calls he received. In one inter-view, within an hour he had around twenty waiting messages. For seekers used to the remote attitudes of local imams, the accessibility of a scholar like Omar is impressive and inspiring. They feel that he cares about them and their need to understand the basis of religious rulings.

Omar is also a gifted orator who utilizes his skills to produce captivating pre-sentations. He is animated and exciting, and he draws out the emotions of audi-ences, something that enhances message receptivity and social movement mobi-lization (Abu Hamza is also animated, but his comparative lack of religious knowledge was decisive for seekers who became al-Muhajiroun activists).[43] Omar's animation is contrasted with many of the other religious figures and speakers in the Muslim community. One activist recounted his early experiences with Salafis during his religious seekership as one of utter boredom: "I tell you, the first time I went to Abu 'Ali's talk, he was like a university lecturer, and I don't like lectures and I fell asleep."[44] It is not as though Omar's lessons are bereft of content. Quite the contrary, they are packed with information, and many ac-tivists note his ability to effectively organize talks like a university lecture so that they are easy to follow. But he adds spice and drama to the talks through clever rhetorical devices to enhance their appeal.

One particularly effective device is his use of humor, something that helps establish likeability and enhances the prospects that a message will be accepted. Whereas some teachers, especially imams, use a dour tone to capture the seriousness of the religious endeavor, Omar feels free to pepper his detailed lectures and talks with humorous stories and jokes.[45] Take the following sarcasm in response to the Blair government's efforts to reach out to the Muslim community during the war in Afghanistan in 2001–2002, as described in *New Statesman*:

"He's Mullah Blair 'cos he says he reads the Koran every day," jokes Bakri. He pauses, waiting for the ripple of giggles to subside. "Mullah Blair says he loves you. But he has some problems: he had to bomb Iraq, bomb Somalia, bomb Afghanistan. But that's because Mullah Blair doesn't like beards." To demonstrate, Bakri pulls down his beard and runs both hands through it. "He sees the beard as an elaborate network to Bin Laden's terrorists. If you have facial hair, you are connected to that network."[46]

Just as important is Omar's ability to communicate in English. When he first arrived in the United Kingdom, Omar did not speak English, so he devoted himself to learning. Initially he only drew Arabic-speaking students, but after two years he had mastered enough English to begin drawing larger crowds. The movement and Omar make sure that all his publications and materials are published in English and made readily available to the public and religious seekers. The availability of such detailed material in English was novel for many seekers who felt thirsty for authentic religious rulings and discussions relevant to their lives.[47]

This was an essential element for building a following in the English-speaking community. For many seekers, Omar enjoyed a virtual monopoly of activist materials within the English-speaking community, unrivaled in sheer volume. For those who were serious about learning from a sheikh, Omar provided a unique opportunity. Individuals could ask him questions directly in English over the phone, through e-mail, on Internet forums, and in face-to-face conversations; and he made himself completely available to those who were interested. His accessibility is extremely broad: he travels around the country to give talks (sometimes multiple talks) every day; he answers the massive volume of e-mails, some of them requiring quite lengthy responses; and he freely gives out his phone numbers.

Omar knows that he is a good salesperson and likes to suggest that if he had not become an Islamic activist, he would have gone into advertising to work for a top marketing firm like Saatchi & Saatchi.[48] For him, it is about selling an ideology by developing a reputation as a credible source of Islamic learning. In the religious marketplace of ideas, seekers view him as a trustworthy source offering an essential spiritual product: the purity of Islam.

MANAGING A PUBLIC PERSONA

Social movements strategically interact with the media as a powerful vehicle for agenda setting, issue framing, and consciousness-raising. The media is an active agent in the social construction of meaning and a site of symbolic contestation, and thus it functions at once as a potential movement resource and a possible discursive competitor.[49] On the one hand, movements utilize media coverage as a mechanism to facilitate message dissemination to a broader audience. Protests and demonstrations are frequently public spectacles scripted to garner attention and transmit particular frames that support movement goals. On the other hand, the media is an assortment of independent entities with interests informed by market pressures, journalistic competition, and editorial choices. Although movement collective action may generate media interest, actors cannot control how they are covered, despite efforts at image management. Negative representations can still help propel issues onto the public agenda, but they often damage public perceptions and attitudes toward a movement and thus its credibility.

Al-Muhajiroun uses media coverage to sell itself as an important and reputable political actor: the volume of coverage is supposed to indicate its relative weight in the Muslim community. Negative representations, however, threaten perceptions about credibility. As a result, the movement is caught between its desire to seem important and disseminate its message to mass audiences, on the one hand, and its desire to carefully manage its public persona to support its credibility and right to sacred authority, on the other.

Al-Muhajiroun openly recognizes the importance of the media as a vehicle for reaching large audiences and disseminating ideas and actively pursues coverage. As Anjem notes, "You cannot address society at large unless you employ the media ... You can't deny the fact that the television, the radio, the magazines, the Internet, have a phenomenal amount of power to structure the ideas that people hold about their surroundings, about the world, about international politics."[50] Media coverage is viewed as one of the primary vehicles for advertising the movement and its basic message, and leaders try to cultivate publicity. At times, al-Muhajiroun seems obsessed with media coverage: prior to September 11 activists collected every newspaper report that mentioned the movement (the upsurge in coverage after the attacks made this practice more difficult, though activists tried to continue the collection). Although the movement believes the media is out to misrepresent the Islamic movement, it sees press coverage as a necessary evil and likens it to the Prophet Mohammed's use of poets (the mass media of his time) for propagation purposes.

The desire to provoke attention and coverage is one of the reasons behind the use of contentious public demonstrations and tactics. Omar Bakri argues that the point of the demonstrations is to raise public awareness and that one of the ways in which to do this is by heightening controversy. Disruptive rhetoric and action make good copy and television, and al-Muhajiroun attempts to incite controversy to open media access for movement leaders.[51] The movement's public events are heated, emotional, and charged with support for violence, enticing elements for the media. As William Gamson and David Meyer argue, "Fire in the belly is fine, but fire on the ground photographs better."[52]

Al-Muhajiroun uses an assortment of attention-seeking antics to tap into the media's seemingly insatiable penchant for covering disruption, confrontation, and "fire on the ground." Typically, these are limited to volatile language that is likely to get coverage in the press. Allusions to violence, veiled threats, and hostile denouncements litter demonstrations and public events. At a protest against President Musharaf of Pakistan, for example, activists invoked slogans and chants like "Musharaf, watch your back, Taliban coming back." As the demonstration unfolded, movement leaders whipped protesters into a frenzy, and the tone of the event became increasingly hostile. Protesters began screaming threats like "Musharaf! We are coming to kill you!" and "Musharaf! We want your blood!" The police were forced to intervene and restore civility. Movement protesters use these kinds of events to push the boundaries of acceptable free speech and raise controversy.

Activists also encourage interviews with the media. Omar Bakri, in particular, warmly welcomes reporters from virtually any news outlet. In fact, despite the anti-Semitic language and vitriolic anti-Israeli position of the movement, Omar shows little hesitancy speaking with Jewish reporters (he would argue that he has nothing against Jews, only Zionism and Israel). His openness has been rewarded with incredible news coverage, including numerous interviews with mainstream outlets like the BBC and the *Guardian*. He has reached out to the Arabic press as well, including the well-known paper *al-Sharq al-Awsat*.

In addition to public activism and interviews, al-Muhajiroun uses press releases to foster attention. Although the movement began issuing press releases sporadically in 1999, overtures to the media did not become consistent and organized until after the September 11 attacks. Only nine press releases were issued between 1999 and 2001, as compared to nearly fifty in the two years following the attacks. The dramatic increase in volume is consistent with the movement's attempt to capitalize on new interest in radical Islam. The vast majority are inflammatory condemnations of Western governments and their insidious plot to undermine Islam and Islamic movements. They often use inflammatory language and headline grabbing titles like "Madrid Today . . . London Tomorrow?" and "Don't Lose Your Head in Iraq!" The first is a reference to the Madrid bombings in March 2004, and the press release warns that London will likely be a target of an al-Qaeda attack if the British government does not change its policies toward the Muslim world.[53] The second release refers to the May 2004 beheading of American Nick Berg, a civilian working in Iraq, and warns non-Muslims to leave Muslim countries.[54] Since September 11, the preponderance of press releases have been related to the war on terrorism, conflicts in Afghanistan and Iraq, and the Israeli–Palestinian conflict.

The movement uses this approach to position itself as an essential source for journalists trying to gain insights into contemporary issues from an Islamic perspective. As Anjem observes, "We are very prolific in our press releases. We are talking about the issues as they happen, so the media can often go to those people who are the first people to quote. So if something happens, and you are the first person to have a press release, or you are the first person to do an action or activity, then inevitably you will be covered."[55] The movement has become a favorite source for journalists reporting on al-Qaeda, Hamas, and other Islamic terrorist organizations.

The movement leadership clearly relishes its public role: "Our coverage since September 11 has been international. We were in every single major media outlet in Britain, and in many European countries, and America, and in the Far East. People from China and Japan were coming down to have interviews. And our ideas were propagated worldwide. I don't think that that can be stopped. People are aware of us en masse in countries."[56]

The attempt to garner media attention has certainly paid dividends. In the year after September 11, the movement's coverage soared (see figure 3.1). Surveying coverage of the four widest circulating newspapers in the U.K. in the eight months prior to the attacks, the movement is only mentioned in three stories, as compared to seventy in the subsequent three and a half months. The upsurge prompted Home Secretary David Blunkett to request that the media limit reporting on such groups.[57] Coverage dwindled a bit after the initial interest but has maintained levels exceeding the pre–September 11 period.

Just as importantly, the movement's press coverage at times exceeded that of the mainstream Muslim Council of Britain (MCB), which represents more than 300 Muslim organizations in the United Kingdom and is considered one of the

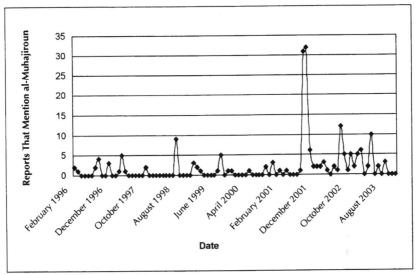

Figure 3.1.   Newspaper Reporting on al-Muhajiroun
Sources: Sun, Guardian, Evening Standard, Financial Times.

country's premier moderate Muslim institutions. Between September 11, 2001, and early 2004, the MCB released ninety-six press releases, about double the volume of al-Muhajiroun, but its press coverage was far from proportional (see figure 3.2). Controversy still receives inordinate media attention.

Al-Muhajiroun's coverage also greatly exceeds that of some other well-known radical groups in the United Kingdom. One of its closest ideological competitors, Hizb ut-Tahrir, for example, has been covered far less in the press, despite the fact that the movement does issue press releases. Between December 19, 2001, and October 17, 2003, Hizb ut-Tahrir issued thirty-one press releases but received only minimal coverage (see figure 3.2).

Despite movement claims to the contrary, the press typically provides an accurate representation of the movement and its ideology by using direct quotes from movement sources, which tend to focus on key ideological elements such as the need to establish an Islamic state, promote good and prevent vice, and wage a defensive jihad against "Crusaders" throughout the world. The quotes only provide ideological snippets, but the movement relishes the opportunity to articulate even partial messages in media forums to reach broad audiences. Leaders tend to fixate on media misrepresentations, but even a cursory survey of the coverage indicates that, by and large, the movement is able to communicate parts of its message.

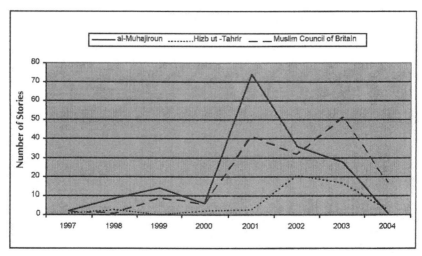

Figure 3.2. Newspaper Reporting on al-Muhajiroun, Hizb ut-Tahrir, and the Muslim Council of Britain
Sources: Sun, Guardian, Evening Standard, Financial Times.

Although the movement can claim success in terms of the volume of coverage and the articulation of some of its central ideas, it has been unable to control its portrayal and image, and this threatens its credibility. The vast majority of news reports represent al-Muhajiroun as a radical fringe group. Stories are typically framed in terms of the overall war on terrorism and al-Qaeda or the rise of radical Islam, thereby situating references to al-Muhajiroun within a broader, generally negative context. Activist statements about jihad and the evils of the West reinforce the association between al-Muhajiroun and terrorism. In many cases, the coverage has prompted public outcry, put pressure on government officials to crack down on the movement, and sparked investigations into the movement's activities. Although the movement views the media as a resource, it is a double-edged sword: the wide coverage invites public and governmental scrutiny, which in turn raises the risks for activists. Even more importantly for attracting religious seekers, negative coverage has the potential to undermine its credibility as a reputable source of religious learning.

Rather than limiting its public persona and the volume of media coverage, al-Muhajiroun has instead gone on the offensive in an attempt to undermine the credibility of the mainstream media (and thus refute negative portrayals of the movement). This strategy generally seems directed at seekers, who might question the movement because of the content of the coverage, rather than the general Muslim community. Most Muslims are unaware of al-Muhajiroun's attacks against the media and as a result are not exposed to any "corrections" or "clarifications."

The Western media is framed as an extension of Crusader and Zionist interests, a propaganda tool mobilized by anti-Muslim forces in a war against Islam. According to the movement, the primary mission of the media is to obfuscate the call to Islam and justice by misrepresenting Islamic movements, distorting the truth, and sowing lies. It is an instrument of Western cultural imperialism, a vehicle for disseminating Western values and supporting Zionist and Crusader industries that weaken resistance to Western assimilation, such as fashion, cosmetics, and pornography. As the leading edge of globalization, the Western media is a powerful instrument for spreading secularism and undermining Islam.[58] It uses negative coverage of al-Qaeda and other radicals to sow discord within the Muslim community, thereby weakening the prospects for a unified *umma* capable of taking on secularism and Western dominance. Through selective and inaccurate reporting, the media perpetuates ignorance about atrocities committed by the West and its global proxies (pliant Arab governments, the Afghan government, Israel, etc.) as well as the righteousness of Islamic movements like al-Qaeda. It is the public face of the international "war on Islam."

As evidence of the insidious intentions of the media, the movement often points to what it claims are factual contradictions. For example, during the U.S.-led war in Afghanistan, the Taliban were clearly routed and dispatched with relative ease, despite the resilience of small groups of fighters operating on the border with Pakistan. For radical Islamic groups, such a state of affairs would clearly represent a startling defeat and challenge the efficacy of rising against allied forces (either in Afghanistan or elsewhere). Studies of rebellion and protest demonstrate that individual calculations about the efficacy of action and the prospects for success are factors in decisions about joining.[59] Perhaps recognizing this phenomenon, al-Muhajiroun attempts to allay concerns about the defeat of the Taliban, even in the face of overwhelming evidence, by challenging Western news source reports about allied successes and Taliban/al-Qaeda defeats. Consider the following line of arguments made by Anjem:

> In the beginning they were saying there were something like 30,000 Taliban, 36,000. Now since then, they have reported about a hundred, twelve hundred, maybe a thousand people being killed, so where are the other 35,000 Taliban? The propaganda machine is such that if there were thousands of people who were killed, CNN and SkyNews would be out there and saying, "Look here are all the

people the American soldiers killed." But they haven't got those examples. There is no example of heavy casualties on the part of the Taliban.

And the Americans have always admitted that the war has only just begun and it is very difficult, [saying that] they [the Taliban and al-Qaeda] have proven to be tough fighters. You can read underneath that: "heavy casualties for the Americans." You don't use strong language like that unless there is something you want to say but is very difficult. If it is just one or two, they would say we have been successful, there is no resistance. Seven soldiers is nothing. You don't have to tell the whole world about that. Why do you want to depress people in America over seven casualties? In the [first] Iraq war, there were many people being killed, and they actually sent Christmas cards on behalf of American soldiers back home because they didn't want people to know people had died.

Look at the Americans. They say that there have been about 20–30 [allied] helicopters that have been downed, and each one in an accident they say a couple of Germans have died. There has actually been no one killed by the Taliban [he says with sarcasm]. There have been so many people killed, and it is like this is an accident because of the weather, it accidentally went into the mountain. This kind of propaganda is taking place all the time. War is about that. In the Second World War, they said that the Germans were eating the babies and stuff like that. It has always been like that. And the truth will probably not appear until at least ten years after.[60]

Activists are quick to point out that the U.S. government lied to its people about casualty numbers during the Vietnam War and argue that it recently lied about weapons of mass destruction in Iraq.

Within this narrative of conspiracy, the movement portrays itself as one of the media's primary victims. Drawing an analogy between the Western media and the "hate campaign" launched by the Quraysh elite in Mecca against the Prophet Mohammed and his companions, al-Muhajiroun argues that "their underlying aims . . . remain the same, namely to divert people from the truth of Islam by silencing those who speak the truth and carry it to the masses and eradicating those who work for its establishment."[61] Activists are seen as following in the footsteps of the Prophet and the companions, brave and steadfast in the face of an overwhelming propaganda machine bent on destroying Islam.

Al-Muhajiroun believes that, just like the Prophet, they have a duty to correct the lies of anti-Muslim detractors so that they might promote the pure message of Islam. So to correct the media "lies and distortions," the movement issues public statements, conducts interviews with reporters, and issues press statements with titles like "If You Want to Lie Don't Claim That the Elephant Flies," "A BBC Christian Reporter Declares His Crusade against Islam and Muslims," "New York Post Joins Western Media Crusade against Muslims," "BBC Lies and Deception in Crusade against Muslims," and "Lies and Fabrications of Reuters Exposed." Most of these focus on reporters' intentions, tying them to the global conspiracy against Islam. For al-Muhajiroun, noting that reporters are Jews or Christians is enough to impugn the neutrality of press reports. Activists make this argument with reference to Qur'anic verses such as "If a *faasiq* (sinner) comes with news verify it" (Qur'an 49:6) and "The Jews and Christians will never be pleased with you until you change your Deen [i.e., Al-Islam]" (Qur'an 3:118) (movement translation). For the movement, the implications are simple: never trust a non-Muslim.

The argument that the media is biased and misrepresents issues related to Islam resonates with many Muslims. Even if they do not accept al-Muhajiroun's entire argument about conspiracy and the righteousness of Islamic fighters, many Muslims accept the more general point that reporting is distorted when it comes to their faith.[62] The media often depicts Islam as a threat to British culture and values. Common stereotypes in reports include statements that Muslims are intolerant, misogynistic, violent or cruel, and strange or different.[63] They are sometimes depicted as irrational and difficult to integrate into British society. And because the press tends to report on Islam during times of crisis such as September 11, negative stories outweigh neutral or positive coverage.[64] Although journalists and editors have made strides in rectifying misrepresentations and inaccuracies, there has been a tendency to demonize Islam.[65] In the control group survey, all of the respondents stated that it is important to address religious biases in the media (90.2 percent believed this is "very important"). For al-Muhajiroun, distrust in the British media increases the likelihood that potential participants will dismiss or overlook negative reporting about the movement as part of the overall trend of negative reporting about Islam in general.

This does not prevent activists from using reports from Western media sources when it suits their purpose. Where reports contradict Western government representations of conflicts involving Muslims, for example, al-Muhajiroun is quick to hold them out as factually accurate. The typical argument is that "even the *kuffar* [unbeliever] press knows the truth." The movement thus cites CNN, the BBC, and other well-known news sources, but only if the stories confirm the movement's worldview and/or arguments. The Western media is uniformly condemned as part of a Crusader war, but specific nuggets of information are adopted as evidence to support al-Muhajiroun arguments.

This strategy of interaction with the media became more difficult in late April 2004 after a series of news sources published reports that Omar Bakri had openly called for jihad and Islamic rule in Europe. The movement responded by sending an appeal to al-Muhajiroun activists "not to speak to any non-Muslim

(Kufr) media bodies following the recent lies and fabrications spread by them about Sheikh Omar Bakri Muhammad and al-Muhajiroun. Rather interviews must only be conducted with Muslims because non-Muslims are biased against Islam and Muslims. . . [E]ven if a Muslim works for a non-Muslim media outlet [he should be avoided] since in this case he will be a slave to the editors' policies."[66] Although the movement views the media as a resource for bolstering its image as an important political actor, it is somewhat circumscribed by possible damage to its credibility.

While the movement combats the Western press, it finds itself embroiled in conflict with Muslim media sources as well. After September 11, mainstream Muslim newspapers and magazines, such as *Q-News* and *Muslim News*, published a number of reports critical of al-Muhajiroun and Omar Bakri. In some instances, the reach and potential influence of the Muslim press are quite substantial. *Muslim News*, for example, gives away 21,000 copies to mosques and Muslim community organizations and sends copies to public opinion makers.[67] Negative coverage in these mediums represents a direct threat to the recruitment and dissemination capacity of the movement, since these outlets target a specifically Muslim readership. In addition, the criticism comes from within the Muslim community itself via newspapers and magazines with substantial credibility among Muslims.

In response, al-Muhajiroun tries to discredit the mainstream Muslim news outlets. Responding to a question about whether it is religiously permissible to buy mainstream Muslim newspapers, such as *Q-News* and *Muslim News*, Omar issued a fatwa prohibiting such purchases. He charged mainstream Muslim media sources with the following:

1. Distorting the image, the profile and reputation of Muslims and Islamic groups such as al-Muhajiroun, Jihadis and Hizb ut-Tahrir which is clearly Haram [religiously forbidden], under their pretext of freedom of expression! 2. Libeling, swearing or backbiting Muslim scholars and activists as terrorists, fundamentalists, lunatics and extremists, which is clearly Haram, under their pretext of freedom of expression! 3. Fooling Muslims, ridiculing Muslims, misquoting Muslims and changing their words, which are clearly Haram and a sin, under their pretext of summarizing and editing! and 4. advertising for Haram things.[68]

While attempting to undermine the reputation and credibility of both the secular and Muslim press in the West, al-Muhajiroun offers itself as a reliable alternative. Until it suffered a massive cyber attack in the spring of 2003, the movement's homepage boasted that "at almuhajiroun.com, we work hard to bring you the latest news from around the world from authentic Muslim sources, void of any lies or misconceptions that are present in Kuffar sources such as the BBC or CNN."[69] It also offered a news section that included reports from jihadi news sources about Islamic struggles throughout the world as well as statements from bin Laden, Mullah Omar, and other radical leaders.

The website also provided several special news sections related to conflicts involving Muslims. Most of these were collages of pictures, presented as definitive, irrefutable proof that Crusaders were slaughtering Muslims across the globe and hiding the atrocities. The special news section on Iraq, for example, claimed to offer pictures of small children and babies "murdered" by British and American forces, proof that "the objectives of the US and UK were not to remove Saddam Hussein, but to murder, kill, rape and butcher more innocent Muslim women and Children, as is their objective in Afghanistan, and all over Muslim countries in the world."[70] The pictures depicted atrocious images of children with organs hanging out of their skin and severe deformities (the images actually appear to be from pictures of children killed during Saddam Hussein's chemical weapon attack against Kurds in Halabja in 1988). Special sections on Jenin, Afghanistan, and Indonesia used similar kinds of grotesque pictures, always claiming that the images were the result of Western handiwork. The more recent version of the website is considerably tamer (as of May 2004) and does not include the pictures, most likely because the government has signaled its willingness to further crack down on the movement.

By challenging the credibility of the media and offering its own news sources, al-Muhajiroun hopes to resolve the tension created by the double-edged nature of the media. The movement accepts and encourages broad coverage to publicize itself, while concomitantly waging a campaign that questions the reliability of negative coverage. Whether this strategy has succeeded is difficult to measure. At a minimum, it helps produce information encapsulation, whereby activists primarily rely on jihadi news sources for the "facts," drawing on the mainstream press only when it confirms al-Muhajiroun's worldview. The result is a conspiratorial mind-set and reliance on extremist news sources.[71]

Media public relations management is a difficult task for the movement. It wants to get attention, both to disseminate its message and to magnify its importance as a movement. The overreporting of al-Muhajiroun gives the impression that it is influential in the Muslim community, enhancing the prospects that seekers will find it a credible source of religious learning. For those who are sampling different fundamentalist groups, in particular, the inordinate attention makes it seem as though al-Muhajiroun is more relevant, thus helping the movement vis-à-vis its intrafundamentalist competitors. Negative coverage, however, can weaken the movement's reputation for some seekers and is a concern. Although it tries to maintain damage control and manage its image, the 2004 appeal to activists to stop speaking with the Western press indicates that this is not always possible.

CONCLUSION

For disaffected religious seekers who are dissatisfied with mainstream religious figures, al-Muhajiroun offers an alternative. Seekers unanimously cite Omar Bakri Mohammed's credibility as a source of religious authority as critical in deciding to pursue religious lessons through the movement rather than another Islamic group. He is seen as knowledgeable, politically aware, and of sound character. Perceptions about credibility are essential for movement recruitment, since they determine whether seekers believe that what Omar says is "real Islam."

These perceptions are not produced in a vacuum; they are in large measure a result of comparative evaluations: Omar seems more knowledgeable and of better character than other alternative sources of religious learning. And he is willing to satisfy intellectual curiosity about the underlying rationale for particular religious rulings by actively engaging audiences in debates and discussions about evidence from the Qur'an and Sunna. This is contrasted with the "mullah mentality" of mosque imams and moderate religious figures, who often exhibit frustration with inquisitive seekers and their questions about the basis of religious interpretations. And while al-Muhajiroun activists still enjoy a good fiery sermon by radicals like Abu Hamza, Omar is seen as a more knowledgeable scholar who deserves to have followers.

Once seekers accept Omar's credibility and right to sacred authority, the way to socialization and culturing is opened. Seekers are more willing to come to regular religious lessons and study circles where the movement can teach them about "proper Islam," understood as the movement's ideology. Activists cast themselves in the role of an ideological vanguard responsible for culturing Muslims about their divine duties to God.

It is the content of the culturing process that encourages risky activism. Students are taught that they must follow Islam in its literalist entirety or risk damnation. This includes edicts to promote violence, struggle to establish Islamic states through military coups, and engage in contentious activism to command good and forbid evil. For seekers inspired by a concern with spiritual destiny (a view encouraged by the movement), the ideology of the movement offers a blueprint or template about how Muslims should behave to ensure salvation on Judgment Day. The content of culturing helps overcome the free rider dilemma by positing individual self-interest as salvation, which is contingent on fulfilling all the divine duties of activism as outlined in the movement ideology. For those who accept Omar's right to sacred authority and the legitimacy of his religious interpretations, a refusal to engage in the risky activism commanded by God is tantamount to jeopardizing self-interest.

NOTES

1. Of course, the message itself and whether it seems logical and well constructed matters for perceptions about the credibility of the source as well. See Michael D. Slater and Donna Rouner, "How Message Evaluation and Source Attributes May Influence Credibility Assessment and Belief Change," *Journalism and Mass Communication Quarterly* 73, no. 4 (1996): 974–91.

2. Carl I. Hovland, Irving L. Janis, and Howard H. Kelly, *Communication and Persuasion* (New Haven: Yale University Press, 1953); William J. McGuire, "Attitudes and Attitude Change," in Gilbert Fiske Lindzey and Elliot Aronson, eds., *Handbook of Social Psychology*, 3d ed. (Reading, Mass.: Random House, 1985); Susan T. Fiske and Shelly E. Taylor, *Social Cognition*, 2d ed. (New York: McGraw-Hill, 1991).

3. David R. Roskos-Ewoldsen, Jacqueline Bichsel, and Kathleen Hoffman, "The Influence of Accessibility of Source Likability on Persuasion," *Journal of Experimental Social Psychology*, March 2002, 137–43.

4. For example, Marvin Goldberg and Jon Hartwick, "The Effects of Advertiser Reputation and Extremity of Advertiser Claim on Advertiser Effectiveness," *Journal of Consumer Research* 17 (1990): 172–79; Anne E. Sartori, "The Might of the Pen: A Reputational Theory of Communication in International Disputes," *International Organization*, Winter 2002, 121–49.

5. See Charlotte Ryan, *Prime Time Activism: Media Strategies for Grassroots Organizing* (Boston: South End, 1991), 85; Robert D. Benford, "Frame Disputes within the Nuclear Disarmament Movement," *Social Forces*, March 1993, 692–93; Robert D. Benford and David A. Snow, "Framing Processes and Social Movements: An Overview and Assessment," *Annual Review of Sociology* 26 (2000): 620–21; Marsha L. Vanderford, "Vilification and Social Movements: A Case Study of Pro-Life and Pro-Choice Rhetoric," *Quarterly Journal of Speech* 75 (1989): 166–82; Dawn McCaffrey and Jennifer Keys, "Competitive Frame Processes in the Abortion Debate: Polarization-Vilification, Frame Saving, and Frame Debunking," *Sociological Quarterly* 41 (2000): 41–46; Robert D. Benford and Scott A. Hunt, "Interactional Dynamics in Public Problems Marketplaces: Movements and the Counterframing and Reframing of Public Problems," in James Holstein and Gale Miller, eds., *Challenges and Choices: Constructionist Perspectives on Social Problems* (New York: Transaction, 2003), 153–86.

6. Benford and Snow, "Framing Processes and Social Movements," 621.

7. Robert Furtell, "Framing Processes, Cognitive Liberation, and NIMBY Protest in the U.S. Chemical-Weapons Disposal Conflict," *Sociological Inquiry* 73 (2003): 380.

8. Furtell, "Framing Processes," 380.

9. Social movement theorists have argued that empirical credibility (how well a frame captures what is going on in the "real world") is important for frame resonance and one could argue that Islamic scholars need to appear grounded in reality as well. For social movement theory arguments along these lines, see David Snow and Robert D. Benford, "Ideology, Frame Resonance, and Participant Mobilization," *International Journal of Social Movement Research* 1 (1988): 208; Benford and Snow, "Framing Processes and Social Movements," 619–20.

10. Omar Bakri Mohammed, interview by author, London, June 2002.

11. Kamran Bokhari, former U.S. al-Muhajiroun spokesperson, telephone interview by author, April 2003. This information is consistent with what I was told and what Omar himself advertised on his personal website.

12. Anjem Choudary, telephone interview by author, June 2002.

13. Anjem Choudary, interview by author, London, March 2002.

14. Anjem Choudary, interview by author, London, March 2002.

15. Anjem Choudary, telephone interview by author, June 2002.

16. Islam, interview by author, London, June 2002.

17. Anjem Choudary, telephone interview by author, June 2002.

18. Anjem Choudary, telephone interview by author, June 2002.

19. Anjem Choudary, telephone interview by author, June 2002.

20. Somali al-Muhajiroun activist, interview by author, London, June 2002.

21. Mohammed al-Massari, interview by author, London, December 2002.

22. Somali al-Muhajiroun activist, interview by author, London, June 2002.

23. Anjem Choudary, telephone interview by author, June 2002.

24. MEMRI, "A New Bin Laden Speech," Special Dispatch Series, no. 539, July 18, 2003.

25. As quoted in Susan Kwilecki and Loretta S. Wilson, "Was Mother Teresa Maximizing Her Utility? An Idiographic Application of Rational Choice Theory," *Journal for the Scientific Study of Religion*, June 1998, 207.

26. Omar Bakri Mohammed, interview by author, London, June 2002.

27. Omar Bakri Mohammed, interview by author, London, June 2002.

28. He made this argument through al-Muhajiroun's list server when questions were raised.

29. He did this, at a minimum, through the movement's *fiqh* forum online.

30. As quoted in *New Statesman*, February 11, 2002.

31. Algerian al-Muhajiroun activist, interview by author, London, June 2002.

32. See, for example, James P. Piscatori, ed., *Islam in the Political Process* (Cambridge: Cambridge University Press, 1983); Quintan Wiktorowicz, *The Management of*

Islamic Activism: Salafis, the Muslim Brotherhood, and State Power in Jordan (Albany: State University of New York Press, 2001), chap. 2; and Seyyed Vali Reza Nasr, *The Islamic Leviathan: Islam and the Making of State Power* (Oxford: Oxford University Press, 2001).

33. James P. Piscatori, "Ideological Politics in Sa'udi Arabia," in Piscatori, *Islam in the Political Process*, 60–61.

34. Omar Bakri Mohammed, *Charity Organisations in Islam: The Islamic Verdict* (London: Al-Muhajiroun Publications, n.d.), 15.

35. Omar Bakri Mohammed, *The Akhaam of Zulm (Oppression) in Islam* (London: Al-Muhajiroun Publications, n.d.), 24.

36. The Shari'ah Court of the U.K., "Fatwa or Divine Decree against General Musharraf-USA," Case no. Pakistan/F135-OBM, September 16, 2001.

37. Omar Bakri Mohammed, *USA at War with Islam: The Losing Battle* (London: MNA Publications, n.d.), 21.

38. Richard E. Petty, Monique A. Fleming, Joseph R. Priester, and Amy Harasty Feinstein, "Individual versus Group Interest Violation: Surprise as a Determinant of Argument Scrutiny and Persuasion," *Social Cognition* 19, no. 4 (2001): 418–42.

39. Omar Bakri Mohammed, interview by author, London, June 2002.

40. Peter Mandaville, *Transnational Muslim Politics: Reimagining the Umma*, 2d ed. (London: Routledge, 2004), 133.

41. Interview by author, London, June 2002.

42. Scott D. Johnson and Ann N. Miller, "A Cross-Cultural Study of Immediacy, Credibility, and Learning in the U.S. and Kenya," *Communication Education*, July 2002, 280–92.

43. Jennifer L. Aaker and Patti Williams, "Empathy versus Pride: The Influence of Emotional Appeals across Cultures," *Journal of Consumer Research*, December 1998, 241–61; James M. Jasper, "The Emotions of Protest: Affective and Reactive Emotions in and around Social Movements," *Sociological Forum* 13, no. 3 (1998): 397–424; Ron Amizade and Doug McAdam, "Emotions and Contentious Politics," in Ronald R. Amizade et al., eds., *Silence and Voice in Contentious Politics* (Cambridge: Cambridge University Press, 2001); and Jeff Goodwin, James M. Jasper, and Francesca Polletta, eds., *Passionate Politics: Emotions and Social Movements* (Chicago: University of Chicago Press, 2001).

44. Interview by author, London, June 2002.

45. For a sense of Omar's joking nature, see Jon Ronson, *Them: Adventures with Extremists* (New York: Simon & Schuster, 2002), chap. 1.

46. *New Statesman*, February 11, 2002.

47. Kamran Bokhari, former al-Muhajiroun U.S. spokesperson, telephone interview by author, April 2003.

48. He made this comment during one of our conversations and made an almost identical statement to reporter Jon Ronson (see Ronson, *Them*, 25).

49. William A. Gamson and David S. Meyer, "Framing Political Opportunity," in Doug McAdam, John D. McCarthy, and Mayer N. Zald, eds., *Comparative Perspectives on Social Movements: Political Opportunities, Mobilizing Structures, and Cultural Framings* (Cambridge: Cambridge University Press, 1996), 287–88.

50. Anjem Choudary, interview by author, London, June 2002.

51. Gamson and Meyer, "Framing Political Opportunity," 288.

52. Gamson and Meyer, "Framing Political Opportunity," 288.

53. Al-Muhajiroun, "Madrid Today . . . London Tomorrow?" press release, March 23, 2004.

54. Al-Muhajiroun, "Don't Lose Your Head in Iraq," press release, May 13, 2004.

55. Anjem Choudary, interview by author, London, June 2002.

56. Anjem Choudary, interview by author, London, June 2002.

57. Press Association, September 21, 2001.

58. Anjem Choudary, interview by author, London, March 2002.

59. Susanne Lohmann, "A Signaling Model of Informative and Manipulative Political Action," *American Political Science Review* 88 (1993): 319–33; Lohmann, "Dynamics of Informational Cascades: The Monday Demonstrations in Leipzig, East Germany, 1989–1991," *World Politics* 47 (1994): 42–101; Karl-Dieter Opp, *The Rationality of Political Protest: A Comparative Analysis of Rational Choice Theory* (Boulder: Westview, 1989); Karl-Dieter Opp, Peter Voss, and Christiane Gern, *Origins of a Spontaneous Revolution: East Germany, 1989* (Ann Arbor: University of Michigan Press, 1993).

60. Anjem Choudary, interview by author, London, March 2002.

61. Al-Muhajiroun, "The Propaganda Machine," press release, n.d. (after September 11).

62. Muslim Council of Britain, "Research Finds That Many Muslims Don't Trust British TV News Following September 11," press release, September 9, 2002.

63. Brian Whitaker, "Islam and the British Press after September 11" (talk presented to a conference on Islam and the media, Central London Mosque, June 20, 2002). Whitaker is Middle East editor for *The Guardian*.

64. For this general argument, see Edward Said, *Covering Islam*, 2d ed. (New York: Vintage, 1997).

65. Elizabeth Poole, *Reporting Islam: Media Representations of British Muslims* (London: Tauris, 2002).

66. Al-Muhajiroun, "An Appeal to All Al-Muhajiroun Members," press release, April 26, 2004.

67. Open Society Institute, "The Situation of Muslims in the UK," *Monitoring the EU Process: Minority Protection*, 2002, p. 426, www.eumap.org/reports/2002/eu/international/sections/uk/2002_m_uk.pdf.

68. Omar Bakri Mohammed, *Questions and Answers, Economic System*, "Can we buy Muslim newspapers like QNews/Muslim News?" n.d.

69. www.almuhajiroun.com, accessed October 16, 2002. After the cyber attack, the movement redesigned the website and no longer included this statement as of February 2004.

70. www.almuhajiroun.com/lnews/misc/special-%20iraq.php, accessed May 22, 2002. The website was shut down and later relocated to http://almuk.com/obm.

71. This emerged in a number of interviews with activists.

4

CULTURING AND COMMITMENT

Even if religious seekers are exposed to al-Muhajiroun and accept Omar Bakri's right to sacred authority, this alone is not enough to overcome the free rider dilemma. Seekers could attend lessons and learn about Islam without committing themselves to risky activism. In this manner, they could free-ride and reap the benefits of an Islamic education without incurring the costs and risks of commitment.

To understand why some individuals eventually commit themselves to the costs and risks outlined in chapter 1, we must understand movement "culturing," or what activists term *tarbiya* (culturing in proper religious beliefs and behaviors). Al-Muhajiroun tries to draw seekers into religious lessons, where they can be cultured in the movement ideology. The ideology, in turn, emphasizes that the only way to achieve salvation and enter Paradise on Judgment Day is to follow the movement's prescribed strategy, which includes high-risk activism. These lessons serve as low-risk forums where, over time, eventual activists are socialized into the ideological template of the movement. Clearly not every individual who is exposed to these lessons accepts the movement ideology as "true" Islam. But for those who become "intellectually affiliated" and adopt movement precepts, al-Muhajiroun offers a rational strategy for advancing spiritual self-interest. This chapter explains the culturing process and how it inspires risky activism.

VANGUARDS OF THE IDEOLOGICAL STRUGGLE

Although some Islamists might eschew the term "ideology" as demeaning religious beliefs, al-Muhajiroun explicitly conceptualizes Islam as an ideology. The

[handwritten note: Ideology = set of shared beliefs that form the basis of a system.]

movement defines *din* (usually translated as religion) as "ideology or way of life. This is distinct from the word 'religion' because religion usually refers to a set of rituals or an aspect of man's relationship with his Creator. Ideology, on the other hand, provides a basis, or in other words a creed, upon which all aspects of life are built."[1]

As a comprehensive system of living, it is seen as directly challenging other dominant ideologies in a cosmic struggle for the soul of humanity. The movement cites two ideological competitors in particular: communism and capitalism. Although a few publications deconstruct and attack the precepts of communism, it is generally dismissed as "dead."[2] In the context of the West, the greater concern is capitalism, which the movement argues is "established on the basis of detaching religion from life's affairs." Capitalism is thus inextricably linked to secularism (and Western culture in general). Democracy is viewed as part of capitalism:

> As for democracy, which is ascribed to this ideology, it arises from man establishing his own system. Therefore, the people are the source of authority, they determine the system, employ the ruler to govern it, deprive him of rule whenever they desire, and put to him the system they want. This is because ruling is an employment contract between the people and the ruler to rule according to the system the people choose for him to apply on them.[3]

For the movement, the freedom of capitalism, as both an economic and political system, is an inherent evil, since it allows humans to follow their desires without restraint, including acts of immorality: "Man is always subject to bias, disparity, differences, contradictions and the influence of his current environment, hardly a basis for complete impartiality and absolute truth. Any man made system will suffer from these same bias, disparity, differences, contradictions, and influence."[4] Islam, in contrast, is portrayed as an ideology based on the immutability of divine law. Since this law is rooted in divine social justice and morality, it is impervious to the whims of shifting human desires and thus superior to man-made systems like capitalism.

The movement is particularly concerned with children who grow up in a Western society without the kind of proper Islamic upbringing necessary to stall, challenge, and reverse capitalist indoctrination:

> A bad upbringing will result in you being narrow-minded. If the way that you are brought up is incorrect then everything that emanates from that will also be incorrect because it is this socialisation process that determines the mentality of a person. The parents are the examples for their children. If they themselves are bad then their children will emulate them and also become bad.[5]

Particular blame for a bad upbringing (socialization) is placed on the educational system in the United Kingdom. State secular schools are framed as institutional agents of capitalism, designed to pull children away from their Islamic identity by emphasizing narrow nationalism (i.e., being British) and nonreligious values. Anjem argues that,

> Western capitalist States imbibe in children all their false ideas such as Nationalism, evolution and the worship of science instead of treating [science] as a means of discovering the creation. Children are taught to conform to a code of dress that shows their nakedness. Islam is taught as a religion just like any other religion such as Christianity and Sikhism. Children grow up idolizing pop-stars and footballers rather than appreciating the Messengers from their creator and worshiping God alone. All of this is also imposed as a National Curriculum with which you cannot disagree or control.[6]

The educational attack on Islam is seen as especially dangerous because of its insidious nature: it saps confidence in Islam as a comprehensive way of life by portraying it as backward and inferior to Western values.[7] Just as importantly, secular education focuses on forging a national British identity intended to supersede global religious bonds.

Muslims and established religious institutions are also blamed for the ideological crisis. Al-Muhajiroun argues that moderates try to pacify Muslims into accepting adherence to ritual as leading to salvation rather than teaching them that Islam is a system of life that includes both beliefs and behaviors or actions.[8] This is contrasted with the movement's own interpretation, which emphasizes the inextricable link between belief and action to establish God's rule on earth. Current religious education in the United Kingdom (and more globally) is therefore insufficient to teach Muslims about Islam and resurrect the power and honor of the *umma*.[9]

For the movement, this secular socialization undermines the natural human inclination to follow Islam. From this perspective, everyone has Islam inside because it is the natural and pure state of being human *(fitra)*. That is why, activists argue, a person in the desert alone will inevitably become a Muslim. Infectious socialization into other ideologies, however, interferes with this natural tendency. This is particularly the case for Muslims living in the West because they are bombarded by non-Islamic beliefs and practices. In the West, then, the central challenge is to "resocialize" Muslims who have adopted alternative ideologies, whether capitalism or the postsecular variant of Islam supported by moderates.[10]

In this struggle for the hearts and minds of Muslims, the movement portrays itself as an intellectual vanguard responsible for properly teaching the Muslim community about "true" Islam. Its self-identified functions are twofold: "1. Carrying Islam as an intellectual leadership to the society by culturing the society about Islam i.e. as a spiritual and political belief; 2. Bonding the Muslim community in the West with the Muslims globally in order to create an unbeatable bond within the Ummah and for them to be part of the preparation for the world-wide Islamic revolution."[11] In this capacity, the movement seeks to facilitate a network of shared meaning predicated on its own interpretation of Islam, thereby fostering a global Islamic identity rooted in its ideological vision. This strategy is identified as "interaction," as opposed to either integration (assimilation) or isolation (withdrawal into Muslim enclaves isolated from the broader British society). Not surprisingly, given the emphasis on culturing and resocialization, lessons and other educational activities are the primary instruments of interaction. Once contacts are convinced that Omar Bakri has sacred authority, the potential exposure to these lessons, and thus movement culturing, increases. In these socialization environments, students are taught a particular understanding of Islam that focuses on the necessity of risky activism for those who are concerned with Judgment Day and salvation. The actual content of socialization or culturing matters for understanding how individuals overcome the free rider dilemma and why they engage in high-risk activism through a group like al-Muhajiroun.

THE CENTRALITY OF *TAWHID*

 Many Islamic fundamentalist movements, including al-Muhajiroun, emphasize the centrality of *tawhid*—belief in the oneness of God. *Tawhid* begins with the *shahada*, or testimony of faith that signals a conversion to Islam: "I testify that there is no God except Allah and that Mohammed is His messenger." Though typologies vary from movement to movement, *tawhid* can generally be broken down into two categories.

The first is *tawhid rububiyya*—the state of being the only true *rabb*, or Lord. God is described as the sole Lord and sovereign of the universe, based on suras (Qur'anic verses) such as "Allah is Creator of all things, and He is Guardian over all things" (Qur'an 39:62). Unlike God, humans cannot create or form something from nothing; they can only use the materials provided by the Lord. And God has ultimate power in controlling, guiding, and directing everything: "No calamity befalleth save by Allah's leave. And whoever believeth in Allah, He guideth his heart. And Allah is Knower of all things" (Qur'an 64:1).

For al-Muhajiroun, this component of *tawhid* includes *tawhid al-asma' wa al-sifat*—belief in the unity of the names and attributes of God (some fundamentalist groups create this as a distinct category of *tawhid*), often referred to as the "ninety-nine names of God." The Qur'an explains that these names and attributes cannot be likened to those of His creations: "He is Allah the One! Allah, the eternally Besought of all! He beggeteth not nor was begotten. And there is none comparable to Him" (Qur'an 112:1–4). Another sura states, "Naught is His likeness, and He is the Hearer, the Seer" (Qur'an 42:11).

Rationalists such as the Mu'tazila read many of God's attributes as metaphors. They argue, for example, that God cannot have sight per se, since this implies that He has eyes. Because God created eyes and cannot share attributes with His creations, this is impossible. Rationalists instead interpret references to God's eyes as His vision.

Islamic groups like al-Muhajiroun, on the other hand, argue that the Qur'an, as the literal word of God, cannot be read in metaphorical terms. God may not have eyes like those of humans, but because the Qur'an mentions His eyes, He has eyes, even if humans cannot comprehend what divine eyes look like. They are part of the *ghayb,* domains beyond human perception and comprehension. Omar Bakri argues, "A quality of the pious, for which they are praised in the Qur'an, is that they believe in the Al-Ghayb without questioning or doubting it, as long as it comes from the Qur'an or the authentic Sunnah. Allah the Creator cannot be subjected to the limited faculties of His creatures."[12] From this perspective, Muslims must avoid distorting, altering, denying, or sharing God's attributes, as expressed in the sources of Islam. In short, humans must have faith in the wisdom of God, who decides what we need to know or understand. Only then does a Muslim truly believe in God.

 The second major element of *tawhid* is *tawhid al-ilah*—worshiping only God. This is based on suras such as, "And the places of worship are only for Allah, so pray not unto anyone along with Allah" (Qur'an 72:18) and hadith such as, "Allah's right upon the creatures is that they worship Him alone without taking any partners with Him."[13] Fundamentalists are unified in their ardent rejection of practices that imply worshiping other than the one true God. This includes praying to intermediaries such as saints, swearing to other than God, or supplicating to a dead or living person. Perhaps the largest body of fundamentalist publications is devoted to undermining popular religious practices seen as violating *tawhid al-ilah*, especially those conducted by Sufis, who are charged with heresy for saint worship and blindly following their Sufi masters. Jews and Christians, considered People of the Book and fellow monotheists, are similarly condemned for blindly following priests, rabbis, and prophets. Fundamentalists cite the following hadith as evidence: "The curse of Allah falls upon the Jews and Christians for they have made their prophet's tombs places of worship."[14]

The opposite of *tawhid* is *shirk*—ascribing partners in worshiping God. This is considered the worst possible deviance, a transgression God does not forgive. The Qur'an is replete with dire warnings about the consequences of *shirk*:

> [A]nd be not one of those who ascribes partners (unto Him). (Qur'an 30:31)

> Lo! Whoso ascribeth partners unto Him, for him Allah has forbidden Paradise. His abode is in the Fire. For evil-doers there will be no helpers. (Qur'an 5:72)

> Lo! Allah forgiveth not that a partner be ascribed Unto Him. He forgiveth (all) save that to who He will. Whoso ascribeth partners to Allah, he hath indeed invented a tremendous sin. (Qur'an 4:48)

Fundamentalists draw a distinction between major and minor *shirk*. The latter includes transgressions that an individual may not realize constitute *shirk*, such as swearing by other than God or showing off in religious rituals to impress others. In such cases, the *mushrik* (someone who has engaged in *shirk*) is sent to hell, though God may choose to forgive him or her. Major *shirk*, on the other hand, constitutes a violation of the basic tenets of the faith, such as worshiping other deities, for which there is no forgiveness or reprieve. A *mushrik* who does not repent before dying faces hellfire for eternity.

For this reason al-Muhajiroun emphasizes the importance of *tawhid* in its lessons. Not only do lessons explain the relevance of *tawhid* for following the straight path of Islam, but they also stress the consequences for those who fail to uphold it:

> Tawheed prevents man from eternally remaining in the Hellfire. The Prophet Mohammed (SAW) stated in an authentic report: Whoever dies and has so much as a mustard seed of faith in his heart shall enter al-Jannah [the garden of Paradise]. Faith here signifies a correct belief in Allah and His Messenger Mohammed (SAW) and all that they instructed, commanded and prohibited for mankind.[15]

In emphasizing rewards and punishments, lessons on *tawhid* are framed in terms of individual self-interest in salvation. (Following *tawhid* also provides benefits in this life because God rewards the true believers and provides for the rightly guided.)[16]

For al-Muhajiroun, the importance of *tawhid* necessitates that all Muslims educate themselves about its demands to avoid hellfire. There is thus an educational imperative for those who desire protection on Judgment Day. Omar Bakri cites Qur'an 14:52: "This is a declaration for the people to be warned and to be aware that there is only one God."[17] It is not enough to simply iterate the *shahada*; a true believer is "aware" of the requirements of *tawhid*: "For Verily, the one who testifies that *'there is no god but Allah'* without having knowledge about it will never save his neck on the day of judgment, rather that the testimony of the *Kalima* necessitates that the person is aware about what *Laa ilaahah* [none has the right to be worshiped] negates (*Nafi*) and what *illalaah* [but God] affirms (*Ithbaat*)."[18] It is therefore "obligatory to know what leads us to kufr [disbelief] and shirk in order not to fall down into the fiery pit."[19]

Because of this imperative, ignorance about *tawhid* is not an excuse that saves an individual on Judgment Day. In fact, God tests Muslims from time to time with *shirk*, disobedience, and evil; the true believers will stand firm against temptation. The real possibility of unconsciously violating *tawhid* and leaving Islam means that "Muslims should be aware of what negates and contradicts Tawheed in order to make a shield for themselves, protecting them from apostasy."[20] This argument is intended to press students to look more deeply into *tawhid* by attending al-Muhajiroun lessons.

To facilitate this education, the movement offers an assortment of publications, audio materials, and events related to *tawhid,* including lessons about the pillars and conditions of *tawhid,* how one becomes a *mushrik,* and the apostasy of rulers in the Muslim world. One common lesson related to *tawhid* focuses on the issue of democracy. For al-Muhajiroun, major *shirk* includes participation in democracy and government in non-Muslim countries.[21] Omar Bakri argues that,

At-Tawheed which means obeying, following, worshiping, and elevating Almighty Allah (SWT) exclusively, without associating with him or his attributes with anyone else, and that conversely associating with God or with any of his attributes is an act of Shirk which makes a person go outside the fold of Islam and this is why at-Tawheed is the fundamental pillar of Islam. One of Allah (SWT)'s attributes is that he is the legislator and the commander and he has the absolute right and power to command and legislate, and no-one shares this absolute power with him.[22]

Furthermore, the verdict for voting is that perpetrators are *kafirs* (unbelievers): "Any Muslim who votes for a person knowing that the Parliament is a body of legislating law is an apostate." Certainly the movement accepts that Muslims may be unaware of their deviance, especially if guided by a "rationalist or secular clergyman," but this is not ceded as an excuse and the individual remains sinful because "believing that Allah (SWT) is the only legislator is a matter known from the Deen of Islam by necessity."

More generally, students are taught that following any kind of human-made law is apostasy because it rejects the idea of sovereignty for God alone *(tawhid al-hakamiyya)*. For al-Muhajiroun, any act is an act of worship. As a result, if the act does not conform to divine law, it is tantamount to worshiping other than God, or *shirk*. This includes not only support for democracy (a human-made system), but other actions that are not sanctioned by the *shari'a* as well. Although there are interpretive differences over the precise content of the *shari'a*, al-Muhajiroun claims its own interpretation as the only "correct" version. This means that any act that does not conform to movement interpretations of Islam is considered heretical. This includes a wide variety of behaviors (see table 4.1).[23]

Based on this argument, the movement gives itself wide latitude to declare other Muslims apostates *(takfir*, the process of declaring a Muslim an unbeliever). All of the leaders of the Muslim world are considered apostates because they obey international law and support the United Nations (a human-made institution), adopt non-Islamic legal codes, ridicule Islam by permitting what God forbids (such as uncovered women), form alliances with non-Muslims, and embrace democracy.[24] President Musharaf, in particular, was declared an apostate

Table 4.1.   Some Examples of Apostasy according to al-Muhajiroun

1. Calling for secularism
2. Thinking that human made law is better or similar to Islam or that Islam is old-fashioned and not suitable for today
3. Thinking that Islam is just ritual and does not include an economic system, foreign policy, social system, etc.
4. Hating the religion
5. Fighting the religion
6. Mocking the religion
7. Rejecting God's commands, including the duty to avoid free mixing of men and women or anything else that is "known by necessity"*
8. Denying the command to have a beard
9. Not understanding the meaning of the testimony of faith; a Muslim must know the meaning and act on this understanding
10. Turning away from Islam by not studying, acting, or caring about the religion
11. Leaving the prayer intentionally, even for one prayer
12. Refusing to call Jews or Christians unbelievers or doubting that they are unbelievers
13. Making alliances with non-Muslims or to love or accompany them against Muslims
14. Becoming a member of a non-Muslim political party
15. Any kind of *shirk*

*Al-Muhajiroun lists 262 items that all Muslims must "know by necessity."

CULTURING AND COMMITMENT

in a formal fatwa issued by Omar Bakri. Al-Muhajiroun has also shown a proclivity to declare moderate Muslims apostates, including the leadership of the Muslim Council of Britain. While most Muslims reject the use of *takfir* since, as the Prophet Mohammed said, "And he who accuses a believer of *kufr* (disbelief) then it is like killing him,"[25] al-Muhajiroun argues that it is actually a *duty*:

We MUST make Takfeer in order to worship Allah and purify our 'Aqeedah [creed]. To say the rulers of Muslim countries are not kafir murtad (apostates) has serious implications. It means that any person can change their deen, kill Muslims, ridicule Allah, his Messenger, the Muslims, the 'Ulama, the Mujaahideen [holy warriors] and still remain Muslim; this means there is no boundaries of kufr [disbelief], a person can do whatever they want and never become kafir. It also means that we must have Wala (alliance) with them, we must defend them, protect them and obey them . . . In order to purify our 'Aqeeda and Tawheed and most importantly, to remain Muslims we must declare them to be murtad or we too may fall under the banner of kufr.[26]

For students who accept the centrality of *tawhid*, the calculus is clear: follow the divine rules and receive a spiritual payoff; remain deviant and suffer eternal consequences. But what are the divine rules and how does an individual Muslim identify proper adherence? Islamic movements offer religious interpretations represented in ideologies as guidelines to answer this question. These ideologies essentially outline strategies for obtaining the spiritual payoff—what individuals must do to ensure salvation.

All Islamic fundamentalist groups base their proffered strategies on the model of the Prophet Mohammed—the Muslim exemplar whose path (Sunna) is considered the perfection of Islam in practice. There are divergences, however, over the specifics of the prophetic paradigm and its application to the contemporary context. Each group believes it is following the proper model and interpretation, and these differences matter in terms of the potential for salvation. The Prophet predicted that the Muslim community would fracture into sects after his death and warned his followers to remain focused on his example and the Qur'an for guidance: "I am leaving you two things and you will never go astray as long as you cling to them. They are the Book of Allah and my Sunnah."[27] Fundamentalist groups like al-Muhajiroun believe there is one correct understanding of the straight path of Islam; all others are deviations and will not receive divine reward. This is based on authentic hadiths, for example, "And this Ummah will divide into seventy-three sects all of which except one will go to Hell and they are those who are upon what I and my Companions are upon."[28] Each group considers itself this "saved sect" *(firqa al-najiyya)* and therefore believes that its activists will be saved on Judgment Day. Al-Muhajiroun argues that Muslims must search for the one saved sect to protect their spiritual destiny.[29]

THE IDEOLOGICAL TEMPLATE

Many differences about strategies for fulfilling God's divine commands and ensuring salvation derive from disagreements about the prophetic model. Although Islamists like to argue that they have located objective truth about proper behavior, there is an inherent subjectivity. Because the Qur'an is silent on many issues, Muslims invariably turn to the Prophet's Sunna for guidance. In essence, they ask what the Prophet would do in particular circumstances if he were alive today. To extrapolate, scholars use *qiyas* (reasoning by analogy) and *ijtihad* (independent judgment), which means searching for analogous situations from the time of the Prophet and reasoning to the contemporary period.

But what is the proper analogical period? Should we liken our situation to the stage at which the Prophet just started preaching? Or is it more analogous to the period after the Prophet established the first Islamic state in Medina? Or are we at a point that is similar to the expansion of the Islamic state through an offensive jihad? The Prophet used different strategies during different stages, and fundamentalist groups draw divergent conclusions about contemporary strategies depending on which analogical period they adopt.

Al-Muhajiroun reasons that today corresponds to the period just prior to the establishment of the first Islamic state, the point at which the Prophet shifted from educating his small group of followers in secret to a public campaign and intellectual struggle—the stage of interaction in which the Prophet and his companions directly challenged the unbelievers. Proselytizing thus moved from secretly approaching friends and family to openly calling all people to the faith. This was designed to sway public opinion in favor of Islam and swell Muslim ranks. During this open campaign, "The Messenger of Allah (SAW) waged an unrelenting and fierce ideological war against injustice, harshness and the slavery that dominated Makkah [sic], and he mocked and attacked their ill-fated concepts and practices."[30] His actions met fierce resistance from the Quraysh elite in Mecca; and Muslims were oppressed, tortured, and persecuted.

During this period, the Prophet met with the Ansar from Medina, who pledged their support. These were men of arms, capable of helping form and protect the first Islamic state in Medina. After the pledge, the Prophet ordered the believers to migrate to Medina in what is known as the Hijra (migration).[31]

For al-Muhajiroun, the prophetic model is one in which Muslims follow this particular history, which is essential for salvation. As Omar Bakri puts it:

The [prophetic] methodology is the only way. If I follow it, I remove the sin from my neck. The only way of accepting His command [God] is by following the methodology of the messenger of the Prophet Mohammed. So the Prophet he cultured society; he exposed man-made law in society (commanding good and forbidding evil); and he sought support from those sincere [Muslims in the army] who accept Islam from him and give him power from the army. This is the only way we can remove the sin from our neck.[32]

According to al-Muhajiroun, then, the model calls for three divine duties, and students are taught that an individual must fulfill all three or risk damnation. First, like the Prophet, Muslims must engage in *tarbiya* (culturing society in proper Islamic belief and behavior) and *da'wa* (propagation). For al-Muhajiroun, this necessitates lessons and activities that teach people about their divine duties and responsibilities as Muslims, according to movement precepts. In lessons, an important component of this is promoting support for jihad against infidels in Muslim lands as an individual Muslim obligation: "any aggression against any Muslim property or land by any Kuffar [unbelievers] or non-Muslim forces whether American, British or Jews of Israel makes Jihad (i.e., fighting) against them an obligation upon all Muslims."[33] This mandates armed struggles against the Russians in Chechnya; the United States in Afghanistan, Iraq, and Saudi Arabia; India in Kashmir; Israel (both in the occupied territories and the state of Israel, which al-Muhajiroun considers Muslim territory); and the United Nations (specifically in Iraq).[34] It also includes struggles to reclaim territory formerly controlled by Muslims, such as Spain. All such cases are considered examples of "defensive jihad," a concept akin to Judeo-Christian just war theory and international law regarding the right to self-defense.

Since *tawhid* demands the full application of divine law, al-Muhajiroun argues that all Muslims are obligated to fulfill their responsibility of jihad or risk jeopardizing salvation. Omar Bakri was explicit about this utility calculation at a conference entitled Terrorism and Osama bin Laden held in East London in 2000: "You all have an obligation to support the jihad. Or you will be punished on the Day of Judgment! You will get a reward for fighting. You must send your children to jihad."[35]

To save themselves and fulfill their duties toward jihad, activists practice what they preach by providing not only verbal support, but financial and physical assistance as well. In the past, al-Muhajiroun openly raised money for struggles throughout the Muslim world, especially for Chechen rebels, jihadis in Kashmir, and Hamas in the Palestinian territories. Recent changes in antiterrorism laws, however, made this fund-raising illegal. Interviews with Omar Bakri indicate that financial support for the struggles might still occur through charity front organizations, which raise money for general "charitable" purposes. A number of activists have actually gone to fight in the struggles, not as representatives of al-Muhajiroun as an organization but as individuals fulfilling their personal duty to God "to support their Muslim brothers and sisters."[36]

The second divine duty is the command to promote virtue and prevent vice (al-amr bi'l-ma-ruf wa'l-nahy 'an al-munkar). This is the Prophet's public campaign to challenge disbelief, and activism to fulfill this obligation is required to follow tawhid and remain a Muslim. The movement cites the following hadith: "There is no prophet that Allah sent before me but he had supporters and companions who did what he said and obeyed his commands. After them there are many successors and they will say what they don't do and do what Allah forbids. Whoever fights them with his hand is a believer, whoever fights them with his tongue is a believer, whoever fights them with his heart is a believer and if you do nothing you can't claim you are a Muslim."[37] The punishment for those who fail to rise is hellfire. The true believers and activists will receive eternal reward. Al-Muhajiroun teaches students that engaging in contentious activism is a divine duty and a necessary condition for salvation.

The third divine duty is to work for the reestablishment of the caliphate (Islamic state). Once again, this duty is posited in terms of individual interest in removing sin to ensure personal salvation. Al-Muhajiroun argues that after the collapse of the caliphate in 1924, its reestablishment was a collective duty (fard kifaya), meaning an obligation that can be fulfilled by some on behalf of the umma (Muslim community). However, after a period of time without an Islamic state, "working to establish the Khilafah [caliphate] [becomes] Fard [a divine duty] upon all Muslims i.e. (Fard Kifayah Muhattam) or a sufficient duty binding immediately without a time limit upon all Muslims and those who engage in it remove the sin and the burden on their necks until they accomplish the task. Whereas those who do not engage in working to establish the Khilafah nowadays are sinful [except for those exempted in shari'a]."[38]

For activists, the proper method for establishing the Islamic state is a military coup. The Prophet received nusra (support) from those with arms (the Ansar); today Muslims must similarly seek the support of militaries capable of establishing an Islamic state. As a result, activists contact members of the military in an attempt to foment a military rebellion to seize power and establish the caliphate. Because the religious sources did not specify a particular locale for the Islamic state, Muslims are obligated to work to establish it wherever they are, including the United Kingdom.

Those who attend lessons and activities are taught that they must fulfill these three divine duties to replicate the model of the Prophet and the *salaf,* and must do so through the vehicle of a group and not as individuals. The movement distinguishes between divine duties that can be fulfilled on an individual basis and those that can only be fulfilled by working with other Muslims. Prayer, for example, is an individual duty (though praying as part of a group is better than doing it alone). The central argument is that the Prophet and his companions worked as individuals when they addressed *individuals* but formed collectivities when addressing *society*:

> The Messenger Mohammed (saw) did not work individually to change society. Rather he worked collectively, with the companions, as a group. Shaikh Taqiudine Al-Nabhani [founder of Hizb ut-Tahrir and still a reference point for al-Muhajiroun] reasons that when Allah (swt) revealed the verse **"Therefore, proclaim openly that which has been revealed to you . . ."** He (swt) was referring to the group becoming public since the message was open right from the beginning. Also, after this verse was revealed, the companions marched around the Ka'bah [the sacred house in the middle of the holy mosque in Mecca] in an organised manner. Shaikh Taqiudine concludes that Allah (swt) was asking for the groups to be proclaimed openly.[39]

Time and again, publications and activists refer to Qur'an 3:104 to justify collective action: "Let there rise from among you group(s) calling society to Islam, commanding society to do what Allah orders and to refrain from what He forbids and these (group(s)) [sic] are the ones who are successful" (al-Muhajiroun translation). For the movement, only qualified groups such as itself are allowed to emerge.

The parallels with other Islamic movements are strong. In Egypt, for example, newly emerging Islamic activists are told by members of the Muslim Brotherhood that they have obligations that require working with a movement: "No individual alone can establish the Islamic state and return the caliphate; rather, there must be a collectivity [*gama'a*] to gather together all these individual efforts in order to fulfill this mighty task."[40] The target of the outreach is told to investigate the different groups and choose the best one in the belief that this will lead him or her to join the Muslim Brotherhood in particular.[41] The difference between this argument and al-Muhajiroun's perspective seems to be that the pitch of the former is more in terms of efficacy than divine duties.

Students are taught that merely joining a group, however, is not enough to remove sin. Those who fail to participate in prescribed activities remain sinful and are not part of the saved sect: group membership alone does not produce the desired spiritual payoff. The group is merely a vehicle for fulfilling individual obligations, so individuals still must engage in the prophetic methodology and fulfill duties to remove the sin from their necks.[42] As Omar Bakri explains,

If any one of them or some of them did a duty or engaged in any duty e.g. political struggle in any part of the world, it does not mean that all of them are rewarded for it, nor does it mean that all the members are fulfilling their duties, rather those who did it alone will be rewarded and will remove the sin from their necks whereas the others remain sinful if they did not fulfill their duties.[43]

This is because, as Omar Bakri argues, "Allah (swt) will account as individuals [on Judgment Day], not as an entity."[44]

Where salvation on Judgment Day is a concern, this ideological precept essentially undermines free-riding inside the group. Each individual must engage in activism since he or she will not benefit from the work of others. Only active participants receive the payoff. Anjem nicely summarizes the spiritual incentive for joining the movement: "The only benefit that they [the activists] have, which is a great benefit unto itself, is that they fulfill a duty and ultimately will be rewarded in the hereafter. We don't pretend they are going to get anything apart from that."[45] A refusal to replicate the model in terms of working with a group or fulfilling the specific duties jeopardizes an individual's status in the hereafter. In effect, such a refusal constitutes a rejection of *tawhid* and is deviance.[46]

In making this argument about the necessity of groups as vehicles for fulfilling individual obligations, the movement faces charges from critics that it is culpable of *hizbiyya*, or sectarianism, something condemned in the Qur'an (6:160): "Lo! As for those who sunder their religion and become schismatics [partisans], no concern at all hast thou with them. Their case will go to Allah, who will then tell them what they used to do." Omar Bakri tries to address this by arguing that prior to references about sectarianism in the Qur'an and hadith, the sources of Islam condemn Jews and Christians for calling each other disbelievers and dividing. "Upon studying the areas in which they disagreed, one finds that they disagreed on the fundamentals or the basis of their deen [religion] . . . Since Allah and His Messenger ordered us not to divide as the people of the book did, then we are to avoid that area in which the disagreement occurred. This means that disagreement on the fundamentals of the deen is condemned."[47] Omar readily recognizes the importance of Qur'an 3:103: "And hold fast altogether by the rope of Allah and divide not." However, he argues that this refers to the fundamentals of the religion rather than disagreements about methods and areas of *ijtihad* (independent reasoning). After all, the companions agreed about the creed but frequently disagreed over implementation. "Sects differ in areas of belief or fundamentals, and this is not permitted, but groups disagree in opinions and this is allowed."[48] For Omar, the prohibition does not refer to groups like al-Muhajiroun, which are necessary to fulfill divine obligations.

In addition to the more general principle that a Muslim must actively fulfill the three divine duties of the prophetic model to follow *tawhid* in its entirety and ensure salvation, there are several other ideological components that help overcome resistance to risky activism. First, in terms of individual calculations, it is irrelevant whether the prospects are likely to succeed. Omar Bakri readily admits that establishing an Islamic state in the United Kingdom is highly unlikely. But students are taught that success does not matter, since individuals are judged on whether they *work* to fulfill divine duties such as the establishment of the caliphate. In other words, salvation does not hinge on whether activists are successful in reaching stated movement goals; they are judged according to whether they worked toward these objectives. The duty is the effort and not the outcome of collective action. The Qur'an emphasizes that divine reward and punishment are meted out according to whether individuals "go forth in the cause of Islam" (i.e., exert effort):

> O ye who believe! What is the matter with you, that, when ye are asked to go forth in the cause of Allah, ye cling heavily to the earth? Do ye prefer the life of this world to the Hereafter? But little is the comfort of this life, as compared with the Hereafter. Unless ye go forth, He will punish you with a grievous penalty, and put others in your place; but Him ye would not harm in the least. For Allah hath power over all things. (Qur'an 9:38–39)

When asked whether a demonstration in front of the Indian embassy attracted much attention and support, Anjem could thus dismiss the importance of a large showing and media coverage as largely irrelevant, since he "had fulfilled [his] duty to command good and forbid evil."[49]

Rational choice studies of rebellion and social movements argue that individuals assess the prospects for success when deciding whether to participate.[50] But in the case of radical Islam, these kinds of calculations are less important. The primary objective is not to establish an Islamic state or hold a successful demonstration. These are ways of fulfilling obligations to God, which in turn is the only way to achieve salvation. In terms of personal calculations, the act of participation itself produces the payoff in the hereafter.

Second, the ideological template tells students that suffering is a sign they are following the straight path and thus saving their souls. The very act of suffering

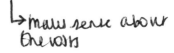

in high-risk activism is a divine signal that the activist is going to achieve his or her preference for salvation. Because the movement's ideology is predicated on an analogy that likens the contemporary period to the one in which the Prophet and his companions initially used *da'wa* and suffered at the hands of the Quraysh, movement activists find reassurance in the risks. One respondent emphasized that regardless of the difficulties the Prophet and his companions spoke out:

> The Prophet [Mohammed] and all the Anbiyya [Prophets], all the Sahabas [Companions], they got tortured, they struggled, they went through pain. For what? Was it because they testified? It was because they implemented in action. The Lord said 'Why do you say something that you do not do, you do not act upon?' When we see the Prophet Mohammed, and the Anbiyya, and the Sahabas, they struggled, they did *da'wa*, they commanded good and forbid evil, they exposed the idolatry of the society, and they introduced the *shahada* [testimony of faith]. But no one is doing that today. This is an obligation that is upon every single Muslim when they see *munkar* (evil). When they see evil and corruption, it becomes an obligation.[51]

This historical precedent creates the basis for contemporary analogical reasoning that interprets hardship as evidence that activists are on the right path. In other words, what rational actor models typically view as risks and costs associated with activism are in fact benefits for those who view them as confirmation of the correctness of belief:

impossible choice → this is

> Al-Muhajiroun says, "Look at the Prophet Mohammed, he went to Taif, and he got stones thrown at him." I think why did he get stones thrown at him and we aren't getting stones thrown at us? So when I see the police and they come to us and speak to us, I say "*alhamdulillah* [praise be to God], we are on the right path." If they didn't come to us and said we are very nice people, we are wrong, because Allah said in the Qur'an: the Jews and Christians will never be happy with you until you follow their way of life.[52]

Students are taught that if the authorities treat them well, it is a sign of deviance. The Prophet was attacked by the authorities of his day. Obviously he was on the straight path as the messenger of God and the authorities were unbelievers. Drawing an analogy to the present, activists believe that police or government accommodation is a sign of incorrect beliefs. This is reflected in al-Muhajiroun's disdain for the Muslim Council of Britain and scholars and movements throughout the Muslim world that cooperate with regimes. The ideology

frames overtures and friendly gestures by the authorities as signs of an insidious plot to destroy the truth of Islam, based on Qur'an 9:8: "Verily if the unbelievers have authority over you, they will not respect you any trust, agreement, or covenant. With their mouths they will have fair words in front of you but their hearts are averse from you and most of them are rebellious, betrayers, and wicked" (al-Muhajiroun translation). As one respondent put it:

> I feel good because I feel that [our way] is the only way, because the only way to be a good Muslim is like this—as long as someone is struggling and finds everything against him, then that person is on the right path. The only way to know that someone is really on the right path is, for example, that all the leaders are against him, all the government people are against him. And they don't compromise. So as long as someone is trying and struggling then hopefully he is on the right path. The Prophet he was like that as well. Everyone was against him. He got kicked out of his homeland, Mecca, and he had to go to Medina. So that is the way we look at it.[53]

Students at lessons are also taught that suffering is part of a general test of certitude and commitment. One activist argued that "it is a test for everyone. And Allah even said that there will be a time when the majority of people will leave Islam or will neglect Islam, and that He will replace people with those who fulfill his command."[54] Others referred to an oft quoted hadith as evidence of the test of will: "Hold all of you fast to the rope of Allah and do not separate yourselves."

As a result, activists revel in their tales of confrontation with the police as proof of their own beliefs and eventual salvation.[55] Suffering is affirmation, and movement participants see themselves as following in the Prophet's shoes, living his experience in modern times. The fact that activists are condemned by the mainstream Muslim community furthers this conviction, since the Prophet and his companions were a minority in a sea of *jahiliyya* (disbelief). This produces a heady sense of purpose and certitude in a mission that is seen as providing activists with necessary strategies for the spiritual payoff.

WHO ARE THE "REAL SALAFIS"?

Al-Muhajiroun is not unique in offering guidance about how to follow the principle of *tawhid* and achieve salvation; most fundamentalist groups in the United Kingdom and elsewhere deal extensively with *tawhid*, emphasize its centrality in belief, and offer strategies. The movement faces competition from a number of similar groups, all vying for the same pool of potential and actual activists. The al-Muhajiroun leadership openly admits that all fundamentalist groups share 95 percent of the same ideological precepts. As a result, the movement operates in a competitive environment in which it must distinguish itself to attract adherents. Given the risks and costs associated with activism, al-Muhajiroun must convince potential joiners that the slight differences among fundamentalist groups are critical in determining whether individuals are actually practicing "real Islam" and will receive a spiritual payoff. Otherwise, most seekers will likely opt for less-risky movements. Much of the movement's culturing through lessons and events is therefore devoted to explaining not only the ideological template outlined above but also the deficiencies of intrafundamentalist community rivals.

One of al-Muhajiroun's most important ideological competitors is the Salafi movement. The term "salafi" is derived from the Arabic *salaf*, which means "to precede." In the Islamic lexicon it refers specifically to *al-salaf al-salih*, the companions of the Prophet Mohammed and virtuous forefathers of the religion. Application of the term *salaf* is generally extended to include not only *al-salaf al-salih*, but also their followers *(al-tabi'un)* and their followers' followers *(tabi 'un al-tabi'in)*. The founders of the four schools of Islamic jurisprudence *(madhhabs)* are all considered part of the *salaf*. Those who call themselves "Salafis" argue that they are following the religious interpretation of the Prophet's companions. "Reformist" Salafis believe in personal and societal transformation through propagation and education, while the "jihadi" Salafis (such as al-Qaeda) emphasize the necessity of violence. In this discussion, I use the term "Salafi" to refer to the reformists, since this is the designation used by al-Muhajiroun. It should be noted, however, that in June 2002 the movement officially announced that it had dropped its earlier Maturidi theological approach, which has rationalist tendencies, in favor of the more literalist Salafi perspective.[56]

Both al-Muhajiroun and the Salafis argue that because the companions learned about Islam directly from the Messenger of God, they commanded a pure, unadulterated understanding of the religion. Subsequent understandings were distorted by innovations, cultural syncretism, and the development of schisms within the Muslim community. From this perspective, only by returning to the purity of Islam as expressed in the Qur'an, Sunna, and *ijma* (consensus) of the Prophet's companions can the Muslim community find the straight path of Islam.

Any action, behavior, or belief that is not sanctioned in the original sources of Islam is considered *bid'a* (innovation in faith) and a distortion of the straight path. For fundamentalists, even acts born from love of God are innovations and evil if they are not supported by religious "evidence" in the Qur'an, Sunna, or *ijma* of the *salaf.* A Muslim who prays more than the five times a day sanctioned in *shari'a* is engaged in *bid'a* and is deviant, even if the intention is to express love for God. The consequences for *bid'a* are severe:

> Those of you who live long after me will see a lot of differences, so hold fast to my Sunnah and to the Sunnah of the Rightly-Guided Khaleefahs [successors] after me. Cling to it tightly and beware of newly-invented matters, for every newly-invented matter is an innovation, and every innovation, and all misguidance is in the Fire.[57]

For al-Muhajiroun, Salafis, and other fundamentalists, there is only one Sunna and correct straight path: "This is My straight path, so follow it. Follow not the other ways, lest ye be parted from His way. This hath He ordained for you that ye may ward off (evil)" (Qur'an 6:154).

In terms of ideological competition, this is a zero-sum game. Either a group is the saved sect and its activists receive a spiritual payoff in the hereafter or it is deviant. In this context, al-Muhajiroun tries to convince students that its ideology expresses pure Islam, in contradistinction to rival ideologies, which although similar are deviant. This leads to extreme boundary activation that divides the world into two camps in Manichean style: the true believers and everyone else.[58]

For this reason, the movement uses many of its lessons and events to attack and undermine the "Salafis" as influential ideological competitors. The Salafis enjoy immense resources and scholarly authority in the Muslim world. The extensive Saudi clerical establishment represents mainstream Salafi thought and commands a great deal of respect among Muslims. The movement is supported by a network of world-renowned *ulama* across space and time, including Abd al-Aziz Bin Baz (d. 1999), Mohammed al-Uthaymin (d. 2001), Salim al-Hilali, Ali Hasan al-Halabi, Mohammed Nasir al-Din al-Albani (d. 1999), and others. Salafis enjoy substantial financial support from wealthy Muslim donors and conservative governments, particularly in the Gulf.

The Salafi *ulama* have widely and explicitly condemned the kind of activism and ideology proposed by al-Muhajiroun, which is seen as fostering *fitna*, or trials and tribulations (strife) within the Muslim community, a serious offense in Islamic law. First, al-Muhajiroun-style demonstrations and protests are viewed as religious innovations without precedent in the Qur'an or Sunna. For the Salafis, the model of the *salaf* did not include public contention. As the Prophet is reported to have explained, "The best jihad is to speak a word of truth to a tyrant."

This is interpreted as advice to leaders about what is and is not religiously sanctioned behavior. Even more specifically, according to mainstream Salafi arguments, Muslims should give this advice in private. As al-Uthaymin argues, "The obligation upon us is to advise as much as we are able. As for competing in protests and staging public demonstrations, then this is in opposition to the guidance of the Salaf."[59] Bin Baz was asked the following question: "Are the demonstrations by men and women done against the rulers to be counted from amongst the means *(wasaa'il)* of *da'wah*?" He provided the following response:

> I do not view the rallies and demonstrations done by women and men to be from the treatment. However, I do see that they are from amongst the causes of *fitan* [trials] and from amongst the causes of evil and from amongst the causes of transgression upon some people and to have enmity towards some people without due right. Rather, *the Sharee'ah* means consist of writing letters, advice and calling to goodness by *Sharee'ah* legislated means that the people of knowledge have explained. And the Companions of the Messenger of Allah *(sallallaahu 'alayhi wa sallam)* and their followers in goodness have all explained these means to be writing letters and speaking with the leader and calling him and advising him and writing to him, without publicizing the affair upon the pulpits that he did such and such and such and such emanated from him. And Allah is the One from whom aid is sought.[60]

Second, the Salafi mainstream ardently rejects the broad use of *takfir* by al-Muhajiroun and similar groups. For the Salafis, *takfir* requires absolute proof about an individual's belief. Consequently, because it is impossible to know with certainty what is in a person's heart, *takfir* is rarely possible. This includes *takfir* against rulers, so long as they establish the *salat* (prayer). If the ruler has a "mustard seed of *iman* [faith]," he is still a Muslim. Groups that use *takfir* and condone violence, like al-Muhajiroun and al-Qaeda, are called "neo-Khawarij" to connote the deviancy of the Khawarij sect that stoked violence among Muslims during the seventh century.

Third, the Salafis dispute the Islamic basis of military coups as the method for establishing an Islamic state. They draw analogies to the early stages of divine revelation when the focus of the Islamic mission was propagation rather than warfare and violence. Today's society is likened to the early community of Muslims who were surrounded by *jahiliyya* (pre-Islamic ignorance). During this initial period, Mohammed spent most of his time in *da'wa* (calling people to Islam), *tarbiya* (education and cultivation to encourage proper Muslim practices), and *tasfiya* (purification). As Mohammed Nasir al-Din al-Albani argues, "History repeats itself. Everybody claims that the Prophet is their role model.

Our Prophet spent the first half of his message making da'wa, and he did not start it with jihad."[61] Instead of waging war, Muslims should use the early model of the Prophet "and train the people to understand the correct Salafi doctrine, which is void of myths and heresies, and to teach them good morals, so that we can emerge with a broad base that embellishes this religion for human beings."[62] Al-Albani warns, "The way to salvation is not, as some people imagine, to rise with arms against the rulers and to conduct military coups. In addition to being among contemporary bidah [innovations], such actions disregard texts of Islam, among which is the command to change ourselves. Furthermore, it is imperative to establish the basis upon which the building will stand."[63]

For Salafis, a prerequisite condition for any kind of political activism is personal and societal transformation according to the model of the *salaf*. Change begins at the individual level. Eventually this transformation will spread to the rest of society. 'Ali Hasan al-Halabi outlines the strategy: "If the Muslims desire good, unity and establishment upon the earth, then they should make their manners and behaviors like that of the *salaf* of this *ummah* and begin by changing themselves. However, he who is unable to change even himself, will not be able to change his family, not to mention change the *ummah*."[64]

Salafis argue that even if one accepts al-Muhajiroun's argument that the leaders are *kafirs* (unbelievers), this still does not legitimate defiance and opposition since it will likely result in a greater evil (like the imprisonment of Islamic scholars). It is not that Salafis disregard the possibility of declaring a leader an apostate and removing him from power, but it can only be attempted (assuming the leader is indeed a *kafir*, which is a point of dispute) if success is inevitable and would result in a better situation for Muslims. As Bin Baz argued, if a group "wishes to replace him with a good righteous leader, without bringing about that which is greater evil and corruption upon the Muslims, and a greater evil than this ruler, then there is no problem."[65]

Fourth, although Salafis do not reject *jihad al-sayf* (struggle of the sword) per se, they argue that other priorities must be fulfilled first. Here again, al-Muhajiroun's view of jihad meets opposition from the powerful Salafis. The central component of the Salafi counterdiscourse on jihad is that unless Muslims follow the straight path of Islam and the Salafi *manhaj* (method for religious interpretation), they will be unable to engage in a successful jihad, since God rewards only the true believers. A lack of effective Salafi propagation means that the Muslim community remains divided and weak, and it strays from Islam. It cannot prepare for jihad properly because it lacks the spiritual preparation. In a debate between al-Albani and a member of the Egyptian Islamic Jihad, al-Albani complained, "We notice the mujahids [those who actively take part in a jihad] call for whatever of the Muslims to join the fight, and when they go to fight they find disagreements among themselves in matters of their faith and the basics of Islam. How do these people get ready for jihad when they are yet to understand what is obligatory on them of aqida [articles of faith]?!"[66] Salafis believe that only when Muslims agree on the true faith, as understood in Salafi doctrine, will unity in jihad endure and Muslims remain united. It is only at this point that triumph becomes an inevitable reward from God to the community of the faithful.

The assault on al-Muhajiroun's call for activism is a direct threat to the movement's capacity to encourage joining and participation. The critique is not issued by fundamentalist outliers; it comes from central and powerful fundamentalist scholars and institutions backed by far-reaching resources and international networks. As a result, it is a challenge that strikes at the heart of al-Muhajiroun recruitment.

In response, the movement directly takes on the Salafi argument at the level of ideology and belief in religious lessons to convince students that al-Muhajiroun truly follows the model of the *salaf.* Its primary strategy is to argue that the self-proclaimed Salafis are deviants because they fail to uphold *tawhid.* For al-Muhajiroun, there are two conditions for *tawhid.* First, an individual must reject *taghout* (anything worshiped other than God). This includes a rejection of human-made legal systems. It also includes use of *takfir* against "non-Islamic" leaders such as al-Saud. Second, after rejecting *taghout,* a Muslim must believe that God alone is worthy of worship. Al-Muhajiroun claims that the first condition is a necessary prerequisite before continuing to the second: "To declare that Allah is the creator or the provider is not enough to become Muslim. You must give up before taking up i.e. give up all kufr, shirk, culture and jaahiliyyah and then take Islam, Eemaan [faith] and Tawheed."[67] This is considered "the Islamic standard" practiced by the Prophet and the *salaf.* Any who fail to openly reject *taghout* violate the principle of *tawhid al-hakamiyya* and are not really Muslim.

This linkage between belief and action is the critical linchpin of al-Muhajiroun's charges against the Salafis, a critique that strikes at the very core of Salafi ideology by questioning adherence to *tawhid.* According to al-Muhajiroun, although the Salafis accept *tawhid rububiyya* [unity of the Lord and His names and attributes], they are delaying fulfillment of *tawhid al-ilah* [unity of worship] by refusing to openly reject un-Islamic leaders and regimes. They are characterized as the "fake Salafiyya" or "as-Salafiyyat ut-Talafiyyah" [those who separate belief from action and thus violate *tawhid*]: "The fake salafis study the Qur'aan, ahadeeth [sing. hadith] and fitrah [natural disposition]. They follow the usool [foundations] of Ahl us-Sunnah wal-Jama'ah [The

People of the Sunna and the Group], claiming to be the protectors of the deen and Ahl ul-Haq [people of Truth], but in conditions they will not enter any struggle against kufr, shirk or taaghout [un-Islamic and evil rule]."[68]

Al-Muhajiroun agrees with the Salafis that rebellion is prohibited if the leader implements Islam. If he is oppressive but establishes the prayer, Muslims cannot rise with the sword. But oppression differs from the implementation of non-Islamic law. The "so-called Muslim leaders," according to the movement, are not simply oppressive; they implement non-Islamic law and are therefore apostates unworthy of obedience. In addition, the secret advice offered to rulers by the Salafis is a practice and obligation reserved for a caliph, which al-Saud certainly is not, so there is no need to give advice.

Even if one accepts the Salafi perspective, the movement argues, open condemnation is still necessary under several conditions: (1) the leader does not respond to secret advice; (2) the evil affects the beliefs of Muslims; (3) the leader knows that he is implementing and enforcing non-Islamic law and does not want to change it; and (4) if Muslims do not openly denounce the leaders and non-Islamic law, the people will think it is *halal* [religiously permitted]. From this perspective, given that leaders flagrantly implement *kufr* law, ignore advice from the *ulama,* and press the people to accept non-Islamic practices, open defiance through demonstrations and protests is not just permissible; it is religiously required.

In its attacks against the Salafis, al-Muhajiroun draws a sharp distinction between following "Salafi" scholars, who can make mistakes, and following the Qur'an, Sunna, and *ijma* of the *salaf.* The true Salafis are those who follow

an idea based on some general and intellectual principles derived from well-preserved sources—the Qur'an, Sunnah, and Consensus (ijma). These principles govern the method of acquiring the Deen and understanding the Qur'an and Sunnah according to the principles agreed upon by the righteous predecessors in Islam (As-Salaf as-Saalih) i.e. those early generations of Muslims who were close to the Prophet of Islam, and who were praised in the Qur'an by Allah (swt) . . . whoever abides by these principles is a Salafi and . . . those people who [can] rightly claim to belong to Ahl Al Sunnah Wal Jama'ah (the people who most correctly follow the teachings of the Prophet of Islam).[69]

In contrast, the movement argues, the self-proclaimed Salafis care more about their scholars than the real model of the *salaf;* if they abandoned their emotional attachment to their teachers and *ulama,* they would free their minds to find the true straight path, an approach that demands both belief and action. Omar Bakri emphasizes that al-Muhajiroun does not follow a particular scholar and warns against identifying correct religious interpretation with only one or a small handful of individuals. He derides the tendency among Salafis to ask other Muslims which sheikhs they follow, arguing that the response should always be "the *salaf.*" Essentially al-Muhajiroun charges Salafis with *taqlid*—blindly following a scholar rather than the sources of Islam. The contentiousness of this charge cannot be understated, since by claiming to refer directly back to the model of the *salaf*, the Salafis consciously frame their religious method as one that explicitly rejects *taqlid.*

The charge is ironic, given al-Muhajiroun's emphasis on Omar Bakri's own credibility as a scholar, but the movement tries to emphasize its focus on ideas and not individuals. Even while expressing respect and admiration for Omar, activists are careful to distinguish between following the man and following his Islamic interpretation as representing the straight path. One activist put it this way: "Omar Bakri is like any other Muslim brothers, but I respect him as well for his effort, and for his honesty. He is a lot of things. You can't really describe him. [But] our model is the Prophet, and is not Omar Bakri, but just to show you how much we care about the guy as a Muslim and as a believer. It is too little to say about him."[70] Activists claim that al-Muhajiroun is just a vehicle to fulfill individual divine duties and that if they found a better scholar or if Omar deviated, they would not hesitate to leave the movement. This is supposed to distinguish them from the Salafis, who are frequently portrayed as victims of an emotional bond to their teachers, incapable of questioning deviant practices, even when they are "known by necessity."

In this manner, the movement tries to appropriate usage of the term "Salafi" for itself by claiming that it alone truly follows the model of the *salaf* through belief and action. In lessons and events, al-Muhajiroun does not usually provide an unbiased and neutral representation of reformist Salafi ideology. Instead, it begins by emphasizing what it sees as deficiencies in the logic of the reformist Salafi argument about duties in Islam, particularly regarding *tawhid.* The movement usually follows this with an explanation of how its own interpretation corrects these deficiencies. It is not that reformist ideology is rejected in its entirety. The basic premise of the model of the *salaf* and emphasis on *tawhid* are shared. But reformist Salafi ideology is framed as incomplete, and the movement offers additional requirements for the devout who wish to truly follow the example of the *salaf* and achieve salvation on Judgment Day.

INTELLECTUAL AFFILIATION

The objective of the culturing sessions is to socialize students to accept the ideological template of the movement. This includes not only salvation as self-

[handwritten margin notes: "Only way" "It" "make it to thar" "one way" "no one's choice"]

interest and the three divine duties of activism as an exclusive path to Paradise, but also al-Muhajiroun as one of the only groups that truly allows individuals to comprehensively follow *tawhid* and the prophetic model. Those who adopt the ideology in its entirety are considered "intellectually affiliated" with the movement. Anjem describes the affiliation as follows:

> Someone is intellectually affiliated, in other words we find that the culture has merged with him in his actions: he propagates the ideas; he attends the stalls; he wants to come to the circles; and basically he carries *da'wa*. He propagates the ideas, and from what he says he seems to understand them as well. He must understand that what he is doing ultimately is fulfilling a duty [through] an organization. He has to understand that to do that collectively is an obligation as mentioned in the Qur'an (3:104): "Let there rise from among you groups calling society to Islam, commanding society to do what Allah orders and to refrain from what He forbids and these groups are the ones who are successful." So he has to understand that these are the fundamental duties of the group and he has to understand what is *maroof* [good] and what is *munkar* [evil] and what is the good and evil that must be propagated, and that the highest good is for Islam to be dominant, to be law and order, and the highest evil is for man-made law to be dominant.[71]

Omar Bakri describes intellectual affiliation in similar terms: "When the thought occupies you, becomes the thought that was behind your action. The thought is manifest in your action, your behavior, your discussion, your debate. Everything you discuss has a link with the objective of the ideology."[72]

The goal of the movement is to promote a network of shared meaning predicated on its understanding of *tawhid* and divine duties, and the basis of this network is intellectual affiliation—individuals adopt and express al-Muhajiroun's ideology. Consequently, formal membership numbers and followings are less relevant than the internalization of the movement ideology by individuals who may or may not be formally or administratively tied to al-Muhajiroun. Affiliated individuals can then reproduce and expand the network of shared meaning as what Omar Bakri calls "life cells." When asked about intrafundamentalist competition for members, Anjem responded,

> Funnily enough, we are not that concerned about the organization and its own continuity as opposed to the propagation of the ideas that we hold. And that is the unique thing about our organization, I suppose. Because you do not need to be a big organization in order to be successful in changing the thoughts and concepts and ideas of the masses. And I suppose this is the dangerous thing about our organization as compared to other organizations. People are more concerned about

their numbers and more concerned about their own continuity, whereas we are concerned about the masses and changing public opinion and public awareness. And I firmly believe that if any cultured one of us goes to any country, we will continue the ideas, we will be a life cell, we will build a body, and we will continue to struggle there. So the numbers are irrelevant and insignificant. The important thing is that you are having an impact on society, and one man can do it.[73]

In terms of activities and whether individuals can participate, there is little distinction between formal members and others with a looser affiliation. In at least a few instances, individuals without formal membership have actually held official positions. In the U.S. branch of the movement in the 1990s, for example, the al-Muhajiroun spokesperson, Kamran Bokhari, was not a formal member. He did not attend the formation meeting that established the branch in 1996, and he lived in Springfield, Missouri, far away from the New York City branch headquarters and the movement leadership. Those who are not intellectually affiliated can still participate in the various activities (apart from formal member-only lessons) to "remove the sin" from their necks, even if they do not fully comprehend all of the ideological intricacies. In addition, individuals may leave al-Muhajiroun as formal members but remain intellectually affiliated. For example, the individuals who split off to form Hizb ut-Tawhid left al-Muhajiroun but continued to take lessons from Omar Bakri.

Although just about anyone is allowed to participate in most activities, only individuals considered intellectually affiliated are eligible to become formal members. The movement uses a screening process to determine whether an individual has fully adopted the ideology and is free of "foreign ideas." This ensures that only the most advanced and committed students become formal members, thereby reducing the prospects of defection. As Omar explains, a member of the movement "is an identical copy of the way I think, and he has my adopted culture, and he teaches it to the people."[74] These activists are qualified to develop and culture others: they are authorized to give *halaqahs* and speak to the public on behalf of the movement. As life cells, formal members are often sent to other countries to establish branches, indicating Omar Bakri's confidence in their ideological internalization. The movement refers to them as *hizbis* (party members). There are 160 *hizbis* in the United Kingdom.

Local leaders and official members are responsible for identifying potential members. Because they work with their local groups on an ongoing basis, they are better situated than Omar to evaluate whether a particular student has fully adopted the ideology and is intellectually affiliated. Typically local leaders recommend someone to the national leader of the movement, who then decides whether the individual is intellectually affiliated. But because Omar resides in the United Kingdom, he makes the ultimate decision, even if he relies extensively on Anjem's evaluation. If Omar does not know enough about the candidate Anjem recommends, he will ask to meet with the prospect. Anjem has the authority to make someone a member without consulting Omar, but this does not happen.

The movement uses the selectiveness of the process as an "incentive" to encourage students to study the ideology in-depth. "Students understand the distinction between a student and the A-team," says Omar. "And that is why they look forward to graduating."[75] The entire process holds out the prospect of special private lessons with Omar at every level of participation: contacts look forward to the closed *halaqahs,* and students look forward to the private *halaqahs* with the "A-team" and "junior *ulama.*"

The numbers reflect the selectiveness of the process. There are thousands of "contacts." Newspapers erroneously report an estimated 7,000 "members." This number probably accurately reflects the number of contacts, but alone it tells very little because it is impossible to determine the level of commitment within this aggregate. Some contacts may come to a single public event. Others may indulge in deeper religious sampling and progress toward becoming actual students.

There are 700 students taking regular lessons with al-Muhajiroun, many of whom refer to themselves as members of the movement, even if the leadership does not recognize them as formal members. Although he had only been studying with the movement for two months, for example, one activist in Slough referred to himself as a *member* of al-Muhajiroun. The leadership seems to encourage this ambiguity to make students feel part of the ideological project. As Omar explains, "We don't tell them that they are not members, but we know. We have some of them; we call them students."[76]

The purposeful obfuscation of what it means to be a member is not unique to al-Muhajiroun. Hizb ut-Tahrir (HT), for example, follows a similar approach. A former HT student explains,

What is a membership? Even the definition of membership in HT is up for grabs. We were told, by our *mushrif,* the director of the *halaqah,* "Look, HT doesn't really discriminate between those who take the oath and those who don't. It is just an administrative difference." You have the [formal] commitment on hand whereas the other person doesn't have the [formal] commitment [but it] doesn't mean he is not a good Muslim. It doesn't mean that he is not committed. It just means he hasn't gone through the formal process. And it is just for administrative purposes. And he [the *mushrif*] says, "For the outside world all of you are members. So if someone asks, you tell them you are a member."[77]

While making the same kind of argument, al-Muhajiroun actually prohibits discussions about the "administration" of the movement, including membership numbers. This is intended to focus participants on the ideas and ideology rather than the movement as an organization. The movement bylaws require that local leaders track the number of contacts, students, and formal members, but this information is not supposed to be shared with outsiders or followers who are not official members.

While downplaying the distinction and encouraging participation, activists use the difference between members and students to create plausible deniability when activists engage in behaviors that violate the ideology. The behavior of such an individual is, in fact, used as evidence that he or she has not been fully cultured and is therefore not intellectually affiliated. Omar explains,

> Not every "member" of al-Muhajiroun is affiliated intellectually. You need to be careful. Someone may say something that does not represent our views. He has himself other previous ideas and previous groups, or he takes from here or there. Or he affiliates only administratively because anybody who believes in the objective, accepts the leadership, he will join. But it doesn't mean he becomes a member. He commits himself. With time he will affiliate intellectually, he must study certain concepts, he must pass certain stages.[78]

This line of argument was used to deny movement connections to Hanif and Sharif, the two suicide bombers, as well as others.

Once an individual becomes a formal member, the culturing process becomes deeper and more complex. Members participate in movement-only lessons that deal with more specific technical elements of the ideology. These more technical elements further solidify an individual's internalization of the values and deepen his or her understanding and commitment to the ideology, so that he or she can effectively debate and persuade other Muslims.

This training takes place under Omar's careful supervision and is bound by certain rules. Member lessons are typically run by the local branch leader of the movement, who is responsible for leading and managing the lessons. Omar provides a list of books for study, and the circles are required to study the books in the order provided, unless there is approval for changes. Additional books can be utilized in the sessions for extra culturing if the local leader considers them appropriate and Omar gives permission, but they cannot be used to replace the adopted books and must serve as supplements to required curricular material.

The local leader can only use a book he has already studied in *halaqah* and is provided a special teaching guide to assist in leading the study circles (the local leader is not permitted to give this book to outsiders or any other members). This is to ensure that there are no deviations from the ideology as understood by Omar. All members are required to attend their weekly lessons, unless Omar excuses them.

These specialized lessons delve into the details of the ideology and train members to reproduce the movement ideology; they also provide some training in rhetoric and debate. In one lesson, for example, Omar outlined how members should respond to particular points and counterpoints during exchanges with activists from other Islamic groups. During fieldwork, I found many of the leading members repeating some of Omar Bakri's particular rhetorical devices and phrasing. Members giving lessons even use some of Omar Bakri's intonations, cadences, and jokes.

Since members by this time have generally internalized the norms of the movement and are therefore self-motivated, there is far less focus on motivation and more on the seriousness of learning. The movement's rules state that "each member must understand that the Halaqah is a serious discussion and not a chat."[79] I was given special permission by Omar to attend one of these private member-only lessons, and the tone confirmed this norm. There were fewer students than at the open lessons, as one would expect, and this particular session was for advanced members. There was none of the characteristic humor and flair of presentation that makes Omar so persuasive at the open lessons. Instead, this was all business. Distractions from the serious content of the material drew rare agitation from Omar, who politely chided students with: "Brothers! Brothers! If you have something to say, then say it!" Consternation especially grew if he felt he was forced to repeat himself because students were not listening or had come unprepared (they were assumed to have mastered the previous material). He never lost his temper or exploded in rage, but this was supposed to be a serious time of learning at the most advanced level. After all, these members were expected to represent the ideology to other students and the public.

The duties and responsibilities for these activists do not change once they become "formal members," since these are "set out in the Qur'an and Sunna."[80] To remove the sin from their necks and fulfill responsibilities to God, members are required to propagate, publicly enjoin good and forbid evil at the *da'wa* stalls, participate in demonstrations, and attend lessons and talks. From the movement's perspective, the only real change, in addition to the specialized training, is that members become important vehicles for expanding the network of shared meaning through outreach. They become, in the words of John Lofland, "deployable agents."[81] Anjem explains:

> The more they understand and the more they interact, the more articulate they will become and the better they will be as public speakers, in debating, in preparing talks, in conferences and lectures. They will develop, and the added responsibility will come because they will be relied upon I suppose to propagate the ideas on behalf of the organization. So that is the only added responsibility really.[82]

These are the hard-core activists of al-Muhajiroun. Most of them have been with Omar for some time, though very few date their relationship to the movement founding in 1996. They also tend to be older. The leaders, for example, are often married with children, generally in their late twenties or early thirties. Contacts and students, in contrast, are usually young university students. The fact that the *hizbis* are older and intellectually affiliated reduces the likelihood of defection at this level. Even with reduced biographical availability because of family- and work-related responsibilities, they have seemingly reconciled themselves to participation in risky activism through al-Muhajiroun. At least according to Omar Bakri and several others in the movement, few formal members have defected. Even when this happens, many retain their intellectual affiliation (and continue to take religious lessons with Omar). This is most likely a result of the selective screening process: only the truly committed are permitted to become formal members.

But defections, although limited, have occurred. Because the movement would not identify defectors and defectors did not identify themselves, data is sparse. There is, however, some limited data that is suggestive. One of the most important examples of this kind of defection came in 1998 after Omar Bakri argued that the al-Qaeda–sponsored U.S. embassy bombings in Africa were supported by Islamic law. He reasoned that the embassies spy on Muslims and therefore constitute instruments of war and legitimate targets. For many activists in the movement, the pronouncement came as a shock. As Kamran Bokhari explains:

> The really big jump and wake-up call for me happened in '98 . . . come '98 and the embassy bombings, it was really an eye opener for me and I said, "What the heck!" I was informed, I got the news just like anyone else. First of all I didn't even know what they [the al-Muhajiroun leadership] said. The media is saying they supported it, they [al-Muhajiroun] are saying that this is what is going to happen if you continue your policies in the Muslim world.

How can you do that? Every day we hammer the jihadis for what they are doing, and here we turn around and say that this is right. And immediately I saw that OBM [Omar Bakri Mohammed] was trying to take political mileage out of it. The group wanted political mileage out of it. They saw it as an incident they could use to catapult their position. And OBM would constantly keep saying these things like "We can't wait like the *Ikhwan* [Muslim Brotherhood] for forty or fifty years." Okay, we are a fresh group and we are not going to go through the stages that HT [Hizb ut-Tahrir] went, and we have to achieve what others achieved in a long period of time.

And I just got really shocked and I said what is going on. And I called him and asked him, and I said at least tell us what is going on. You are surprising your own members. And he said you are right and we shouldn't do that. And I said this is really sticky, and I don't agree with it. And it is a fast one being pulled on me. And I just got a really sour taste in my mouth.

For the longest time we said we are unique, we don't do this, we do not fight, we do not pick up weapons, we are for peaceful political change, we are through intellectual change. And all of a sudden this is being thrown upon us. It was sort of downhill from there. I just sort of fell to the wayside. I stopped listening and stopped calling, and soon they realized I was no longer with the party.[83]

In his recount, the 1998 episode led a number of members to leave the movement. This included the worldwide spokesperson and several other "big names," key individuals who had represented the movement in public as speakers and leaders.

Some members left the movement after September 11. Media reports, new terrorism laws, and so on raised the risks for participating in al-Muhajiroun. Immense pressures from families in the aftermath of the attacks led several activists to leave the movement. Others left after being arrested and fined. According to Omar Bakri, none of those who left the movement after the attack had been with him since the founding of the movement in 1996. In his estimation, the majority had only been members a few weeks or months prior to the attacks, implying that their ideological training may have been limited or incomplete. But several others had been with the movement two or three years and still left.

Three activists left the movement and joined Abu Hamza's Supporters of Shariah. The catalyst was a disagreement over *takfir*. In his lessons, Omar emphasizes that evidence of apostasy is needed (though this can be based on actions as well as beliefs). The three individuals in question, however, had used *takfir* without sufficient evidence, and Omar demanded that they apologize since it was an attack on personal honor and lacked religious evidence. They refused, and Omar issued a fatwa that Muslims could speak to the men (presumably to "correct" their beliefs) but could not listen to them. The three turned to Abu Hamza, who welcomed them to his movement and told them that Omar should never have issued the fatwa. Abu Hamza made one of the men the movement spokesperson on his first day in Supporters of Shariah.[84] Subsequently, Supporters of Shariah began holding the same kinds of demonstrations as al-Muhajiroun, indicating that there may have been some influence from the new members.

Other activists became gradually disillusioned with Omar and the overall project of the movement over time. Both Kamran Bokhari and the former leader of the women's section in the U.K. were disappointed, in particular, by the lack of specificity about how an Islamic state would actually function. Although the movement outlines the *structure* of governance in a newly established Islamic state (i.e., the various administrative offices and departments), it provides few details about how the system would actually *govern*.[85] The former head of the women's section describes an incident that deeply impacted her views about al-Muhajiroun:

> His [Omar's] biggest mistake was approving a national project that we [the women's section] had presented and putting me in charge. Conference on Citizen of the Khilafah. Nazli and I went and booked, of all places, the Royal Albert Hall. I can't help but laugh when I think about it. We must have been mad! The idea behind this was to bring the call to a new phase, from the need for Khilafah to a vision of the specifics. When I arranged for OBM to do intensive sessions with the members on the details of the Islamic state, I was shocked to see him regurgitate the basic framework that we had known from [the] HT [Hizb ut-Tahrir] days. It then struck a lot of us that there were no specific details. That came as a massive blow and a turning point . . . the conference got cancelled because of OBM's obsession with the name al-Muhajiroun being plastered all over the media. The whole experience left me with a bitter taste in my mouth.[86]

After six years as the head of the women's division, she dropped out of the movement with two other women. In addition to this disillusionment, there may have been some difficulties with male chauvinism in the movement.[87]

All of these examples lead to three general observations. First, cognitive openings are recurrent and can catalyze reconsiderations that might lead to defection. Introspection is most likely when the previously accepted ideology cannot resolve new issues or where exogenous conditions reveal inconsistency or limitations to the ideological template, thus prompting a participant to think about whether the ideology as a whole is "the truth." These kinds of cognitive openings may lead individuals to continue religious seeking and draw them to experiment with or explore new ideologies. In other cases, frustration or disillusionment may prompt the individual to simply abandon the ideology and religious seeking altogether. Some such individuals remain religious but no longer engage in activism or participate in a movement. Others are turned off by religious conservatism and instead lead more secular lives. These kinds of processes can lead individuals to defect from a movement like al-Muhajiroun. If they no longer believe in the movement precepts or are not certain about its "truth," continued high-risk activism becomes less likely. In most instances, fully cultured activists will use the movement ideology to resolve the issues that emerge as a result of the opening, but where the ideology provides an insufficient remedy, defection becomes more likely.

Second, movement consistency matters. Where a leader or a movement seems inconsistent or hypocritical, defections become more likely. Leaders may be seen as betraying the very cause they claim to represent. This could lead to disenchantment with the mission and ideological precepts of the movement. In addition, a sense that the movement is not really working toward its stated purpose (such as a real vision of how an Islamic state would actually function) could lead some to question the consistency between rhetoric and action.

And third, risks and costs can change over time, thereby influencing individual calculations about participation. Just as importantly, in the face of increased risks, activists may reevaluate their self-interest and priorities and decide that there are more important things to consider, such as family.

What is more striking than the defections, however, is the fact that they are so few. Although many members have families and children to consider and face increased risks from antiterrorism legislation, very few seem to have left the movement. Many question whether Islam supports attacks like September 11 yet remain committed to a movement that supports an assortment of violent causes. And though there have been issues of inconsistency, the vast majority of members have remained part of al-Muhajiroun.

If one takes the ideological beliefs of the committed activists seriously, a plausible explanation is that the movement culturing was effective. From this perspective, so few members leave, despite several factors that should undermine persistent commitment, because they see risky activism as a necessary strategy for fulfilling self-interest in salvation. They feel confident that they are following *tawhid* and engaging in the divine method in a manner that ensures a spiritual payoff, especially when compared to fundamentalist competitors.

CONCLUSION

Max Weber draws a distinction between instrumental and value rationality. The former is described as the pursuit of self-interest, such as material preferences.

Value rationality, in contrast, is the pursuit of a value. For Weber, "Examples of pure value-rational orientation would be the actions of persons who, regardless of possible cost to themselves, act to put into practice their convictions of what seems to them to be required by duty, honor, the pursuit of beauty, a religious call ... In our terminology, value-rational action always involves 'commands' or 'demands' which, in the actor's opinion, are binding on him."[88] In value rationality, individuals are willing to accept risks and costs to remain faithful to the value, as opposed to means/end instrumental rationality.

It is tempting to describe the rationality of radical Islamic activists, such as those in al-Muhajiroun, in terms of value rationality. The argument in this chapter, however, indicates that high-risk Islamic activism is at once the pursuit of a value and self-interest. As part of the self-proclaimed ideological vanguard in the struggle between Islam and other ideologies, especially capitalism, al-Muhajiroun uses religious lessons to culture students in "true" Islam. The cornerstone of the culturing process is the initial premise that one must fulfill God's command and follow *tawhid* or risk individual salvation. For the movement, God's commands include risky activism. Socialized to deeply believe this premise, individuals who internalize the norms are likely to accept high-risk activism. Serving God is the only way to this salvation, and the ideology maps out how this service should be done to ensure Paradise. Participation in the movement remains rooted in the self-interest of the activist who participates to protect his or her spiritual destiny. In fact, for individuals who become "intellectually affiliated" (i.e., have accepted the movement ideology), deviations from the ideological template will jeopardize their prospect of salvation and thus self-interest. In short, *inaction violates self-interest.* Action is indeed influenced by belief in a set of religious values and all the accompanying divine commands, but individuals are still driven by spiritual self-interest.

This challenges perspectives that dismiss the possible usefulness of a rational actor approach to Islamic activism. Roxanne Euben, for example, argues that "even the most austere version of rational actor theory has very little to say about fundamentalism because, given its basic assumptions, it concludes only that fundamentalists have a revealed preference for fundamentalism."[89] As this chapter indicates, this kind of argument confuses religious methods with goals or interests. Fundamentalism is not a preference; it is a strategy or method for obtaining the preference of salvation as an end. It is a way of approaching religious interpretation that emphasizes literalism and strict adherence to *tawhid*. Activists follow this interpretive approach because they view it as an exclusive strategy for the pursuit of Paradise. If we recognize that value and instrumental rationalities are frequently related, radical Islamic activism becomes intelligible within a rational actor framework.

NOTES

1. Omar Bakri Mohammed, *The Role of the Mosque* (London: ALM Publications, n.d.), 5 n. 5.

2. Al-Muhajiroun, *The Intellectual Leadership* (London: Al-Muhajiroun Publishing, n.d.).

3. Al-Muhajiroun, *Intellectual Leadership*, 8–9.

4. *Mankind's Greatest Question* (MNA Publications, n.d.), 11.

5. *Dheeq Ul-Ofouq: Narrow-mindedness* (n.p., n.d.), 1.

6. Anjem Choudary, *Human Rights: Comparison between the Declaration of Human Rights and Divine Rights in Islam* (London: Al-Muhajiroun Publications, n.d.), 16.

7. Omar Bakri Mohammed, *The Islamic Education System* (London: Al-Muhajiroun Publications, n.d.), 25.

8. Al-Muhajiroun, *The Post-Secular Attack*. Leaflet, n.d.

9. Al-Muhajiroun, *Knowledge*. Leaflet, n.d.

10. Mohammed, interview by author, June 2002.

11. Al-Muhajiroun, *Administration*, n.d.

12. Omar Bakri Mohammed, *Kitab ul-Imaan*. Movement training manual, n.d., 20.

13. As cited in Muhammad al-Jibali, *Allah's Rights upon His Servants* (Cincinnati, Ohio: Al-Qur'an Was-Sunnah Society of North America, 1995), 24.

14. Omar Bakri Mohammed, *Kitab*, 13.

15. Omar Bakri Mohammed, *Kitab*, 17.

16. Omar Bakri Mohammed, *Al-Fareed Fee Mukhtasar Al-Tawheed: A Summary of the Unique Tawheed* (London: Al-Muhajiroun Publications, n.d.). This version was published as a web book without pagination.

17. Omar Bakri Mohammed, *Al-Fareed*.

18. Omar Bakri Mohammed, *Al-Fareed*.

19. Al-Muhajiroun, *How to Become a Mushrik! Can a Person Become a Kaafir Unknowingly?* Leaflet, n.d.

20. Omar Bakri Mohammed, *Al-Fareed*.

21. Even use of the term "democracy" is considered forbidden. See Abu Abdullah [Omar Bakri Mohammed], *It Is Prohibited (Al-Mahzoor) to Use the Word Democracy* (1424 AH, sometime between 2003 and 2004). For more, see Omar Bakri Mohammed, *The Islamic Verdict on Sharing Power with Kufr Regimes* (London: Al-Muhajiroun Publications, n.d.).

22. Shari'ah Court of the U.K., "Islamic Verdict (Fatwa) against Voting for Man-Made Law," Fatwa no. L/221, May 15, 2001.

23. Al-Muhajiroun, *How to Become a Mushrik!*

24. Al-Muhajiroun, "6 Reasons Why All the Rulers Are Kafir," *Shari'ah Magazine* 1, no. 13 (n.d.): 1.

25. Reported by al-Bukhari.

26. Al-Muhajiroun, "6 Reasons," 1.

27. As quoted in Jam'iat Ihyaa' Minhaaj Al-Sunnah, *A Brief Introduction to the Salafi Da'wah* (Ipswich, U.K.: Jam'iat Minhaaj Al-Sunnah, 1993), 5.

28. Jam'iat Ihyaa' Minhaaj Al-Sunnah, *Brief Introduction*, 3.

29. Al-Muhajiroun, *Sectarian Divisions*. Leaflet, n.d.

30. From a book distributed by al-Muhajiroun entitled *Makkah to Medina*, 13. No author is identified, and it is unclear whether the book was written by someone in the movement.

31. This narrative comes from *Makkah to Medina*.

32. Omar Bakri Mohammed, interview by author, London, December 2002.

33. Shari'ah Court of the U.K., "Fatwa against the Illegitimate State of Israel," Case no. Israel/M/F50, October 2, 2000.

34. See, for example, Shari'ah Court of the UK, Case no. Russia/F41, "Fatwa Concerning the Russian Aggression," n.d.; Shari'ah Court of the UK, "Fatwa on Jihad against the Illegitimate State of Israel"; Shari'ah Court of the UK, "Fatwa against Those Who Ally with the Disbelievers against Muslims," September 11, 2003; al-Muhajiroun press release, "The United Nations: A Legitimate Target?" August 25, 2003.

35. Aaron Klein, "My Weekend with the Enemy," *Jerusalem Post*, May 30, 2000.

36. Al-Muhajiroun, press release, November 5, 2001.

37. Omar Bakri Mohammed, *Jihad: The Method for the Khilafah?* (London: MNA Publications, n.d.), 19.

38. Omar Bakri Mohammed, Questions and Answers, "Are we obligated to work for the Khilafah?" n.d.

39. Omar Bakri Mohammed, *Groups and Parties in Islam: The Islamic Verdict* (London: Al-Muhajiroun Publications, n.d.), 16.

40. Carrie Rosefsky Wickham, *Mobilizing Islam: Religion, Activism, and Political Change in Egypt* (New York: Columbia University Press, 2002): 145.

41. Wickham, *Mobilizing Islam*, 145–46.

42. That group participation is about individual duties to God is made clear by how al-Muhajiroun conceptualizes a group: "in Islam a group is not an entity rather it is individuals following the opinions of their Ameer" (OBM, Questions and Answers, "Is the Group an Entity?" n.d.). What connects individuals to one another in a "group" is an ideology and a religious belief. In the case of al-Muhajiroun, the criterion for determining whether an individual belongs to the group is whether he or she adopts the ideological precepts about a comprehensive *tawhid* that combines belief and action through specified divine duties.

43. Omar Bakri Mohammed, "Is the Group an Entity?"

44. Omar Bakri Mohammed, "Is the Group an Entity?"

45. Anjem Choudary, telephone interview by author, June 2002.

46. Under many understandings of Islamic law, the ultimate sanction for an individual convicted of apostasy is death, though this is rarely enforced.

47. Omar Bakri Mohammed, *Groups and Parties*, 20.

48. Omar Bakri Mohammed, *Groups and Parties*, 22.

49. Anjem Choudary, telephone interview by author, June 2002.

50. Susanne Lohmann, "A Signaling Model of Informative and Manipulative Political Action," *American Political Science Review* 88 (1993): 319–33; Lohmann, "Dynamics of Informational Cascades: The Monday Demonstrations in Leipzig, East Germany, 1989–1991," *World Politics* 47 (1994): 42–101; Karl-Dieter Opp, *The Rationality of Political Protest: A Comparative Analysis of Rational Choice Theory* (Boulder: Westview, 1989); Karl-Dieter Opp, Peter Voss, and Christiane Gern, *Origins of a Spontaneous Revolution: East Germany, 1989* (Ann Arbor: University of Michigan Press, 1993); Bert Klandermans, "Mobilization and Participation: Social-Psychological Expansions of Resource Mobilization Theory," *American Sociological Review* 49 (1984): 583–600.

51. Somali member, interview by author, London, June 2002.

52. Somali member, interview by author, London, June 2002.

53. Sixteen-year-old member, interview by author, London, June 2002.

54. Islam (local leader), interview by author, London, June 2002.

55. I observed this in several instances, including a large gathering of members prior to a lesson where they swapped stories about confrontations with police.

56. Omar's leaning toward the Salafis dates back to at least 1997, according to my interview with Kamran Bokhari, April 2003. For more on the Maturidi sect, see W. Madelung, "Maturidiyya," *Encyclopedia of Islam*, CD-ROM ed. (London: Brill, 2002).

57. Hadith cited in Muhammad Ibn Jameel Zaynoo, "Methodology of the Saved Sect," *Al-Ibaanah*, April 1996, 32–33.

58. For the importance of boundary activation, particularly in collective violence, see Charles Tilly, *The Politics of Collective Violence* (Cambridge: Cambridge University Press, 2003).

59. http://www.troid.org/articles/ibaadah/jihaad/algerianaffairibnbaaz.htm

60. http://www.troid.org/articles/ibaadah/jihaad/algerianaffairibnbaaz.htm

61. *Munatharah ma' Tantheem alJjihad al-Islami*, audiocassettes, n.d., transcript posted at www. allahuakbar.net/scholars/albanni/debate_on_jihad.htm.

62. Usamah Siddiq Ali Ayyub, an Egyptian Salafi who gained political asylum in Germany in 1999, as quoted in *al-Sharq al-Awsat*, October 12, 1999, 3, in FBIS-NES-1999-1013. Ayyub is considered one of the most wanted Salafis in Egypt.

63. As quoted in 'Ali Hasan al-Halabi, *Fundamentals of Commanding Good and Forbidding Evil according to Shayk Ul-Islam Ibn Taymiyya* (Cincinnati, Ohio: Al-Qur'an Was-Sunnah Society of North America, 1995), 2.

64. 'Ali Hasan al-Halabi, "Tarbiyah: The Key to Victory," *Al-Ibaanah*, August 1995, 16.

65. Fatwa by Abd al-Aziz Bin Baz, as reproduced at www.troid.org/articles/ibaadah/jihaad/algerianaffair3.htm.

66. *Munatharah ma' Tantheem alJjihad al-Islami*, audiocassettes, n.d., transcript posted at www. allahuakbar.net/scholars/albanni/debate_on_jihad.htm.

67. Al-Muhajiroun, *The 10 Types of People in the Muslim Ummah Today*. Leaflet, n.d.

68. Al-Muhajiroun, *The 10 Types of People*.

69. Al-Muhajiroun, "London Islamic Conference Review: The 'Salafiyya' Onslaught," January 25, 2004.

70. Interview by author, London, June 2002.

71. Anjem Choudary, telephone interview by author, June 2002.

72. Omar Bakri Mohammed, interview by author, London, June 2002.

73. Anjem Choudary, telephone interview by author, June 2002.

74. Omar Bakri Mohammed, interview by author, London, December 2002.

75. Omar Bakri Mohammed, interview by author, London, December 2002.

76. Omar Bakri Mohammed, interview by author, London, December 2002.

77. Kamran Bokhari, former al-Muhajiroun U.S. spokesperson, telephone interview by author, April 2003.

78. Omar Bakri Mohammed, interview by author, London, June 2002.

79. Al-Muhajiroun, *Administration*.

80. Anjem Choudary, telephone interview by author, June 2002.

81. John Lofland and Rodney Stark, "Becoming a World-Saver: A Theory of Conversion to a Deviant Perspective," *American Sociological Review*, December 1965, 862.

82. Anjem Choudary, telephone interview by author, June 2002.

83. Kamran Bokhari, telephone interview by author, April 2003.

84. Omar Bakri related this story to me in December 2002.

85. See Omar Bakri Mohammed, *The First 24 Hours after the Establishment of the Islamic State: How Can We Transform the Present Ruling Systems and Government Departments into an Islamic System and Islamic Departments?* (London: Al-Muhajiroun Publications, n.d.).

86. Former head of the U.K. women's section, e-mail, October 7, 2003. Name withheld to protect the identity of the former activist.

87. In her e-mail, she indicates that during the conflict over the Citizens of the Khilafah conference, she "got so much rubbish and attitude from the brothers loyal to the leadership purely because they could not take a woman being in charge."

88. As quoted in James V. Spickard, "Rethinking Religious Social Action: What Is 'Rational' about Rational-Choice Theory?" *Sociology of Religion* 59, no. 2 (1998): 104.

89. Roxanne L. Euben, *Enemy in the Mirror: Islamic Fundamentalism and the Limits of Modern Rationalism* (Princeton: Princeton University Press, 1999), 33.

CONCLUSION

Like other radical Islamic groups, al-Muhajiroun is an identity movement. It promotes a network of shared meaning predicated on a particular interpretation of Islam as the basis of community and "being Muslim." In doing so, it draws stark boundaries between the community of true believers, on the one hand, and the deviants, hypocrites, and unbelievers on the other. It offers an exclusive identity of salvation by claiming to monopolize the religious truth necessary to fulfill divine duties and enter Paradise. All other interpretations are seen as religious transmogrifications that obstruct eternal reward in the hereafter. Activism, in this context, is predominantly about drawing initial interest and convincing others that the movement commands a pure form of Islam capable of guiding Muslims along the straight path of Islam.

As they reach out to others, activists try to live in accordance with the movement ideology to set an example and ensure salvation. They view themselves as vanguards of a future society guided by movement precepts. As with many new social movements, activists seek to "practice in the present the change they are struggling for: they redefine the meaning of social action for the whole society."[1] Al-Muhajiroun activists are living embodiments of a particular religious interpretation—faith in action.

This form of identity-based activism involves high risks. The ideology that constitutes the foundation of the network of shared meaning demands risky activism as a necessary condition for the spiritual payoff in the hereafter. From the movement's perspective, the straight path of Islam requires that Muslims struggle to establish an Islamic state via a military coup wherever there are Muslims, publicly demonstrate and call for jihad, and educate others about their Islamic duties, including support for violence. These duties command risky contention, irrespective of the consequences in a post–September 11 period characterized by tightened security, heightened legal repercussions for Islamic radicalism, and general societal disdain for militant Islam.

In addition, the al-Muhajiroun identity itself entails risk. As Verta Taylor and Nicole C. Raeburn argue, "The fact that in identity politics, individuals' personal lives, work, and activism all become sites of political expression means that activists who engage in this style of movement participation literally 'put their bodies on the line for the cause.' As a result, they become easy targets of stigma, harassment, retaliation, and even more extreme sanctions such as loss of a job, injury, or death—effects that have been shown to weigh heavily on individual's decisions to become involved in unpopular causes."[2] In short, being an al-Muhajiroun activist means countenancing negative consequences.

So why participate in the movement? On the surface, the choice seems irrational: the risks are high and the guarantee of spiritual salvation is intangible and nonverifiable (i.e., there is no way to know whether those who follow al-Muhajiroun's interpretation and die actually make it to Paradise). And there are plenty of less risky alternatives that guarantee the same spiritual outcome. This includes a plethora of less risky Islamic fundamentalist groups that share many of al-Muhajiroun's ideological precepts. Is participation in the movement, then, the choice of the irrational?

Certainly where exogenous conditions are static and an individual is satisfied it would seem illogical to join a radical group—some kind of grievance is necessary to provide impetus for joining. Exogenous conditions, however, change and can impact individual satisfaction. Typically cited changes include deteriorating economic conditions, political repression, and cultural alienation. In this book, I have added personal conditions to capture idiosyncratic experiences that engender grievances or dissatisfaction, such as a death in the family.

In some cases, grievances are severe enough to prompt a cognitive opening in which the affected individual is open to alternative belief systems and ways of looking at the world. For many of those who became al-Muhajiroun activists, cognitive openings were produced by a sense of cultural alienation and exclusion. In the United Kingdom, many young Muslims do not feel accepted by the majority society. While growing up in a British system that preaches tolerance and multiculturalism, they experience both racial and religious discrimination (most Muslims are from ethnic minorities). At the same time, they do not identify with their parents' generation, which tends to practice a nonintellectual form of Islam in ethnic enclave communities separated from the broader British society. Trapped between two worlds, these young Muslims lack a sense of belonging and community. For some, this creates openness to new identities, communities, and ideologies.

Al-Muhajiroun works to foster cognitive openings through outreach activism intended to generate a sense of crisis. This is accomplished through collective action like protests and propagation stalls that focus on the "oppression of Muslims" in places like Palestine, Kashmir, and Chechnya. The movement uses graphic images and rhetoric to highlight the various "genocides" being perpetrated against Muslims worldwide. The objective is to convince audiences that immediate action is needed to protect fellow Muslims, to induce a sense of moral shock and outrage, and to underscore the ineffectiveness of mainstream approaches to addressing the crises.

Activists also foster cognitive openings through individual propagation. They approach individuals in their social network and initiate conversations about Islam and problems in society and the world. Many of these conversations are sculpted to fit the particular concerns of the individual propagation target so as to facilitate interest and discussion about possible solutions. In this context, activists try to shake the target's certitude in mainstream prognostications, thereby opening him or her to the possibility that alternative ways of looking at problems and new solutions may be needed. This kind of outreach is directed toward strangers as well, though activists must spend more time identifying the target's interests because a relationship and familiarity have yet to be established.

For the movement, the hope is that cognitive openings, whether prompted by an identity crisis, contact with the movement, or some other catalyst, will initiate a process of religious seeking whereby affected individuals seek to address their grievances and concerns through a religious idiom. Most of these "religious seekers" initially turn to community religious figures for Islamic meaning. They seek knowledgeable individuals in their own networks and communities for guidance. Those who turned to al-Muhajiroun, however, found these figures wanting: they seemed unable, unwilling, and ill-equipped to answer the kinds of questions that interested eventual activists, particularly questions pertaining to politics. As a result, these disaffected seekers began looking outside the mainstream Muslim community.

The process of religious seeking can be self-initiated or guided. In the former, individuals seek religious answers without help from anyone affiliated with al-Muhajiroun or other movements. This includes attending various mosques, Islamic lectures, and activities sponsored by any number of Muslim organizations. This is a relatively rare trajectory of joining. The more common pattern is that disaffected seekers are guided by someone already in the movement, particularly where the cognitive opening is facilitated by movement outreach in the first place or the seeker already knows someone in the movement. In these cases, an al-Muhajiroun activist guides seekers as they begin to explore the different religious perspectives. In essence, the guide helps seekers "shop around" the marketplace of ideas.

The movement tries to take advantage of this process of seeking through its local branches and front organizations. These offer an assortment of activities and lessons for those interested in learning more about Islam. Many are explicitly designed to cater to the particular concerns of disaffected seekers. Whereas mainstream figures often eschew the kinds of sensitive and political topics that interest disaffected seekers, al-Muhajiroun tackles these directly through its dense organizational network, thereby filling a void.

Although this helps explain how individuals are initially exposed to the movement and its activities, it does not explain why an individual, once exposed, decides to learn about Islam from al-Muhajiroun. This decision hinges on perceptions about the movement's sacred authority: does it have the right to interpret Islam and does it seem to be a credible source of religious learning? Activists consistently cite Omar Bakri Mohammed's status as a scholar as critical in their earlier decision to become students of the movement. Perceptions about Omar's level of knowledge, character, and personality were important for convincing seekers that he is in a position to teach them about "real Islam." This was a comparative evaluation born from the process of seeking: Omar seemed more credible as a source of Islam than alternatives did (including mainstream moderates as well as other fundamentalists). They trusted his credentials to properly interpret Islam. Al-Muhajiroun actively works to foster this image, often challenging negative media representations of the movement to protect seeker perceptions about its sacred authority. Once seekers accept Omar's authority as an Islamic scholar, they are more willing to attend movement religious lessons and study circles, where they can be socialized into the movement ideology.

During the process of socialization or "culturing," students learn several key ideological tenets that help overcome obstacles to high-risk activism. First, obedience to God is paramount if an individual desires salvation. This includes rigid adherence to the concept of *tawhid*, or oneness of God, which is central to the movement's ideology. Lessons teach students that the unity of God means worshiping God alone by following *all* divine commands, even those that entail risk. Second, the model of the Prophet Mohammed includes educating fellow Muslims about their divine duties (including jihad), challenging humanly made law and institutions through contentious collective action, and seeking to establish an Islamic state through a military coup wherever there are Muslims (including the United Kingdom). Because the Prophet and his companions pursued these activities as a group, Muslims must do likewise and join a movement like al-Muhajiroun. Those who follow this model are the true Salafis (followers of the Prophet and his companions [*salaf*]) and will receive divine reward. All others are deviants. And third, the divine commands necessitate high-risk activism, but the burdens are evidence that activists are on the straight path since the Prophet and his companions suffered to spread Islam. Those who wish to enter Paradise must endure the risks in the here-and-now or jeopardize salvation. Those who accept these arguments and the movement ideology are considered "intellectually affiliated" with al-Muhajiroun and are eligible for formal membership. Some "intellectually affiliated" activists have left the movement, but most remain committed to high-risk activism.

For those who become intellectually affiliated with the movement, engaging in high-risk activism through al-Muhajiroun is a rational choice. Though it may seem like blind fanaticism to outsiders, there is an inherent logic in militant Islamic activism. Individuals do not view costs and benefits in terms of material gain, social consequences, or personal freedom (i.e., arrest). The calculus is instead organized according to which choices and actions maximize the prospects of salvation on Judgment Day. For those who internalize al-Muhajiroun's ideology, risky activism is a utility-maximizing choice in that activists believe it is an efficient strategy for salvation. In fact, for those who accept the movement's religious interpretation, it is the only choice that produces a spiritual payoff—an exclusive path to salvation as part of the "saved sect" of Islam.

So what does this tell us about radical Islam more generally? First of all, radicals defy the caricatures of the "wild-eyed fanatics" often depicted in the media and popular books on Islamic movements. Those who have interviewed radical Islamic activists in depth recognize that they are quite sane and logical. Certainly their logic operates according to a distinct set of ideological and religious precepts, but this does not mean that they are devoid of reason. Radicals are still driven by self-interest and calculations about cost and benefit, though informed by religious and ideological beliefs. Whereas recent studies of terrorism emphasize the rationality of radicalism at the group level, where individual self-sacrifice benefits movement goals, this book emphasizes the rationality of radical activism at the individual level, where self-sacrifice benefits individual spiritual self-interest.

Second, the processes that draw individuals toward participation in radical groups are not all that different from those that lead individuals to join moderate Islamic movements. In both cases, individuals must be willing to consider alternative beliefs and often experience a cognitive opening as a result of exogenous conditions or movement outreach. Eventual joiners frequently engage in religious seeking as they look to redress their grievances through religion. Individuals are exposed to moderate and radical movement activities as a result of activist outreach to friends and strangers alike. Moderates and radicals mobilize resources to provide points of interaction and encourage participation. They also try to establish their credentials as reputable sources of religious learning. And both moderate and radical groups hold religious lessons and educational activities to promote their particular religious interpretations and encourage activism.

The differences are in terms of exposure to movement activities and the content of the socialization process. In terms of exposing individuals to the movement, moderate groups have an inherent advantage over radicals. Because they are less repressed, moderates can more effectively use outreach and propagation and thus expose religious seekers to their movements. Moderate movements tend to be larger and enjoy broader social networks that can be used to draw initial interest. And because many such movements are legal or semilegal, they can openly mobilize resources and engage the public. Radicals, on the other hand, must be more circumspect. They can rarely work and mobilize resources in the open to the same extent as moderates and must be careful in using network ties or creating new social relationships because of the possibility of government infiltration.

The differences in the content of culturing are important as well. Moderates cast a broader net for potential joiners by offering a more inclusive ideology than the radicals. And whereas the radical culturing process inculcates values of violence and risky activism, this is not usually the case for moderates, who tend to emphasize peaceful instruments of religious activism. What individuals are taught during religious lessons impacts the patterns of activism that result from socialization. In Short, ideas matter.

Third, and finally, the dynamics of radical Islamic groups are not all that different from those of non-Islamic social movements. These other movements use social networks, foster moral shock, mobilize resources, and try to frame arguments to encourage support and participation; and individual activists from these movements calculate cost and benefit when deciding whether to participate. This indicates that the *dynamics, process, and organization* of radical Islamic activism can be understood as important elements of contention that transcend the specificity of radical Islam as a system of meaning, identity, and basis of collective action. Though the ideational components and inspiration of radical Islam as an ideological worldview differentiate it from other examples of contention, the collective action itself and concomitant mechanisms that draw interest and participation demonstrate consistency across movement types. In other words, Islamic activism is not sui generis.[3]

This is not to argue that the ideological distinctiveness of radical Islamic groups is irrelevant. A central contention of this book, in fact, is that this difference is essential for understanding why individuals engage in high-risk Islamic activism when it seems to jeopardize their self-interest. Studies of social movements rarely delve into the specifics of movement ideologies and the process of socialization and instead rely on other variables to explain progression to high-risk activism, such as network ties and biographical availability. This book, in contrast, emphasizes a role for ideas. Ideas shape patterns of contention by rendering some choices imaginable and thus ideologically available.[4] The peace movement, for example, would be hard-pressed to mobilize a campaign of violence because such a strategy violates the core principles of its ideology. For radical Islamic movements, high-risk activism is inspired by an ideology that privileges the motivating promise of salvation and the necessity of risky behavior for those who aspire to enter Paradise.

In making this argument, this book is not meant to be definitive. It may, in fact, raise more questions than it answers. The point of the book, however, is to use a detailed case study, which draws upon comparative social movement research and theory, to produce insights into the processes that encourage individuals to engage in high-risk activism. The comparative theoretical foundation of the study implies that the explanation derived from the al-Muhajiroun case study can help us better understand other radical Islamic groups. Though avoiding claims of generalizability, the book strives to offer an explanation that contributes to theoretically informed research on radical Islam.

NOTES

1. Alberto Melucci, "An End to Social Movements? Introductory Paper to the Sessions on 'New Social Movements and Change in Organizational Forms,'" *Social Science Information* 23, no. 4–5 (1984): 830.

2. Verta Taylor and Nicole C. Raeburn, "Identity Politics as High-Risk Activism: Career Consequences for Lesbian, Gay, and Bisexual Sociologists," *Social Problems,* May 1995, 254.

3. For an elaboration of this argument, see Quintan Wiktorowicz, "Introduction: Islamic Activism and Social Movement Theory," in *Islamic Activism: A Social Movement Theory Approach* (Bloomington: Indiana University Press, 2004).

4. See, for example, Russell J. Dalton, *The Green Rainbow: Environmental Groups in Western Europe* (New Haven: Yale University Press, 1994).

EPILOGUE

On October 7, 2004, after this book was completed, Omar Bakri Mohammed surprised observers by officially dissolving al-Muhajiroun. The movement shut down its website, closed its branch offices, discontinued its member-only activities, and released members from their administrative duties and responsibilities. It has discontinued all *da'wa* stalls, demonstrations, and public activities. Omar continues to give religious lessons and lectures, but they are open to the general public. British authorities suspect that the movement has gone underground, raising concerns about the possibility of new terrorist activities by former members and activists.

To understand the dissolution, one must appreciate the impact of the war on terror for al-Muhajiroun's ideological outreach. As this book details, antiterror legislation and stepped-up security crackdowns have directly affected the ability of the movement to mobilize. After September 11, it encountered greater difficulty booking venues for events, securing permits for rallies and protests, and raising revenues. All of this circumscribed al-Muhajiroun's resource mobilization capacity, but it was not responsible for its dissolution. For Omar, the constancy of Salafi principles means that it is religiously prohibited to alter the divinely sanctioned strategies for fulfilling God's will simply because activists encounter difficulties. As discussed in chapter 4, difficulties are interpreted as proof that activists are on the straight path and will receive divine reward in Paradise.

According to Omar, the movement was instead responding to the "culture of jihad" that has emerged among Muslims. This term denotes the overwhelming preoccupation with issues related to warfare. In the current climate, activists find that audiences and outreach targets are almost entirely concerned with jihad and thus uninterested in the movement's broader message and ideological precepts. As Omar explains,

> Whenever we invite non-Muslims to Islam and work collectively, people are no longer interested during the time of war to talk about the purpose of life, Islam as providing everything for mankind, as an economic, social, and political system, etc. People now, in the [da'wa] stalls, in the debates, in the discussions, they ask you two questions. Do you condemn or condone? Do you condemn 9/11 or do you condone 9/11? Do you condone the kidnapping of Mr. So-and-So or do you condemn it? Do you condone [the attack] in Beslan [by Chechen rebels] in the school or condemn it?[1] In other words, people are no longer interested to know about Islam as a way of life, as an economic, social, political ruling system.[2]

For Omar, this preoccupation with jihad signifies the extent of the crisis in the Muslim world. Although he has always argued that the Western occupation of Muslim land and the war on terror are the most pressing issues facing the Muslim community, al-Muhajiroun's inability to propagate other parts of its ideology and message is seen as indicating a qualitative change in the severity of the crisis. Western attacks on Muslims are now viewed as existential threats to Islam itself.

During this time of war, Omar argues, it is a religious obligation to unite under a single global leader. He bases this on a hadith in which the Prophet predicted "a day of calamities upon calamities" when the enemy would divide the Muslims and occupy their land. Asked what the Muslims should do on that day, the Prophet called for them to unite under a leader. Omar thinks that this day has come and that the priority is now jihad.

Given this shift in priority and the need for unity, Omar believes that al-Muhajiroun no longer serves the purpose of divine obligations. "Every time has its own divine obligation," he muses. "And every obligation has its own circumstances." The initial purpose of the movement was to emerge as an ideological vanguard to command good and forbid evil, in accordance with Qur'an 3:104. Although it functioned to promote the call for jihad, this was not its primary raison d'être. Circumstances, however, now call for a focus on jihad. This does not mean that every *individual* Muslim must participate in jihad, but that all *organizations* must focus on this issue as the priority. So organizations must either work for this purpose exclusively or dissolve themselves. Since al-Muhajiroun was not formed for this reason and is limited by the "covenant of security," which prevents activists from attacking in the United Kingdom as long as they are legal residents (citizens or otherwise), it must dissolve itself.

Moreover, Omar argues, if al-Muhajiroun had continued to function, it would represent an alternative leadership and detract from the jihadi struggle against the West, something he believes is religiously forbidden during a time of crisis. This assessment is based on his interpretation of Qur'an 3:103–4:

> And hold fast by the covenant of Allah all together and be not disunited, and remember the favor of Allah on you when you were enemies, then He united your hearts so by His favor you became brethren; and you were on the brink of a pit of fire, then He saved you from it, thus does Allah make clear to you His communications that you may follow the right.

> And from among you there should be a party who invite to good and enjoin what is right and forbid the wrong, and these it is that shall be successful.

Omar emphasizes that the call to unite Muslims, particularly during a time of crisis, supersedes the call to rise as a group to command good and forbid evil. This means that once the crisis is resolved, Qur'an 3:104 again becomes an operative rule. "Then, *inshallah* [God willing], I will rise again with a group," Omar predicts, "whether al-Muhajiroun or any group, in order to continue my Islamic obligation." But until that time, Muslims must unite behind a leader in the jihad, and organizations that do not focus on fighting must dissolve themselves to preserve unity of purpose.

Omar claims he has altered his activism. While former members continue to ask his advice about Islamic rulings, he no longer has authority over them, other than that of a spiritual guide (as opposed to an *amir*). He no longer gives special culturing sessions and his public activities have diminished substantially. He now focuses on writing and publishing, though he gives some public lectures that are open to everyone. Since he lives under the covenant of security, Omar believes he has a divine permit not to actually engage in fighting and therefore focuses on commanding good and forbidding evil as an *individual* Muslim (rather than as the *amir* or member of an organization). While the conflict rages, Omar waits for the "dark cloud to pass," after which he will reemerge as a leader and continue to pursue the three divine duties that served as the principal foundations of al-Muhajiroun—propagation, public demonstrations (commanding good and forbidding evil), and struggling to establish an Islamic state via a military coup.

As for the individual activists of al-Muhajiroun, Omar argues that they are still bound by certain individual Muslim responsibilities. As *individuals* they must still propagate and command good and forbid evil. But they cannot do this as part of an organization, since all organized efforts must prioritize the jihad.

What drove Omar to dissolve al-Muhajiroun is ambiguous. He cites the state of crisis in the Muslim world, but how does the current situation differ from what it was, say, a year ago? His conclusions about the level of crisis are likely the culmination of U.K. crackdowns, the almost myopic concern with jihad among his followers and audiences at movement events, the Iraq crisis, and the Saudi crackdown on radicals after the 2003 bombings. All of this made it difficult for the movement to effectively operate as an ideological vanguard.

So what does the future hold for Omar and the former al-Muhajiroun activists? It is, of course, difficult to be prescient, particularly since this epilogue was written only one week after the dissolution, but let me speculate. It is likely that former al-Muhajiroun activists will take different paths. Omar himself speculates, "Some of them want to adhere to the covenant of security [and remain in the United Kingdom and command good and forbid evil]. Some may decide to leave and go to the Muslim land to give them [the jihadis] physical support. Some of them are really waiting like me until the situation is settled." At least some of them are likely to become more directly involved in jihad. An internal movement survey conducted a few years ago indicated that a substantial minority of activists wanted to turn to violence.[3] Now that Omar no longer functions as an *amir,* his restraining effect on some of the more violence-prone activists has been severely diminished. Having noted this possibility, I suspect that the vast majority of former activists will follow their mentor's example and remain on the sidelines until the war is over. Many of them continue to operate through the platforms, indicating that "plan B" is under way.[4]

Omar himself has become radicalized since September 11, and there is no reason to believe that he will moderate in the short to medium term. He has expressed strong support for some of the most radical jihadi scholars underlying the al-Qaeda network, such as Ali bin Khudayr al-Khudayr, Nasir Hamad al-Fahd, Suleiman Alwan, and Hammoud al-Uqla al-Shuaybi (d. January 2002): in his own words, "I agree with them completely." He admits that he "follows" bin Laden, arguing that God is guiding bin Laden as the leader of the righteous fighters:

> I do not follow him because he is a scholar. I follow him because he is the most guided person who knows the right path in the time of crisis. And Allah comments that whoever fights for our sake we will guide him to the right path. So he is on the right path. And anything he says, even if it is *kufr* [disbelief], [he is] always guided as if he is the greatest scholar of his time.

Omar does not necessarily support the tactics of al-Qaeda and its affiliates, such as beheadings and killing civilians, but when faced with a stark choice during a time of crisis between bin Laden and the infidels, he chooses bin Laden. For Omar, it is a struggle for Islam's survival, and he believes Muslims cannot remain on the fence: equivocation leads to disunity among Muslims, and disunity leads to defeat and the annihilation of the faith by the infidels. Regardless of Omar's own personal distaste for some of the jihadi attacks that kill innocent civilians, he refuses to condemn the jihadis completely because, in his view, the crisis is at such a level that terrorism has become religiously permitted. To support his position, he turns to Qur'an 47:4: "When you encounter the unbelievers, strike off their heads. Until you have made a wide slaughter among them tie up the remaining captives." Omar believes this means escalating the level of killing until the infidels retreat. He is trying to make a distinction between his own personal feelings about these tactics and an "objective" jurisprudential position, but the nuances are likely to be lost on most observers: it still seems like encouragement for an "anything goes" form of jihad.

If Omar forms a group after "the dark clouds pass," it will likely resemble a more radical version of al-Muhajiroun. He may resurrect the three divine duties for the new organization, but it is difficult to imagine the resurrection will not encompass his newly found jihadi leanings. This may link any new organization more directly to various radical jihadi groups in the future. Although observers have, I believe, erroneously speculated a connection between al-Muhajiroun and al-Qaeda, their speculations may prove more accurate for any new incarnation.

NOTES

1. He is referring to the Chechen rebel takeover of a school in Beslan in September 2004. More than 300 civilians were killed when Russian forces and rebels exchanged gunfire. Several bombs exploded in the school during the exchange. Most of the casualties were children.

2. Omar Bakri Muhammed, telephone interview by author, October 19, 2004. All quotes are from this interview, which was conducted to address the dissolution. The dissolution itself was announced in a press release dated October 7, 2004.

3. Omar Bakri Muhammed, conversation with author, London, December 2002.

4. For example, see www.islamicthinkers.com, which posts Omar's books (without his name listed) and the images previously posted on al-Muhajiroun's web site. Accessed April 7, 2005.

BIBLIOGRAPHY

Aaker, Jennifer L., and Patti Williams. "Empathy versus Pride: The Influence of Emotional Appeals across Cultures." *Journal of Consumer Research*, December 1998, 241-61.

Abedin, Maham. "Al-Muhajiroun in the UK: An Interview with Sheikh Omar Bakri Mohammed." *Terrorism Monitor*, March 23, 2004, 1-13.

Alexander, Christopher. "Opportunities, Organizations, and Ideas: Islamists and Workers in Tunisia and Algeria." *International Journal of Middle East Studies*, November 2000, 465-90.

Allen, Christopher, and Jørgen S. Nielsen. *Summary Report on Islamophobia in the EU after 11 September 2001*. Vienna: European Monitoring Centre on Racism and Xenophobia, 2002.

AlSayyad, Nezar, and Manuel Castells, eds. *Muslim Europe or Euro-Islam: Politics, Culture, and Citizenship in the Age of Globalization*. Lanham, Md.: Lexington, 2002.

Amizade, Ron, and Doug McAdam. "Emotions and Contentious Politics." In Ronald R. Amizade et al., *Silence and Voice in Contentious Politics*. Cambridge: Cambridge University Press, 2001.

Anderson, Lisa. "Fulfilling Prophecies: State Policy and Islamist Radicalism." In John L. Esposito, ed., *Political Islam: Revolution, Radicalism, or Reform?* Boulder: Lynne Rienner, 1997.

Anonymous [Rita Katz]. *Terrorist Hunter*. New York: HarperCollins, 2003.

Ansari, Hamied N. "The Islamic Militants in Egyptian Politics." *International Journal of Middle East Studies*, March 1984, 123-44.

Antoun, Richard. *Muslim Preacher in the Modern World: A Jordanian Case Study in Comparative Perspective*. Princeton: Princeton University Press, 1989.

Argo, Nichole. "Understanding and Defusing Human Bombs." Paper presented at the International Studies Association Annual Meeting, 2004.

Al-Azmeh, Aziz. *Islams and Modernities.* London: Verso, 1993.

Bainbridge, William Sims. *Satan's Power.* Berkeley: University of California Press, 1978.

Barry, Brian. *Sociologists, Economists, and Democracy.* New York: Macmillan, 1978.

Benford, Robert D. "Frame Disputes within the Nuclear Disarmament Movement." *Social Forces,* March 1993, 677–701.

Benford, Robert D., and Scott A. Hunt. "Interactional Dynamics in Public Problems—Marketplaces: Movements and the Counterframing and Reframing of Public Problems." In James Holstein and Gale Miller, eds., *Challenges and Choices: Constructionist Perspectives on Social Problems,* 153–86. New York: Transaction, 2003.

Benford, Robert D., and David A. Snow. "Framing Processes and Social Movements: An Overview and Assessment." *Annual Review of Sociology* 26 (2000): 611–39.

Berman, Eli, and David D. Laitin. "Rational Martyrs vs. Hard Targets: Evidence on the Tactical Use of Suicide Attacks." In Eva Meyersson Milgrom, ed., "Suicide Bombings from an Interdisciplinary Perspective." Manuscript.

Berman, Sheri. "Islamism, Revolution, and Civil Society." *Perspectives on Politics,* June 2003, 257–72.

Blackaby, David, Derek Leslie, Philip Murphy, and Nigel O'Leary. "Unemployment among Britain's Ethnic Minorities." *Manchester School,* January 1999, 1–20.

Burgat, François. *Face to Face with Political Islam.* London: Tauris, 2003.

Burgat, François, and William Dowell. *The Islamic Movement in North Africa.* Austin: Center for Middle Eastern Studies, University of Texas at Austin, 1993.

Checkel, Jeffrey T. "Why Comply? Social Leaning and European Identity Change." *International Organization,* Summer 2001, 553–88.

Chong, Dennis. *Collective Action and the Civil Rights Movement.* Chicago: University of Chicago Press, 1991.

Clark, Janine. *Islam, Charity, and Activism: Middle-Class Networks and Social Welfare in Egypt, Jordan, and Yemen.* Bloomington: Indiana University Press, 2004.

———. "Islamist Women in Yemen: Informal Nodes of Activism." In Quintan Wiktorowicz, ed., *Islamic Activism: A Social Movement Theory Approach,* 164–84. Bloomington: Indiana University Press, 2004.

Clark, Janine Astrid, and Jillian Schwedler. "Who Opened the Window? Women's Activism in Islamist Parties." *Comparative Politics,* April 2003, 293–312.

Cohn, Steven F., Steven E. Barkan, and William A. Halteman. "Dimensions of Participation in a Professional Social-Movement Organization." *Sociological Inquiry,* August 2003, 311–37.

Crenshaw, Martha. "Political Violence in Algeria." *Terrorism and Political Violence,* Autumn 1994, 261–80.

Cuthbertson, Ian. "Whittling Liberties: Britain's Not-So-Temporary Antiterrorism Laws." *World Policy Journal,* Winter 2001–2002, 27–33.

Dalton, Russell J. *The Green Rainbow: Environmental Groups in Western Europe.* New Haven: Yale University Press, 1994.

Dekmejian, R. Hrair. "The Rise of Political Islamism in Saudi Arabia." *Middle East Journal,* Autumn 1994, 627–43.

Della Porta, Donatella, and Dieter Rucht. "Left-Libertarian Movements in Context: A Comparison of Italy and West Germany, 1965–1990." In Craig C. Jenkins and Bert Klandermans, eds., *The Politics of Social Protest.* Minneapolis: University of Minnesota Press, 1995.

Donohue, Laura K. *Counter-Terrorist Law and Emergency Powers in the United Kingdom, 1922–2000.* Dublin: Irish Academic Press, 2001.

Doran, Michael. "The Pragmatic Fanaticism of al Qaeda: An Anatomy of Extremism in Middle Eastern Politics." *Political Science Quarterly* 117, no. 2 (2002): 177–90.

Downton, James, Jr., and Paul Wehr. "Persistent Pacifism: How Activist Commitment Is Developed and Sustained." *Journal of Peace Research* 35, no. 5 (1998): 531–50.

Dwyer, Claire. "Negotiating Diasporic Identities: Young British South Asian Muslim Women." *Women's Studies International Forum,* July–August, 475–86.

Eickelman, Dale F., and James Piscatori. *Muslim Politics.* Princeton: Princeton University Press, 1996.

Emerson, Steven. *American Jihad: The Terrorists Living among Us.* New York: Free Press, 2003.

Esposito, John L. *Islam and Politics.* 4th ed. Syracuse: Syracuse University Press, 1998.

Esposito, John L., and John O. Voll. *Islam and Democracy.* New York: Oxford University Press, 1996.

Euben, Roxanne L. *Enemy in the Mirror: Islamic Fundamentalism and the Limits of Modern Rationalism.* Princeton: Princeton University Press, 1999.

El Fadl, Khaled Abou. "Islamic Law and Muslim Minorities: The Juristic Discourse on Muslim Minorities from the Second/Eighth to the Eleventh/Seventeenth Centuries." *Islamic Law and Society* 1, no. 2 (1994): 141–87.

———. "Legal Debates on Muslim Minorities: Between Rejection and Accommodation." *Journal of Religious Ethics,* Spring 1994, 127–62.

———. "Striking a Balance: Islamic Legal Discourse on Muslim Minorities." In Yvonne Yazbeck Haddad and John L. Esposito, eds., *Muslims on the Americanization Path?* 47–64. New York: Oxford University Press, 2000.

Fahmy, Ninette S. "The Performance of the Muslim Brotherhood in the Egyptian Syndicates: An Alternative Formula for Reform?" *Middle East Journal,* Autumn 1998, 551–62.

Faksh, Mahmud A. *The Future of Islam in the Middle East.* Westport, Conn.: Praeger, 1997.

Ferree, Myra Marx, and Frederick D. Miller. "Mobilization and Meaning: Toward an Integration of Social Psychological and Resource Perspectives on Social Movements." *Sociological Inquiry,* Winter 1985, 38–61.

Finkel, Steven E., Edward N. Muller, and Karl-Dieter Opp. "Personal Influence, Collective Rationality, and Mass Political Action." *American Political Science Review,* September 1989, 885–903.

Fireman, Bruce, and William A. Gamson. "Utilitarian Logic in the Resource Mobilization Perspective." In Mayer N. Zald and John McCarthy, eds., *The Dynamics of Social Movements: Resource Mobilization, Social Control, and Tactics.* Cambridge: Winthrop, 1979.

Fiske, Susan T., and Shelly E. Taylor. *Social Cognition.* 2d ed. New York: McGraw-Hill, 1991.

Furtell, Robert. "Framing Processes, Cognitive Liberation, and NIMBY Protest in the U.S. Chemical-Weapons Disposal Conflict." *Sociological Inquiry* 73 (2003): 359–86.

Gamson, William A., and David S. Meyer. "Framing Political Opportunity." In Doug McAdam, John D. McCarthy, and Mayer N. Zald, eds., *Comparative Perspectives on Social Movements: Political Opportunities, Mobilizing Structures, and Cultural Framings,* 287–88. Cambridge: Cambridge University Press, 1996.

Goldberg, Marvin, and Jon Hartwick. "The Effects of Advertiser Reputation and Extremity of Advertiser Claim on Advertiser Effectiveness." *Journal of Consumer Research* 17 (1990): 172–79.

Goodwin, Jeff. "The Lidinal Constitution of a High-Risk Social Movement: Affectual Ties and Solidarity in the Huk Rebellion, 1946 to 1954." *American Sociological Review,* February 1997, 53–69.

Goodwin, Jeff, and James M. Jasper. "Caught in a Winding, Snarling Vine: The Structural Bias of Political Process Theory." *Sociological Forum* 14, no. 1 (1999): 27–54.

Goodwin, Jeff, James M. Jasper, and Francesca Polletta, eds. *Passionate Politics: Emotions and Social Movements.* Chicago: University of Chicago Press, 2001.

Goodwin, Jeff, and Theda Skocpol. "Explaining Revolutions in the Contemporary Third World." *Politics and Society* 17 (1989): 490.

Gould, Robert V. *Insurgent Identities: Class, Community, and Protest in Paris from 1848 to the Commune.* Chicago: University of Chicago Press, 1995.

Grünewald, Klaus. "Defending Germany's Constitution." *Middle East Quarterly,* March 1995.

Haddad, Yvonne Yazbeck. "Islamists and the 'Problem of Israel': The 1967 Awakening." *Middle East Journal,* Spring 1992, 266–85.

Haddad, Yvonne Yazbeck, and I. Qurqmaz. "Muslims in the West: A Select Bibliography." *Islam and Christian Muslim Relations* 11, no. 1 (2000): 5–49.

Haddad, Yvonne Yazbeck, and Jane I. Smith, eds. *Muslim Minorities in the West: Visible and Invisible.* Walnut Creek, Calif.: AltaMira, 2002.

Hafez, Mohammed M. *Why Muslims Rebel: Repression and Resistance in the Islamic World.* Boulder: Lynne Rienner, 2003.

Al-Halabi, 'Ali Hasan. *Fundamentals of Commanding Good and Forbidding Evil according to Shayk Ul-Islam Ibn Taymiyya.* Cincinnati, Ohio: Al-Qur'an Was-Sunnah Society of North America, 1995.

———. "Tarbiyah: The Key to Victory." *Al-Ibaanah,* August 1995, 15–19.

Hall, Deana. "Managing to Recruit: Religious Conversion in the Workplace." *Sociology of Religion* 59, no. 4 (1998): 393–410.

Harrison, Mark. "The Logic of Suicide Terrorism." Paper presented at the conference Weapons of Catastrophic Effect: Confronting the Threat, London, February 12–14, 2003.

Heirich, Max. "Change of Heart: A Test of Some Widely Held Theories about Religious Conversion." *American Journal of Sociology*, November 1977, 653–80.

Hepple, Bob, and Tufyal Choudhury. *Tackling Religious Discrimination: Practical Implications for Policy-Makers and Legislators*, 4–5. Home Office Research Study 221, Home Office Research, Research and Statistics Directorate, February 2001.

Hermassi, Mohammed Elbaki. "La Société Tunisienne au Miroir Islamiste." *Maghreb-Machrek*, January-March 1984, 1–54.

Hirsch, Eric L. "Sacrifice for the Cause: Group Processes, Recruitment, and Commitment in a Student Social Movement." *American Sociological Review*, April 1990, 243–54.

Hoffman, Valerie J. "Muslim Fundamentalists: Psychosocial Profiles." In Martin E. Marty and R. Scott Appleby, eds., *Fundamentalisms Comprehended*. Chicago: University of Chicago Press, 1995.

Hovland, Carl I., Irving L. Janis, and Howard H. Kelly. *Communication and Persuasion*. New Haven: Yale University Press, 1953.

Hunter, Shireen T., ed. *Islam, Europe's Second Religion: The New Social, Cultural, and Political Landscape*. Westport, Conn.: Praeger, 2002.

Hunter, Shireen T., and Huma Malik, eds. *Islam in Europe and the United States: A Comparative Perspective*. Washington, D.C.: Center for Strategic and International Studies, 2002.

Iannaccone, Laurence R. "The Market for Martyrs." Paper presented at the annual meeting of the American Economic Association, San Diego, Calif., January 3–5, 2004.

Ibrahim, Saad Eddin. "Anatomy of Egypt's Militant Islamic Groups: Methodological Notes and Preliminary Findings." *International Journal of Middle East Studies*, December 1980, 423–53.

——. "The Changing Face of Egypt's Islamic Activism." In *Egypt, Islam, and Democracy*. Cairo: The American University in Cairo Press, 1996.

Irons, Jenny. "The Shaping of Activist Recruitment and Participation: A Study of Women in the Mississippi Civil Rights Movement." *Gender and Society*, December 1998, 692–709.

Jam'iat Ihyaa' Minhaaj Al-Sunnah. *A Brief Introduction to the Salafi Da'wah*. Ipswich, U.K.: Jam'iat Minhaaj Al-Sunnah, 1993.

Jasper, James M. *The Art of Moral Protest: Culture, Biography, and Creativity in Social Movements*. Chicago: University of Chicago Press, 1997.

——. "The Emotions of Protest: Affective and Reactive Emotions in and around Social Movements." *Sociological Forum* 13, no. 3 (1998): 397–424.

Jasper, James M., and Jane Poulsen. "Recruiting Strangers and Friends: Moral Shocks and Social Networks in Animal Rights and Anti-Nuclear Protests." *Social Problems*, November 1995.

Al-Jibali, Muhammad. *Allah's Rights upon His Servants*. Cincinnati, Ohio: Al-Qur'an Was-Sunnah Society of North America, 1995.

Johnson, Scott D., and Ann N. Miller. "A Cross-Cultural Study of Immediacy, Credibility, and Learning in the U.S. and Kenya." *Communication Education*, July 2002, 280–92.

Kahani-Hopkins, Vered, and Nick Hopkins. "'Representing' British Muslims: The Strategic Dimension to Identity Construction." *Ethnic and Racial Studies*, March 2002, 288–309.

Kalyvas, Stathis N. "Wanton and Senseless? The Logic of Massacres in Algeria." *Rationality and Society* 11, no. 3 (1999): 245.

Kaplan, D. E. "Made in the USA." *U.S. News & World Report*, June 10, 2002.

Keddie, Nikki R. "The Revolt of Islam, 1700 to 1993: Comparative Considerations and Relations to Imperialism." *Comparative Studies in Society and History*, July 1994, 463–87.

Kepel, Gilles. *Muslim Extremism in Egypt: The Prophet and the Pharaoh*. Berkeley: University of California Press, 1993.

Khan, Kafar. "Muslim Presence in Europe: The British Dimension—Identity, Integration, and Community Activism." *Current Sociology*, October 2000, 29–43.

Kim, Hyojoung, and Peter S. Bearman. "The Structure and Dynamics of Movement Participation." *American Sociological Review*, February 1997, 70–93.

Klandermans, Bert. "Mobilization and Participation: Social-Psychological Expansions of Resource Mobilization Theory." *American Sociological Review* 49 (1984): 583–600.

———. *The Social Psychology of Protest*. Oxford: Blackwell, 1997.

Klandermans, Bert, and Dirk Oegema. "Potentials, Networks, Motivations, and Barriers: Steps toward Participation in Social Movements." *American Sociological Review*, August 1987, 519–31.

Knoke, David. "Networks of Political Action: Toward Theory Construction." *Social Forces*, June 1990, 1041–63.

Kornhauser, William. *The Politics of Mass Society*. Glencoe, Ill.: Free Press, 1959.

Kwilecki, Susan, and Loretta S. Wilson. "Was Mother Teresa Maximizing Her Utility? An Idiographic Application of Rational Choice Theory." *Journal for the Scientific Study of Religion*, June 1998, 205–21.

Langhor, Vicky. "Of Islamists and Ballot Boxes: Rethinking the Relationship between Islamisms and Electoral Politics." *International Journal of Middle East Studies*, November 2001, 591–610.

Lebor, Adam. *A Heart Turned East: Among the Muslims of Europe and America*. New York: St. Martin's, 1997.

Lia, Brynjar. *The Society of Muslim Brothers in Egypt: The Rise of an Islamic Mass Movement, 1928–1942*. Ithaca, N.Y.: Ithaca Press, 1998.

Lichbach, Mark Irving. *The Rebel's Dilemma*. Ann Arbor: University of Michigan Press, 1995.

Lofland, John. "'Becoming a World-Saver' Revisited." *American Behavioral Scientist,* July–August 1977, 805–18.

Lofland, John, and Rodney Stark. "Becoming a World-Saver: A Theory of Conversion to a Deviant Perspective." *American Sociological Review,* December 1965, 862–75.

Lohmann, Susanne. "Dynamics of Informational Cascades: The Monday Demonstrations in Leipzig, East Germany, 1989–1991." *World Politics* 47 (1994): 42–101.

———. "A Signaling Model of Informative and Manipulative Political Action." *American Political Science Review* 88 (1993): 319–33.

Loveman, Mara. 1998. "High-Risk Collective Action: Defending Human Rights in Chile, Uruguay, and Argentina." *American Journal of Sociology,* September 1998, 477–525.

Lust-Okar, Ellen M. "The Decline of Jordanian Political Parties: Myth or Reality?" *International Journal of Middle East Studies,* November 2001, 545–69.

Madelung, W. "Maturidiyya." *Encyclopedia of Islam.* CD-ROM ed. London: Brill, 2002.

Malik, Iftikhar H. *Islam and Modernity: Muslims in Europe and the United States.* London: Pluto, 2004.

Mandaville, Peter. "Europe's Muslim Youth: Dynamics of Alienation and Integration." In Shireen Hunter and Huma Malik, eds., *Islam in Europe and the United States: A Comparative Perspective,* 22–27. Washington, D.C.: Center for Strategic and International Studies, 2002.

———. *Transnational Muslim Politics: Reimagining the Umma.* 2d ed. London: Routledge, 2004.

Martinez, Luis. *The Algerian Civil War.* New York: Columbia University Press, 2000.

McAdam, Doug. *Political Process and the Development of Black Insurgency, 1930–1970.* Chicago: University of Chicago Press, 1982.

———. "Recruitment to High-Risk Activism: The Case of Freedom Summer." *American Journal of Sociology,* July 1986, 64–90.

McAdam, Doug, and Roberto M. Fernandez. "Microstructural Bases of Recruitment to Social Movements." *Research in Social Movements, Conflict, and Change* 12 (1990): 1–33.

McAdam, Doug, John D. McCarthy, and Mayer N. Zald. "Introduction: Opportunities, Mobilizing Structures, and Framing Processes—Toward a Synthetic, Comparative Perspective on Social Movements." In *Comparative Perspectives on Social Movements: Political Opportunities, Mobilizing Structures, and Cultural Framings.* Cambridge: Cambridge University Press, 1996.

McAdam, Doug, and Ronnelle Paulsen. "Specifying the Relationship between Social Ties and Activism." *American Journal of Sociology,* November 1993, 640–67.

McCaffrey, Dawn, and Jennifer Keys. "Competitive Frame Processes in the Abortion Debate: Polarization-Vilification, Frame Saving, and Frame Debunking." *Sociological Quarterly* 41 (2000): 41–46.

McGuire, William J. "Attitudes and Attitude Change." In Gilbert Fiske Lindzey and Elliot Aronson, eds., *Handbook of Social Psychology.* 3d ed. Reading, Mass.: Random House, 1985.

Melucci, Alberto. *Challenging Codes: Collective Action in the Information Age.* Cambridge: Cambridge University Press, 1996.

——. "An End to Social Movements? Introductory Paper to the Sessions on 'New Social Movements and Change in Organizational Forms.'" *Social Science Information* 23, no. 4–5 (1984): 819–35.

——. *Nomads of the Present: Social Movements and Individual Needs in Contemporary Society.* Philadelphia: Temple University Press, 1989.

Merali, Arzu, and Massoud Shadjareh. *Islamophobia: The New Crusade.* Islamic Human Rights Commission, May 2002. www.ihrc.org.uk/file/ISLAMOPHOBIAthenewcrusade.pdf.

Meyer, David S. "Opportunities and Identities: Bridge-Building in the Study of Social Movements." In David S. Meyer, Nancy Whittier, and Belinda Robnett, eds., *Social Movements: Identity, Culture, and the State.* Oxford: Oxford University Press, 2003.

Mishal, Shaul, and Avraham Sela. *The Palestinian Hamas: Vision, Violence, and Coexistence.* New York: Columbia University Press, 2002.

Modood, Tariq. "British Asian Muslims and the Rushdie Affair." *Political Quarterly,* April 1990, 143–60.

——. "The Place of Muslims in British Secular Multiculturalism." In Nezar AlSayyad and Manuel Castells, eds., *Muslim Europe or Euro-Islam: Politics, Culture, and Citizenship in the Age of Globalization.* Lanham, Md.: Lexington, 2002.

Modood, Tariq, Richard Berthoud, Jane Lakey, James Nazroo, Patten Smith, Satnam Virdee, and Sharon Beishon. *Ethnic Minorities in Britain.* London: Policy Studies Institute, 1997.

Modood, Tariq, and Pnina Werbner, eds. *The Politics of Multiculturalism in the New Europe: Racism, Identity, and Community.* London: Zed, 1997.

Moghadam, Assaf. "Palestinian Suicide Terrorism in the Second Intifada: Motivations and Organizational Aspects." *Studies in Conflict and Terrorism,* March–April 2003, 65–92.

Mufti, Malik. "Elite Bargains and the Onset of Political Liberalization in Jordan." *Comparative Political Studies,* February 1999, 100–129.

Munson, Henry, Jr. "The Social Base of Islamic Militance in Morocco." *Middle East Journal,* Spring 1986, 267–84.

Munson, Ziad. "Islamic Mobilization: Social Movement Theory and the Egyptian Muslim Brotherhood." *Sociological Quarterly,* Fall 2001, 487–510.

Muslim Council of Britain. *National Survey of Muslim Council of Britain Affiliate Organizations on Proposed Military Action against Iraq.* London: Muslim Council of Britain, September 2002.

Nasr, Seyyed Vali Reza. *The Islamic Leviathan: Islam and the Making of State Power.* Oxford: Oxford University Press, 2001.

Nepstad, Sharon Erickson, and Christian Smith. "Rethinking Recruitment to High Risk/Cost Activism: The Case of Nicaragua Exchange." *Mobilization: An International Journal* 4, no. 1 (1999): 25–40.

Noakes, John A. "Official Frames in Social Movement Theory: The FBI, HUAC, and the Communist Threat in Hollywood." *Sociological Quarterly*, Fall 2000, 657–80.

Oberschall, Anthony. *Social Conflict and Social Movements*. Englewood Cliffs, N.J.: Prentice Hall, 1973.

Olsen, Mancur. *The Logic of Collective Action*, 133–34. Cambridge: Harvard University Press, 1965.

Opp, Karl-Dieter. *The Rationality of Political Protest: A Comparative Analysis of Rational Choice Theory*. Boulder: Westview, 1989.

Opp, Karl-Dieter, and Christiane Gern. "Dissident Groups, Personal Networks, and Spontaneous Cooperation: The East German Revolution of 1989." *American Sociological Review* 58 (1993): 659–80.

Opp, Karl-Dieter, Peter Voss, and Christiane Gern. *Origins of a Spontaneous Revolution: East Germany, 1989*. Ann Arbor: University of Michigan Press, 1993.

Pape, Robert. "The Strategic Logic of Suicide Terrorism." *American Political Science Review* 97, no. 2 (2003): 343–62.

Payne, Sebastian. "Britain's New Anti-Terrorist Legal Framework." *Rusi Journal*, June 2002, 44–52.

Paz, Reuvan. "Middle East Islamism in the European Arena." *Middle East Review of International Affairs*, September 2002, 67–76.

———. "Qa'idat al-Jihad: A New Name on the Road to Palestine," May 7, 2002. www.ict.org.il/articles/articledet.cfm?articleid=436.

Pedersen, Lars. *Newer Islamic Movements in Western Europe*. Brookfield: Ashgate, 1999.

Petty, Richard E., Monique A. Fleming, Joseph R. Priester, and Amy Harasty Feinstein. "Individual versus Group Interest Violation: Surprise as a Determinant of Argument Scrutiny and Persuasion." *Social Cognition* 19, no. 4 (2001): 418–42.

Pfaff, Steven. "Collective Identity and Informal Groups in Revolutionary Mobilization." *Social Forces*, September 1996, 91–118.

Pipes, Daniel. *Militant Islam Reaches America*. New York: Norton, 2003.

Piscatori, James P., ed. *Islam in the Political Process*. Cambridge: Cambridge University Press, 1983.

Platt, Gerald M., and Rhys H. Williams. "Ideological Language and Social Movement Mobilization: A Sociolinguistic Analysis of Segregationists' Ideologies." *Sociological Theory*, November 2002, 328–59.

Poole, Elizabeth. *Reporting Islam: Media Representations of British Muslims*. London: Tauris, 2002.

Richardson, James T. "The Active vs. Passive Convert: Paradigm Conflict in Conversion/Recruitment Research." *Journal for the Scientific Study of Religion* 24 (1985): 163–79.

———. *Introduction to Positive Political Theory*. Englewood Cliffs, N.J.: Prentice Hall, 1973.

Riddle, Donald W. *The Martyrs: A Study in Social Control*. Chicago: University of Chicago Press, 1931.

Riker, William, and Peter Ordeshook. *Introduction to Positive Political Theory*. Englewood Cliffs, N.J.: Prentice Hall, 1973.

———. "A Theory of the Calculus of Voting." *American Political Science Review* 62 (1968): 25–42.

Robinson, Glenn. "Can Islamists Be Democrats? The Case of Jordan." *Middle East Journal*, Summer 1997, 373–88.

Ronson, Jon. *Them: Adventures with Extremists*. New York: Simon & Schuster, 2002.

Roskos-Ewoldsen, David R., Jacqueline Bichsel, and Kathleen Hoffman. "The Influence of Accessibility of Source Likability on Persuasion." *Journal of Experimental Social Psychology*, March 2002, 137–43.

Roy, Olivier. *The Failure of Political Islam*. Translated by Carol Volk. Cambridge: Harvard University Press, 1994.

———. *Globalised Islam: The Search for a New Ummah*. London: Hurst, 2004.

Runnymede Trust. *Islamophobia: A Challenge for Us All*. London: Runnymede Trust, 1997.

Rutten, Rosanne. "High-Cost Activism and the Worker Household: Interests, Commitment, and the Costs of Revolutionary Activism in a Philippine Plantation Region." *Theory and Society*, April 2000, 215–52.

Ryan, Charlotte. *Prime Time Activism: Media Strategies for Grassroots Organizing*. Boston: South End, 1991.

Sageman, Marc. *Understanding Terrorist Networks*. Philadelphia: University of Pennsylvania Press, 2004.

Said, Edward. *Covering Islam*. 2d ed. New York: Vintage, 1997.

El-Said, Sabah. *Between Pragmatism and Ideology: The Muslim Brotherhood in Jordan*. Policy paper no. 3. Washington, D.C.: Washington Institute for Near East Policy, 1995.

Sartori, Anne E. "The Might of the Pen: A Reputational Theory of Communication in International Disputes." *International Organization*, Winter 2002, 121–49.

Schneider, Cathy Lisa. *Shantytown Protest in Pinochet's Chile*. Philadelphia: Temple University Press, 1995.

Schwedler, Jillian. "The Islah Party in Yemen: Political Opportunities and Coalition Building in a Transitional Polity." In Quintan Wiktorowicz, ed., *Islamic Activism: A Social Movement Theory Approach*. Bloomington: Indiana University Press, 2004.

Scott, James. *Domination and the Arts of Resistance: Hidden Transcripts*. New Haven: Yale University Press, 1990.

———. *Weapons of the Weak: Everyday Forms of Peasant Resistance*. New Haven: Yale University Press, 1986.

Sherkat, Darren E., and John Wilson. "Preferences, Constraints, and Choices in Religious Markets: An Examination of Religious Switching and Apostasy." *Social Forces*, March 1995, 993–1026.

Sikkink, David, and Rory McVeigh. "Who Wants to Protest?" Working Paper and Technical Report Series no. 2001-10. Notre Dame, Ind.: Notre Dame, Department of Sociology, 2001.

Singerman, Diane. "The Networked World of Islamist Social Movements." In Quintan Wiktorowicz, ed., *Islamic Activism: A Social Movement Theory Approach*. Bloomington: Indiana University Press, 2004.

Slater, Michael D., and Donna Rouner. "How Message Evaluation and Source Attributes May Influence Credibility Assessment and Belief Change." *Journalism and Mass Communication Quarterly* 73, no. 4 (1996): 974–91.

Smelser, Neil J. *Theory of Collective Behavior*. New York: Free Press, 1962.

Smith, Benjamin. "Collective Action with and without Islam: Mobilizing the Bazaar in Iran." In Quintan Wiktorowicz, ed., *Islamic Activism: A Social Movement Theory Approach*. Bloomington: Indiana University Press, 2004.

Smith, Christian. *The Emergence of Liberation Theology: Radical Religion and Social Movement Theory*. Chicago: University of Chicago Press, 1991.

Snow, David A., and Robert D. Benford. "Ideology, Frame Resonance, and Participant Mobilization." In Bert Klandermans, Hanspeter Kriesi, and Sidney Tarrow, eds., *From Structure to Action: Comparing Movement Participation Across Cultures*. Vol. 1, *International Social Movement Research*. Greenwich, Conn.: JAI Press, 1988.

——. "Master Frames and Cycles of Protest." In Aldon Morris and Carol McClurg Mueller, eds., *Frontiers in Social Movement Theory*. New Haven: Yale University Press, 1992.

Snow, David A., and Richard Machalek. "The Convert as a Social Type." *Sociological Theory* 1 (1983): 259–89.

——. "The Sociology of Conversion." *Annual Review of Sociology* 10 (1984): 167–90.

Snow, David A., Louis A. Zurcher Jr., and Sheldon Ekland-Olson. "Social Networks and Social Movements: A Microstructural Approach to Differential Recruitment." *American Sociological Review*, October 1986, 787–801.

Spickard, James V. "Rethinking Religious Social Action: What Is 'Rational' about Rational-Choice Theory." *Sociology of Religion* 59, no. 2 (1998): 99–115.

Sprinzak, Ehud. "Rational Fanatics." *Foreign Policy*, September-October 2000, 66–73.

Stark, Rodney, and William Sims Bainbridge. "Networks of Faith: Interpersonal Bonds and Recruitment to Cults and Sects." *American Journal of Sociology*, May 1980, 1376–95.

Steward, Charles J., Craig Allen Smith, and Robert E. Denton Jr. *Persuasion and Social Movements*. 4th ed. Prospect Heights, Ill.: Waveland, 2001.

Sullivan, Denis J. *Private Voluntary Organizations in Egypt: Islamic Development, Private Initiative, and State Control*. Gainesville: University of Florida Press, 1994.

Taji-Farouki, Suha. *A Fundamental Quest: Hizb al-Tahrir and the Search for the Islamic Caliphate*. London: Grey Seal, 1996.

Taylor, Verta, and Nicole C. Raeburn. "Identity Politics as High-Risk Activism: Career Consequences for Lesbian, Gay, and Bisexual Sociologists." *Social Problems*, May 1995, 252–73.

Tilly, Charles. *The Politics of Collective Violence*. Cambridge: Cambridge University Press, 2003.

Tindall, David B. "Social Networks, Identification, and Participation in an Environmental Movement: Low-Medium Cost Activism within the British Columbia Wilderness Preservation Movement." *Canadian Review of Sociology and Anthropology*, November 2002, 413–52.

Turner, Ralph H., and Lewis Killian. *Collective Behavior*. Englewood Cliffs, N.J.: Prentice Hall, 1957.

Vanderford, Marsha L. "Vilification and Social Movements: A Case Study of Pro-Life and Pro-Choice Rhetoric." *Quarterly Journal of Speech* 75 (1989): 166–82.

Waltz, Susan. "Islamist Appeal in Tunisia." *Middle East Journal*, Autumn 1986, 651–70.

White, Jenny B. *Islamist Mobilization in Turkey: A Study in Vernacular Politics*. Seattle: University of Washington Press, 2002.

Wickham, Carrie Rosefsky. "Islamic Mobilization and Political Change: The Islamist Trend in Egypt's Professional Associations." In Joel Beinin and Joe Stork, eds., *Political Islam*. Berkeley: University of California Press, 1997.

———. *Mobilizing Islam: Religion, Activism, and Political Change in Egypt*. New York: Columbia University Press, 2002.

Wiktorowicz, Quintan. "Framing Jihad: Ideology and Sacred Authority in the Muslim World." *International Review of Social History*, Supplement, 49 (2004): 159–77.

———. "The GIA and GSPC in Algeria." In Magnus Ranstorp, ed., *In the Service of al-Qaeda: Radical Islamic Movements*. Forthcoming.

———. "Introduction: Islamic Activism and Social Movement Theory." In *Islamic Activism: A Social Movement Theory Approach*. Bloomington: Indiana University Press, 2004.

———. *The Management of Islamic Activism: Salafis, the Muslim Brotherhood, and State Power in Jordan*. Albany: State University of New York Press, 2001.

Wiktorowicz, Quintan, ed. *Islamic Activism: A Social Movement Theory Approach*. Bloomington: Indiana University Press, 2004.

Wiltfang, Gregory L., and Doug McAdam. "The Costs and Risks of Social Activism: A Study of Sanctuary Movement Activism." *Social Forces*, June 1991, 987–1010.

Winthrop, Ronald. "Can Suicide Bombers Be Rational?" Manuscript, 2003.

Wood, Elisabeth Jean. *Insurgent Collective Action and Civil War in El Salvador*. Cambridge: Cambridge University Press, 2003.

Yavuz, M. Hakan. "A Typology of Islamic Social Movements: Opportunity Spaces in Turkey." In Quintan Wiktorowicz, ed., *Islamic Activism: A Social Movement Theory Approach*. Bloomington: Indiana University Press, 2004.

Zald, Mayer N. "Culture, Ideology, and Strategic Framing." In Doug McAdam, John D. McCarthy, and Mayer N. Zald, eds., *Comparative Perspectives on Social Movements: Political Opportunities, Mobilizing Structures, and Cultural Framings*, 261–74. Cambridge: Cambridge University Press, 1996.

Zald, Mayer N., and John D. McCarthy. "Social Movement Industries: Competition and Conflict among SMOs." In *Social Movements in an Organizational Society*, 161–80. New Brunswick, N.J.: Transaction, 1987.

Zald, Mayer N., and John D. McCarthy, eds. *Social Movements in an Organizational Society*. New Brunswick, N.J.: Transaction, 1987.

Zaynoo, Muhammad Ibn Jameel. "Methodology of the Saved Sect." *Al-Ibaanah,* April 1996, 32–33.

INDEX

activism: within al-Muhajiroun, 45–50, 79n12; cognitive opening for, 5, 20, 21, 24, 85, 92–98, 206, 209–10; definition of, 10; demographic profile for, 12; family opposition to, 55–56, 81n33; framing and, 15–16, 18, 136, 137, 162n9, 210; by Marxists, 55; network of shared meaning for, 17, 23, 135, 195–96, 205; Paradise for, 6, 28, 99, 172, 190–91, 200, 205, 213; political issues for, 25–26, 100, 104; in radical Islamic movement, 3, 5–6, 46–47, 206; recruitment for, 4, 5–6, 8, 14–15, 23, 48, 72, 85, 91, 117–18, 192–194; religious training for, 47; risk/cost/reward of, 46–47, 200, 205–6, 209, 211; social networking for, 6, 11–12, 15, 17–19, 24, 27, 57, 58–59, 60, 85, 93, 105–6, 169, 207, 208
activists: deportation of, 8, 9, 46, 63, 65–66, 144; fines for, 53; marginalization of, 54; risk/cost/reward for, 46–47, 200, 205–6, 209, 211; salvation for, 6, 28–29, 167, 170, 178, 190–91, 200, 203n55, 211; self-employment for, 52;

social role of, 6, 11–12, 15, 17–19, 24, 27, 57, 58–59, 60, 85, 93, 105–6, 169, 207, 208; welfare for, 52–53
Afghanistan: Blair and, 2–3, 71; British Muslims in, 2–3, 71; jihadi cause in, 3; *shari'a* angle for, 75. *See also* Taliban
Agence France Presse, 75
Ahmed, Lord, 60
Algeria, GIA rebellion in, 13
Ali, Iftikhar, 69, 76
Allenby Bridge crossing, 1
Alwan, Suleiman, 216
Amin, Nadeem, 50–51
amir (commander, religious leader), 8, 9, 51, 106
ammonium nitrate fertilizer, 3
Anderson, Donald, 9
Anderson, Lisa, 12
Anjem Choudary. *See* Choudary, Anjem
Ansar al-Islam, 3
anti-Semitism, 65, 67, 69, 70, 119
Anti-Terrorism, Crime, and Security Act, 63, 67, 81n58
apostasy, 58, 173–74, *174,* 197–98, 202n46
al-Aqsa intifada, 2, 13, 18

3–4, 31, 45, 46, 48, 59, 64, 75, 88,
112, 138; as war on Islam/Muslims,
109, 120, 131n64
wasta (connections), 12
wealth, distribution of, 93–94, 95
Weber, Max, 199–200
website: for al-Muhajiroun, 158–59,
165nn69–70; Paltalk on, 56; for al-
Qaeda, 48, 79n9
Wehr, Paul, 19
West Bank: Allenby Bridge crossing into,
1; al-Qassem Brigade in, 1; suicide
bombing within, 1
Western Crusade, 92
*What All Muslims Should Know by
Necessity* (leaflet), 113

Whine, Michael, 67
Wickham, Carrie, 18, 22, 27, 28
Wiltfang, Gregory L., 19, 46
World Trade Centers: September 11
attack on, 3–4, 31, 45, 46, 59, 64, 75,
88, 112, 138

Yemen, proselytizing in, 23
Young Muslims U.K., 147

Zald, Mayer, 16
Zalluom, Abdul Qadeem: as HT *amir*, 8,
9; al-Zarqawi, Abu Mussab, 65. *See
also* al-Qaeda
Zawahiri, Ayman, 64
zealots, behavior of, 45

ABOUT THE AUTHOR

Quintan Wiktorowicz is the author of *The Management of Islamic Activism: Salafis, the Muslim Brotherhood, and State Power in Jordan; Global Jihad: Understanding September 11;* and numerous articles and book chapters on radical Islamic groups in Jordan, Egypt, Algeria, and Europe. He is also editor of *Islamic Activism: A Social Movement Theory Approach.*

Printed in Great
Britain
by Amazon